When Face Recognition Goes Wrong

When Face Recognition Goes Wrong explores the myriad ways that humans and machines make mistakes in facial recognition.

Adopting a critical stance throughout, the book explores why and how humans and machines make mistakes, covering topics including racial and gender biases, neuropsychological disorders, and widespread algorithm problems. The book features personal anecdotes alongside real-world examples to showcase the often life-changing consequences of facial recognition going wrong. These range from problems with everyday social interactions through to eyewitness identification leading to miscarriages of justice and border control passport verification.

Concluding with a look to the future of facial recognition, the author asks the world's leading experts what are the big questions that still need to be answered, and can we train humans and machines to be super recognisers? This book is a must-read for anyone interested in facial recognition, or in psychology, criminal justice and law.

Catriona Havard is Professor of Psychology in the School of Psychology & Counselling at The Open University, UK.

When Face Recognition Goes Wrong

Catriona Havard

Routledge
Taylor & Francis Group

LONDON AND NEW YORK

Designed cover image: Getty images

First published 2025
by Routledge
4 Park Square, Milton Park, Abingdon, Oxon OX14 4RN

and by Routledge
605 Third Avenue, New York, NY 10158

Routledge is an imprint of the Taylor & Francis Group, an informa business

© 2025 Catriona Havard

The right of Catriona Havard to be identified as author of this work has been asserted in accordance with sections 77 and 78 of the Copyright, Designs and Patents Act 1988.

British Library Cataloguing-in-Publication Data
A catalogue record for this book is available from the British Library

Library of Congress Cataloging-in-Publication Data
A catalog record has been requested for this book

ISBN: 978-1-032-01096-0 (hbk)
ISBN: 978-1-032-01095-3 (pbk)
ISBN: 978-1-003-17712-8 (ebk)

DOI: 10.4324/9781003177128

Typeset in Optima
by Taylor & Francis Books

Contents

Illustrations

Figures

Table

Boxes

Acknowledgments

There are lots of people I would like to thank for helping me in various ways which led to the creation of this book. Firstly, I would like to thank Meg-John Barker for encouraging me to write the book and for advice on approaching publishers. If they had not encouraged me right from the off then this book might not have happened.

My lovely friend Rebecca Charles deserves special thanks as she has read drafts of several of the chapters and given me constructive feedback. I thank her also for allowing me to use photographs of her face in some of the figures in the book.

There is also Zoe Walkington, Scott Lannigan, Archie Havard and Gary Vasey, who all allowed me to use photographs of their faces for other images in the book.

I would like to thank Stephen Lindsay for putting me in touch with Don Read, who suggested readings for Chapter 3 of this book, making it more interesting and better researched.

For Chapter 12, I need to thank all the researchers who replied to my questions and made the chapter possible. Thank you to Anna Bobak, Mike Burton, Graham Hole, Sarah Laurence, Reuben Moreton, Eilidh Noyes, Graham Pike, Cathy Mondloch, Romina Palermo, Clare Sutherland and Colin Tredoux for providing such thought-provoking answers. Thanks also for the great feedback I received from many of you on the draft of Chapter 12.

I also want to thank my family Scott and Archie for putting up with my heavy typing, at very odd times of the day and night. Thanks also to my parents, Kate and Denis Havard, who let me work up in the Scottish Highlands at their kitchen table.

Finally, I want to thank my publishers and editors at Routledge for their patience, as I totally underestimated how long it would take me to complete writing this book.

I have thoroughly enjoyed doing the research for this book and it has generated new ideas for my own future research. I hope those reading the book also find the topics as fascinating as I do.

1 Introduction

Introduction

The focus of this book is about when face recognition goes wrong, but before looking at research that has investigated this issue and also real-life examples of when this has happened, we need to look at why recognising faces is important. Being able to recognise a face and identify who it belongs to is important for a variety of everyday tasks and some more unusual occurrences that may happen to you throughout your life. Many aspects of daily life rely on face recognition, such as identifying a friend in a cafe or pub, and greeting colleagues at work. Face recognition is also used as a means of verifying a person's identity, for example comparing a person to their passport or driving licence, or identifying a criminal from a police lineup. However, face recognition isn't 100% accurate and we have all had embarrassing incidents when perhaps we haven't recognised someone we have met before, or they seem familiar, but we can't think where from. You may also have gone up to someone to say hello and then realised that actually they aren't the person you thought they were. Generally, when we make errors of face recognition in social situations, it is embarrassing, but doesn't usually have any serious consequences. However, when face recognition is an integral part of a criminal justice process, errors can have serious costs. This book will cover a variety of topics about face recognition, including the types of errors people make and errors in face recognition technology. This chapter serves as a general introduction to face recognition research, describing some of the early

DOI: 10.4324/9781003177128-1

research and methods that have been employed to investigate how accurate we are at recognising faces.

Research investigating face recognition has been conducted since the 1960s, with the first review of face recognition studies published in the 1970s (Ellis, 1975). This was no mean feat considering that there was no Google Scholar, PsychInfo, Web of Science or even the internet to search for papers and collate all of the published studies (Davies & Young, 2017). In the review, Ellis (1975) found very high rates of correct recognition in a standard face recognition paradigm (over 90%). In any typical face recognition study, participants are presented with a series of faces one at a time during the study phase, then they are presented with a larger set of faces (often twice as many) during a test phase, and they must decide which of these faces were seen during the study phase (old) and which are novel (new). The high rates of accuracy found in face recognition studies were at odds with miscarriages of justice that were occurring during the 1970s as a result of misidentifications of innocent suspects by eyewitnesses, suggesting that face recognition was not as accurate as the research claimed (Young & Burton, 2017). It wasn't until Bruce's (1982) study that compared using the identical photographs of faces from study to test, with photographs that varied in expression and viewpoint, responses became much less accurate, dropping from 90% to 60%, but more akin to real-life face recognition. Bruce (1982) suggested that when identical images were used from study to test phase participants were engaged in picture or image recognition rather than face recognition, and since this research many researchers in the field recommend that different images should always be used from study to test phases when investigating face recognition (Young & Burton, 2017). Interestingly, in a further study Bruce (1982) found that when the faces presented were personally familiar to the participants (lecturers at their university) they were easier to recognise as compared to unfamiliar faces. Furthermore, unfamiliar faces were still recognised despite changes in expression and viewpoint.

Familiar versus unfamiliar faces

Bruce's (1982) research demonstrates that recognising a familiar face, such as a work colleague, friend or family member, is quite different from recognising an unfamiliar person that you have briefly seen, such as a shopkeeper who just served you at the checkout. In the face recognition literature, researchers make the distinction between familiar faces and unfamiliar faces. Familiar faces can be personally familiar, like friends, work colleagues, neighbours and family, or publicly familiar such as famous celebrities (e.g. Barack Obama, David Attenborough or Angelina Jolie). When it comes to recognising familiar faces it is relatively easy, even if that person changes their hairstyle, or we see them in different lighting or from a different angle. However, when it comes to recognising someone who is not familiar to us that we've only seen briefly, then this becomes a much more difficult task, and this is where many of the errors with face recognition arise.

In order to investigate how accurate people could be at recognising familiar and unfamiliar faces, Burton et al. (1999) set up two different experiments. In Experiment 1 they showed two different groups of participants video clips of CCTV footage of psychology lecturers walking down the corridor. In one group they had psychology students who should have been familiar with the lecturers (familiar group), and in the other group students who had not studied psychology and were not familiar with the lecturers (unfamiliar group). In the study phase of the experiment participants were shown ten clips from the CCTV video and then in the test phase they were shown 20 high-quality images one at a time; half had previously been presented and half were new, and they were asked to rate each photo on a 1–7 scale, with 1 being the person definitely wasn't in one of the clips and 7 being the person was definitely in one of the clips already seen. Participants were shown twice as many faces in the test phase to determine whether they could not only recognise faces that they had previously seen, but determine that some faces had not been seen before. The findings revealed participants in the familiar group gave much higher ratings to faces they had seen before (6.5) as compared to faces they had not seen before (1.5). The unfamiliar group gave lower ratings to seen faces (4.5) and higher ratings to unseen faces (3), and the difference between the unseen and seen faces was not as great as for the familiar group. Burton and colleagues found that the familiar group were much more accurate at determining which faces had been seen and unseen as compared to the unfamiliar group.

When Burton et al. (1999) discussed the results from Experiment 1, as the CCTV footage was of poor quality, they suggested that instead of using people's faces maybe the familiar group were using other cues from the lecturers they recognised, such as their clothing, gait or body shape. They set up a second experiment to test this. In Experiment 2, one group of psychology students who hadn't taken part in Experiment 1 were presented with a series of CCTV video clips of people walking along a corridor, some were psychology lecturers that should be familiar and some other persons that should be unfamiliar to the students. To investigate which cues were important for person recognition, the clips were presented so that they either had the head (face) masked, or the body masked, or unedited. After viewing the clip the participants were asked to identify the person, either by their name or some other distinguishing information (e.g. they are my cognitive psychology lecturer), or saying 'I don't recognise that person'. Burton et al. found that participants were very accurate at correctly identifying familiar individuals and also accurate at saying when they didn't recognise unfamiliar individuals. The results from the study by Burton et al. (1999) demonstrated that when the face was masked this dramatically reduced how accurate people were at correctly identifying the person from the video, whereas masking the body of a person had less influence in reducing correct identifications, and cues such as body shape and gait were not useful for correctly identifying individuals. The results from Burton et al. (1999) show that not only is the face the most important part of the person for identification, but that people can recognise faces, even from quite poor-quality CCTV footage, if they are familiar persons. However, when it comes to trying to recognise faces that belong to unfamiliar persons, the task becomes much more difficult and error prone.

Research that has investigated how accurate we are at recognising familiar versus unfamiliar faces has found that we can easily recognise familiar faces from low quality video footage (Burton et al., 1999); however, even when viewing high-quality images, identifying unfamiliar faces can be difficult and error prone (Bruce et al., 2001). Furthermore, if there are any changes in the way the faces are viewed, such as changes in viewpoint, expression and lighting, this has little effect on the recognition of familiar faces, but can dramatically reduce the recognition of unfamiliar faces (Hill & Bruce, 1996; O'Toole et al., 1998; Patterson & Baddeley, 1977). These studies seem to suggest that unfamiliar face recognition may be more to do with picture recognition than face recognition if the performance can be reduced in the differences in image properties (Hancock et al., 2000). You may be asking yourself, when would you need to recognise an unfamiliar face? The rest of the chapter will look at some examples of when people must do this in real life, either as part of a job or because they witnessed an incident that involves making an identification. In some cases, face recognition (that is relying on the memory of someone's face that you have seen) isn't necessary, as you may have two pictures of a person already.

Face matching

Face matching – that is, deciding whether two different face images are the same person or two different people – is important for a variety of tasks where you need to verify someone's identity. Examples of face matching include deciding whether a person at a border is the same person as depicted on the passport they are holding, deciding that a person matches their ID when they are trying to buy restricted products such as alcohol, or matching offenders who are in custody to CCTV footage (for a review on face matching see Fysh & Bindemann, 2017). There has been a large amount of research that has investigated how accurately people can verify identities matching multiple faces. Face matching usually presents participants with two faces side by side and they have to decide if they are the same person (match), or two different people (mismatch). There are a number of face matching tests that researchers have developed using this method, such as the Glasgow Face Matching Test (Burton et al., 2010), the Kent Face Matching Test (Fysh & Bindemann, 2018) and the Oxford Face Matching test (Stantic et al., 2022). Figure 1.1 illustrates the typical types of stimuli that are used in face matching tests. The faces have been cropped to remove any cues from the background or clothing, and they have been converted

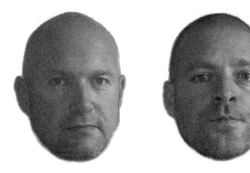

Figure 1.1 An example of a face matching task.

to greyscale to remove any differences in colours. The idea is that you can only use facial information when trying to decide if they are the same person or two different people. Do you think that the two faces belong to the same person or two different people?

Research that has compared familiar versus unfamiliar face matching has found that familiar faces can two different images; however, matching unfamiliar faces can be error prone. When you think about it, why should this task be so difficult? It doesn't rely on memory of a face as the faces are both present. However, research has shown that even with high-quality images on average a wrong decision is made on average 20% of the time (Burton et al., 2010). Although some research has shown that errors on mismatch trials that can increase to 50% if the person doing the matching task has to do it for a long time (Alenezi et al., 2015).

Face matching in applied settings (e.g. passport control) involves matching faces that are unfamiliar, and research with Western participants has found that external features (hair, face shape) appear to be more useful for matching unfamiliar faces than internal features (eyes, nose, and mouth), although internal features can be useful for familiar faces (Bonner et al., 2003; Bruce et al., 1999; Ellis et al., 1979; Young et al., 1985). However, research comparing Western participants and Middle Eastern participants on unfamiliar face matching and recognition tasks found an internal feature advantage for Middle Eastern participants, contrasting with the external feature advantage with Western participants (Megreya et al., 2012; Megreya & Bindemann, 2009; Wang et al., 2015). Megreya and Bindemann (2009) suggest that this advantage is due to a processing advantage from seeing women in the Middle East wearing headscarves that mask the external features. In contrast, research with Western participants found that when unfamiliar faces were presented with the hair masked or removed, it can increase errors by 35% (Bruce et al., 1999); when hairstyles are changed they can also reduce face recognition accuracy and make people more likely to say they haven't seen a previously seen face (Bartel et al., 2018). When a person changes their hairstyle it can also affect whether people are able to verify their identity if their identification has a different hairstyle; see the box describing a real-life example of my personal experience of this.

Personal real-life example

When I was a teenager, I used to have to get a bus and train to school across north London, and I had a bus pass with a photograph on it. This could be used as photo ID to prove that I was under the age of 16 and therefore could get a child fare, rather than paying the higher amount for an adult fare. At the time I had shoulder-length dark blonde hair. Then one weekend I decided to cut and dye my hair black (I was a teenager and it seemed like a good idea at the time!). The next time I got on the bus, the conductor didn't believe that I was the person on the bus pass as I looked so different with black hair and they made me pay for a full adult fare. Have a look at Figure 1.2; what do you think? Do

Figure 1.2 The author with two different hairstyles and colours.

they look like the same person or two different people?

I learnt my lesson: I went and got another photo card with black hair, and then the problem was solved. I kept my other blonde card just in case I dyed my hair back to blonde. One day my friend Kate was on the bus and she forgot her own bus pass. She had dark blonde hair. Although we did not really look alike at all, we decided she would try my blonde-haired bus pass, and when the bus conductor came along she showed it to him and he didn't even bat an eyelid! This is interesting, as not only did the conductor assume that it was Kate's face on the bus pass, but the person who was depicted on the bus pass was present too and he didn't seem to realise at all.

My personal experience of not being identified as the person on my bus pass illustrates that people are just not very good at matching images of unfamiliar individuals if they change their hair colour. Some of my own research also found that removing external features of a face including the hair can reduce face matching accuracy, especially when it comes to faces that are a different race to the person who has to make the decision (Havard, 2021). The issue of race in face recognition will be discussed later in this book (see Chapter 4). Changing one's hairstyle also has implications for other situations where photographic identity cards are used as a source of verification.

In the applied setting of a supermarket, Kemp, Towell and Pike (1997) conducted a study investigating whether supermarket cashiers could accurately decide if a shopper at the till was the same person as a photograph on a credit card. For half of the time the shopper was the person on the credit card (valid card) and for the other half of the time there was a different person on the credit card (fraudulent card). When the shopper had their own photograph on the credit card, it was either unchanged appearance, that is they looked the same as they did in the store, or it was a changed appearance photograph, with a different hairstyle, or the removal of facial hair. When the shopper had a credit card that had a photograph of a different person, the photo was either a matched foil, that is someone who was similar in appearance, or an unmatched foil, someone who was judged to be not similar in appearance, but the same race and gender as the person on the card. When the shoppers visited the tills, the cashiers could either accept the card or reject it if they thought the person in front of them was not the person on the credit card. The results from the study showed that the cashiers falsely accepted the fraudulent cards more than 50% of the time, and this was especially the case for the matched foil cards. Interestingly the cashiers also falsely rejected some of the cards when they had the photograph of the shopper on them, in some cases even when their appearance was unchanged (Kemp et al., 1997).

The study by Kemp and colleagues and my own experience of when someone makes an error trying to match a face to a photographic image both seem to illustrate that people are not very accurate when it comes to matching unfamiliar faces in real-life settings. However, in both scenarios it could be argued that the people who were tasked with the matching were not trained to do so, unlike in other professions, such as passport control, where border force officers check travel documents of passengers. It begs the question that if people are trained and conduct face matching tasks on an everyday basis, are they more accurate than most other people? This is exactly the question that White et al. (2014) hoped to answer in their research employing Australian passport officers. In their study a group of passport officers had to decide if people who approached their desk one at a time were the same persons as shown in on-screen photographs that were either the same person (valid ID) or different persons (invalid ID). They found that 10% of the time the passport officers made an error, that was either accepting an invalid ID, or rejecting a valid ID. Interestingly the length of service in the passport office didn't increase performance on the task.

In a second study, White et al. (2014) compared passport officers and students on a task where they had to decide whether two photos were the same person or two different people. The photo pairs were presented at the same time, with a high-quality image of the target on the left and then either a match (same person) or mismatch (different person), which was either a two-year-old photo, or an official ID photo (e.g. driving license or passport). They found that when the faces were the same person, errors were made 30% of the time. When the photographs were two different people, the performance was more accurate; however, 10% of the time wrong decisions were made that the faces were the same person. This finding is rather worrying considering that the most common type of passport fraud is when persons use someone else's passport as a means to gain entry across borders (Stevens, 2021). There was little difference in the matching accuracy between the students and the passport officers, suggesting that even though the passport offices were trained for this task they didn't seem to perform more accurately than those who had not been trained. The issue of training will be considered in the final chapter of this book (Chapter 12) and whether providing training to individuals who need to use face recognition or matching for their employment can improve face recognition accuracy.

What is interesting from studies that have compared how well people can match different images of the same or different people is that performance is fully dissociable accuracy, that is how well you do on one task (deciding that two faces are the same person) doesn't appear to be related to how well you do on the other task (deciding that two faces are two different people) (Kokje et al., 2018; Megreya & Burton, 2007). This suggests that deciding two faces are the same person is a cognitively different process from deciding that two face images are two different people; however, as mentioned earlier, the variability between images of people can also influence how well

Figure 1.3 An example of the type of stimuli used by Jenkins et al. (2011).

you can recognise them. Have a look at Figure 1.3. How many different people do you think are in shown in the photographs?

Figure 1.3 is based on a study by Jenkins et al. (2011) and illustrates the variability between different images of the same person. In their novel sorting task Jenkins and colleagues investigated how accurately people could 'tell faces together' that is decide that different images were the same person, although the appearance could vary from photo to photo. Participants were given 40 different photographs of faces and asked to sort them into one pile per identity; there were only two identities in total. Those who were not familiar with the faces thought there were many more identities and placed them in 3 to 16 different piles, with 9 piles being the most common. Interestingly, participants rarely confused the two different identities as being the same person and placed them in the same pile only 1% of the time. This study illustrates that there is a huge amount of variation between different images of the same person, for example differences in lighting, viewpoints, expression, and sometimes more so than between different persons (Jenkins et al., 2011). This study also demonstrates that to try and understand why face recognition goes wrong we should be using images that show natural variability, than being too controlled. It has been argued that one of the problems with face recognition research is that the stimuli used are too tightly controlled and artificial, and therefore may not generalise to how we recognise faces in real life (Burton, 2013).

Eyewitness identification

Another aspect of face recognition where there is often variability between unfamiliar faces is eyewitness identification. Eyewitness identification is extremely persuasive evidence in criminal cases; however, as with other tasks that rely on face recognition, it is not as accurate as the prosecution lawyers would have us believe. When someone witnesses a crime involving one or more people, the police will interview the witness to get a description of the culprit and then if the police later arrest someone they suspect as being the assailant, they might ask the witness to come to the police station to see if they can pick the suspect out of a lineup.

In the UK traditionally lineups or parades used to be 'live' and involved placing the suspect among a group of other similar-looking individuals, and the witness had to try and identify the person they had seen previously, usually from behind a glass screen. On the day the parade was due to be shown to the witness the police would go out onto the street and try and find volunteers who looked like the suspect to stand in the lineup as foils. As you could imagine, this was often a difficult task for the police to do, especially if the suspect looked distinctive in any way, and then there was the risk that the lineup could be biased if the suspect stood out as compared to the other members of the lineup. It's therefore not surprising that research found that 52% of the time live lineups were cancelled due to the suspect not turning up, the witness not appearing or a lack of suitable volunteers to take part in the lineup (Pike et al., 2002).

Currently in the UK, video lineups have replaced live lineups, meaning that lots of problems, such as the suspect not turning up and the lack of suitable volunteers to stand in the lineup have been eliminated. In a video lineup a witness is shown a series of nine moving clips, one at a time. One clip will be the suspect and the other eight are similar-looking foils or fillers that have been taken from a large database of volunteer images. Each clip is 15 seconds long and begins with the person looking straight to the camera and then turning their head to the right and then to the left, so that the front of the face is shown along with both profiles. On average a witness would see nine of these video clips and then the whole lineup is shown twice, following police legis-lation PACE code D in England and Wales (Home Office, 2017). However, video lineups are not used universally throughout the world; some countries still use live lineups and others use still photographs, such as in the USA (for a review of eyewitness iden-tification around the world see Fitzgerald et al., 2020).

Psychological research investigating the reliability of eyewitness identification has tended to use experimental and also survey methods. Surveys from the UK have found that suspects are picked out of a lineup on average 40% of the time. This does not necessarily mean that the suspect is always the perpetrator of the crime, as innocent people can be placed in police lineups and falsely recognised by witnesses; this is explored later in the book (see Chapter 3). Furthermore, surveys have also found that 40% of the time witnesses choose someone from a lineup that the police knew was an innocent foil, which does suggest that eyewitness identification is less than reliable (Horry et al., 2012; Memon et al., 2011).

When an eyewitness identifies a suspect from a police lineup this can be compelling evidence for obtaining a conviction in court. However there have been occasions where innocent people have been placed in lineups as they were in the wrong place at the wrong time and vaguely matched the suspect's description. In the USA there is an organisation called the Innocence Project who use DNA evidence to exonerate people who have been wrongfully convicted of crimes they did not commit. At the time of writing, 375 people have been exonerated by the Innocence Project, including 21 who served time on death row. There are still many more people who are incarcerated claiming they have been wrongfully convicted and who the Innocence Project are trying to help. Of the 375 cases that the Innocence Project has exonerated, 70% (that is 269 people) were falsely convicted and imprisoned based on eyewitness misidentification. On average people who had been wrongfully convicted had spent 14 years in prison before being released after exoneration. The real-life example in the box describes just one of the most famous cases of wrongful conviction due to eyewitness misidentification. If you are interested in reading more about the Innocence Project, please see their website (https://innocenceproject.org) for information on other cases.

Real-life example of misidentification

In 1984 a man broke into the apartment of Jennifer Thompson-Cannino and sexually assaulted her at knifepoint; then later that night the same man broke into another apartment and sexually assaulted another woman. Jennifer Thompson-Cannino was a 22-year-old college student at the time and after the attack she helped the police artist create a composite of the attacker. She was then shown a photo lineup and picked Ronald Cotton, a 22-year-old man who looked like her sketch and who had had a previous run-in with the police. She was then shown a live lineup and picked Ronald again. Ronald insisted he was innocent and that Jennifer was mistaken in identifying him. The only other evidence against Ronald was that he had a torch that matched the description of the one the perpetrator had used, and that the sole of his shoe had rubber that was consistent with the rubber found at the crime scene. However, despite having an alibi supported by family members, Ronald was convicted of rape and burglary, and sentenced to life in prison.

While serving his sentence in North Carolina Central Prison, a new inmate arrived called Bobby Poole. He looked very much like Ronald, and other inmates and prison staff mistook them for one another due to their similar appearance. A fellow inmate told Ronald that he'd heard Bobby admit to the rape of Jennifer Thompson-Cannino and the other woman that night. Ronald Cotton won a new trial and Bobby Poole was taken to the court; however, when Jennifer saw him she didn't recognise him as being her attacker. To make matters worse for Ronald, the second victim, who had previously identified someone else, now identified Ronald as her attacker and he was now convicted of both rapes and received another life sentence.

In 1995 Ronald's defence team were given access to all the evidence from the trial and as there had been some scientific advances, DNA tests were conducted on the swabs taken from the victims. The results showed conclusively that the DNA did not match with Ronald Cotton but was a match for Bobby Poole. After over a decade of imprisonment Ronald Cotton was exonerated and released. In 1997 Jennifer and Ronald met each other, and eventually became friends and travelled around the country talking about wrongful convictions, especially for eyewitness identification procedures. If you want to read more about this case, Jennifer and Ronald have written a book based on their experiences at the time (Thompson-Canino, Cotton & Torneo, 2010).

Source: Details from Innocence Project website
(https://innocenceproject.org)

There are several issues with the way the police conducted the identification procedures that resulted in Ronald Cotton being misidentified. In the first photo lineup that Jennifer saw, the real perpetrator Bobby Poole wasn't there, and the only person who resembled the perpetrator was Ronald Cotton. When Jennifer picked Ronald, the police officer said, 'we thought that was him', so this helped to reinforce Jennifer's decision that she was correct to select Ronald from the lineup. Jennifer was then shown the live lineup, which again didn't have her real attacker present; she identified Ronald again and was now confident in her decision that it was Ronald who was her attacker. This phenomenon is called unconscious transference, where the memory of Ronald Cotton's face had replaced that of Bobby Poole's face in Jennifer's memory; this issue will be explored further in Chapter 3. This also ensured that Jennifer was a confident witness in court, which made her evidence more convincing to the jury. One issue that the police could not have controlled was that Ronald was Black and Jennifer was white, and there is a large amount of evidence that has shown that people are worse at recognising faces that belong to someone who is from a different race. This issue will be discussed further in Chapter 4.

Misidentifications via police lineups do not occur only in the USA. There have been several innocent people also convicted through faulty eyewitness identification in the UK. One prominent example was Andrew Malkinson, who was convicted of rape in 2004 after being identified by the victim from a police lineup. At the time there was no DNA evidence to prove his innocence, so he spent 17 years in prison for a crime he did not commit. Andrew's case was twice rejected by the Criminal Cases Review Commission (CCRC), the public body that is meant to investigate miscarriages of justice, in 2012 and 2020. It wasn't until 2023 that he was finally declared innocent by the Court of Appeal as DNA evidence proved that he was not the attacker. Cases such as those of Andrew Malkinson and Ronald Cotton show the fallibility of eyewitness identification and psychologists have investigated why innocent people are mistakenly chosen from lineups using experimental research.

Psychological research that has investigated how accurate people are at making identifications from lineups, has tried to simulate what it is like for eyewitnesses who are tasked with making an identification. In the typical eyewitness paradigm, there is a study phase where participants (witnesses) are shown some type of event, e.g. a mock crime of a thief stealing a laptop or handbag. The event might occur in a live setting with actors, or more often through watching a video. Then after a delay is the test phase where lineups are shown to the participants (witnesses) and they must try and identify the person they saw previously from a group of people. There are also two types of possible lineups that are used in this research. The lineup can be either target present (TP), which contains the person that has been seen previously, and the aim is to see if that target can correctly identified as the previously seen person. Alternatively, the witness might see a target absent (TA) lineup where the person they have seen previously is replaced by a similar looking foil (innocent suspect) and the aim here is to simulate the situation that the police have arrested the wrong person, and to see if a witness chooses someone regardless of whether the person they have seen previously is in a lineup, i.e. making a false identification or misidentification.

Psychological research has also highlighted another important aspect of showing a lineup to a witness and that is whether the person administering the lineup knows the identity of the suspect. In the UK (at this time of writing) there are no regulations about whether the person administering the lineup is aware of the identity of the suspect and in many cases they might know who the suspect is as they may well have encountered them prior to the lineup. There is a wealth of research that has suggested that the person administering a lineup to a witness should not know in advance who the suspect is and therefore the lineup is called 'double blind' as neither the witness or the person administering the lineup knows in advance the identity of the suspect (Wells et al., 2020). More often a lineup is administered 'single blind', where the person showing the lineup knows who the suspect is, and research has shown that when this is the case the person showing the lineup can exhibit behaviour (even unconsciously) that indicates to the witness who the suspect is and increases the chances the suspect is chosen. Increasing the likelihood that a suspect is chosen can be beneficial if the suspect is guilty of the offence; however, single blind administration has also been found to increase misidentification of innocent suspects (Kovera

& Evelo, 2020). Witnesses might be more likely to choose the suspect even though they do not necessary recognise anyone due to demand characteristics of seeing a lineup, as the police are often convinced that the suspect is the culprit of a crime and the witness's role is to choose that suspect. The witness may assume that the police have conducted their investigation effectively and the real culprit is in the lineup and therefore they should choose someone.

Another aspect of showing a witness a lineup, that occurs not only in experiments but also in real police procedures, is that prior to seeing the lineup, a witness is given unbiased instructions and told 'the person you saw commit the offence may or may not be in the lineup'. This instruction is an important aspect of showing a lineup, as research found that witnesses who were not given these instructions were much more likely to choose someone from a lineup, and make a false identification of an innocent person from a target absent lineup (Clark, 2005). The unbiased instructions are included in the guidelines in the UK and witnesses are always told the person they saw 'may or may not be present' (COPFS, 2019; Home Office, 2017). This does not guarantee that innocent persons will not be mis-identified from lineups, and there are lots of other factors that can influence when face recognition goes wrong. That is the focus of most of the chapters in this book.

Conclusion

Face recognition is important for lots of different tasks including social interactions when we need to recognise familiar people we know such as friends, family and work colleagues and for verifying a person's identity such as determining whether a person is the same identity as the photo on a passport or driving license. Research has shown that familiar faces are more easily recognised than unfamiliar faces, whereas when faces are unfamiliar, face recognition is much more likely to go wrong. Face recognition research has used various experimental methods to investigate face recognition, from memory recognition and face matching experiments to eyewitness paradigms, all of which have shown that people make mistakes when it comes to identifying unfamiliar faces. When face recognition goes wrong in real life, such as mis-identifications of innocent individuals from police lineups, there can be serious consequences resulting in miscarriages of justice. Although there are some measures that can be put in place to try and reduce misidentifications, there are still many other factors that can influence whether a face is correctly recognised or not, and they will be explored further in the rest of this book.

(Answer to Figure 1.1: they are two different people.)

References

Alenezi, H. M., Bindemann, M., Fysh, M. C., & Johnston, R. A. (2015). Face matching in a long task: Enforced rest and desk-switching cannot maintain identification accuracy. *PeerJ, 2015*(8). https://doi.org/10.7717/peerj.1184.

Andrews, S., Jenkins, R., Cursiter, H., & Burton, A. M. (2015). Telling faces together: Learning new faces through exposure to multiple instances. *Quarterly Journal of Experimental Psychology*, 68(10), 2041–2050. https://doi.org/10.1080/17470218.2014.1003949.

Bartel, S. J., Toews, K., Gronhovd, L., & Prime, S. L. (2018). 'Do I know you?' Altering hairstyle affects facial recognition. *Visual Cognition*, 26(3), 149–155. https://doi.org/10.1080/13506285.2017.1394412.

Bonner, L., Burton, A. M. and Bruce, V. (2003). Getting to know you: How we learn new faces. *Visual Cognition*, 10(5), 527–536. https://doi.org/10.1080/13506280244000168.

Bruce, V. (1982). Changing faces: Visual and non-visual coding processes in face recognition. *The British Journal of Psychology*, 73(1), 105–116.

Bruce, V., Henderson, Z., Greenwood, K., Hancock, P. J. B., Burton, A. M., & Miller, P. (1999). Verification of face identities from images captured on video. *Journal of Experimental Psychology: Applied*, 5(4), 339–360. https://doi.org/10.1037/1076-898X.5.4.339.

Bruce, V., Henderson, Z., Newman, C., & Burton, A. M. (2001). Matching identities of familiar and unfamiliar faces caught on CCTV images. *Journal of Experimental Psychology: Applied*, 7(3), 207–218. https://doi.org/10.1037/1076-898X.7.3.207.

Burton, A. M. (2013). Why has research in face recognition progressed so slowly? The importance of variability. *Quarterly Journal of Experimental Psychology*, 66(8), 1467–1485. https://doi.org/10.1080/17470218.2013.800125.

Burton, A. M., White, D., & McNeill, A. (2010). The Glasgow face matching test. *Behavior Research Methods*, 42(1), 286–291. https://doi.org/10.3758/BRM.42.1.286.

Burton, A. M., Wilson, S., Cowan, M., & Bruce, V. (1999). Face recognition in poor-quality video: Evidence from Security Surveillance. *Psychological Science*, 10(3), 243–248. https://doi.org/10.1111/1467-9280.00144.

Clark, S. E. (2005). A re-examination of the effects of biased lineup instructions in eyewitness identification. *Law and Human Behavior*, 29 (4), 395–424. https://doi.org/10.1007/s10979-005-5690-7.

COPFS. (2019). Lord Advocate's guidelines on the conduct of visual identification procedures. www.copfs.gov.uk/publications/lord-advocate-s-guidelines-visual-identification-procedures/html/.

Davies, G. M., & Young, A. W. (2017). Research on face recognition: The Aberdeen influence. *British Journal of Psychology*, 108(4), 812–830. https://doi.org/10.1111/bjop.12243.

Ellis, H. D. (1975). Recognizing faces. *British Journal of Psychology*, 66(4), 409–426. https://doi.org/10.1111/j.2044-8295.1975.tb01477.x.

Ellis, H. D., Shepherd, J. W., & Davies, G. M. (1979). Identification of familiar and unfamiliar faces from internal and external features; some implications for theories of face recognition. *Perception*, 8, 431–439.

Fitzgerald, R., Rubinova, E., & Juncu, S. (2020). Eyewitness identification around the world. In J. M. Smith, A. M. Toglia & M. Lampinen (eds), *Methods, measures, and theories in eyewitness identification tasks*. Routledge.

Fysh, M. C., & Bindemann, M. (2017). Forensic face matching: A review. *Face Processing: Systems, Disorders and Cultural Differences*, September, 1–20.

Fysh, M. C., & Bindemann, M. (2018). The Kent Face Matching Test. *British Journal of Psychology*, 109(2), 219–231. https://doi.org/10.1111/bjop.12260.

Hancock, P. J. B., Bruce, V., & Burton, A. M. (2000). Recognition of unfamiliar faces. *Trends in Cognitive Sciences*, 4(9), 330–337. https://doi.org/10.1016/S1364-6613(00)01519-9.

Havard, C. (2021). The importance of internal and external features in matching own and other race faces. *Perception*. https://doi.org/10.1177/03010066211043464.

Hill, H., & Bruce, V. (1996). Effects of lighting on the perception of facial surfaces. *Journal of Experimental Psychology: Human Perception and Performance*, 22(4), 986–1004. https://doi.org/10.1037/0096-1523.22.4.986.

Home Office. (2017). CODE D Revised Code of Practice for the identification of persons by police officers. www.tso.co.uk.

Horry, R., Memon, A., Wright, D. B., & Milne, R. (2012). Predictors of eyewitness identification decisions from video lineups in England: a field study. *Law and Human Behavior*, 36(4), 257–265. https://doi.org/10.1037/h0093959.

Jenkins, R., White, D., Van Montfort, X., & Mike Burton, A. (2011). Variability in photos of the same face. *Cognition*, 121(3), 313–323. https://doi.org/10.1016/j.cognition.2011.08.001.

Kemp, R., Towell, N., & Pike, G. (1997). When seeing should not be believing: photographs, credit cards and fraud. *Applied Cognitive Psychology*, 11(3), 211–222. https://doi.org/10.1002/(sici)1099-0720 (199706)11:3<211:aid-acp430>3.3.co;2-f

Kokje, E., Bindemann, M., & Megreya, A. M. (2018). Cross-race correlations in the abilities to match unfamiliar faces. *Acta Psychologica*, 185 (January), 13–21. https://doi.org/10.1016/j.actpsy.2018.01.006.

Kovera, M. B., & Evelo, A. J. (2020). Improving eyewitness-identification evidence through double-blind lineup administration. *Current Directions in Psychological Science*, 29(6), 563–568. https://doi.org/10.1177/0963721420969366.

Megreya, A. M., & Bindemann, M. (2009). Revisiting the processing of internal and external features of unfamiliar faces: The headscarf effect. *Perception*, 38(12), 1831–1848. https://doi.org/10.1068/p6385.

Megreya, A. M., & Burton, A. M. (2007). Hits and false positives in face matching: A familiarity-based dissociation. *Perception & Psychophysics*, 69(7), 1175–1184.

Megreya, A. M., Memon, A., & Havard, C. (2012). The headscarf effect: Direct evidence from the eyewitness identification paradigm. *Applied Cognitive Psychology*, 26(September 2011), 308–315.

Memon, A., Havard, C., Clifford, B., Gabbert, F., & Watt, M. (2011). A field evaluation of the VIPER system: a new technique for eliciting eyewitness identification evidence. *Psychology, Crime & Law*, 17(8), 711–729. https://doi.org/10.1080/10683160903524333.

O'Toole, A. J., Edelman, S., & Bülthoff, H. H. (1998). Stimulus-specific effects in face recognition over changes in viewpoint. *Vision Research*, 38(15–16),2351–2363. https://doi.org/10.1016/S0042-6989(98)00042-X

Patterson, K. E., & Baddeley, A. D. (1977). When face recognition fails. *Journal of Experimental Psychology: Human Learning and Memory*, 3 (4), 406–417. https://doi.org/10.1037/0278-7393.3.4.406.

Pike, G., Brace, N., & Kynan, S. (2002). *The visual identification of suspects: Procedures and practice*. London: Home Office.

Stantic, M., Brewer, R., Duchaine, B., Banissy, M. J., Bate, S., Susilo, T., Catmur, C., & Bird, G. (2022). The Oxford Face Matching Test: A non-biased test of the full range of individual differences in face perception. *Behavior Research Methods*, 54(1), 158–173. https://doi. org/10.3758/s13428-021-01609-2.

Stevens, C. (2021). Person identification at airports during passport control. *Forensic Face Matching: Research and Practice*, 1–14. https://doi. org/10.1093/OSO/9780198837749.003.0001.

Thompson-Canino, J., Cotton, R. & Torneo, E. (2010). *Picking cotton: Our memoir of injustice and redemption*. New York: St Martin's Griffin.

Wang, Y., Thomas, J., Weissgerber, S. C., Kazemini, S., Ul-Haq, I., & Quadflieg, S. (2015). The headscarf effect revisited: Further evidence for a culture-based internal face processing advantage. *Perception*, 44 (3), 328–336. https://doi.org/10.1068/p7940.

Wells, G. L., Kovera, M. B., Douglass, A. B., Brewer, N., Meissner, C. A., & Wixted, J. T. (2020). Policy and procedure recommendations for the collection and preservation of eyewitness identification evidence. *Law and Human Behavior*, 44(1), 3–36. https://doi.org/10.1037/lhb0000359.

White, D., Kemp, R. I., Jenkins, R., Matheson, M., & Burton, A. M. (2014). Passport officers' errors in face matching. *PLoS ONE*, 9(8). http s://doi.org/10.1371/journal.pone.0103510.

Young, A. W., & Burton, A. M. (2017). Recognizing faces. *Current Directions in Psychological Science*, 26(3), 212–217. https://doi.org/ 10.1177/0963721416688114.

Young, A. W., Hay, D. C., McWeeny, K. H., Flude, B. M., & Ellis, A. W. (1985). Matching familiar and unfamiliar faces on internal and external features. *Perception*, 14(6), 737–746. https://doi.org/10.1068/p140737

2 I recognise your face but who are you?

Everyday face recognition errors

Introduction

As you read in Chapter 1, face recognition is important for a variety of social interactions; however, it is not always 100% accurate, and there are times when people make mistakes. Have you ever had an embarrassing incident where you have not recognised someone you've met before, or you've forgotten someone's name? This often seems to happen just when you are about to try to introduce them to someone else. Have you ever waved and said 'hello' to someone only to realise that it wasn't the person you thought it was, but in fact a total stranger? These errors can be common, and I will describe a couple of examples of embarrassing everyday errors in face recognition that I have personally made. I once saw someone who I mistakenly thought was the woman whose house I had bought, so I ran across the street to say hello to her and talk to her about the house, but as soon as I began speaking to her and she spoke back to me in a French accent I realised that I didn't know her at all, and she was someone who just looked similar to the person I knew. I then apologised for my mistake and went on my way, although I got the distinct impression she thought I was completely bonkers. There was another awkward incident at a party I attended many years ago; I saw the side profile of a man's head and thought he was my boyfriend, so I sat on his knee; however, when I looked at his face I realised that he wasn't my boyfriend at all and both of us got a fright! Fortunately, he was a very understanding chap, although I don't think my boyfriend at the time was overly happy!

DOI: 10.4324/9781003177128-2

There have also been instances where I haven't instigated the interaction, but people recognise me and say hello or wave at me from cars as they drive past, and I have no idea who they are but they seem to know who I am.

This chapter will explore the everyday errors we make when recognising faces and trying to identify people, the psychological research that has been conducted to investigate these mistakes, and theories that have been developed to try to explain why we make these errors. It will begin by looking at some seminal research on everyday memory errors for faces that have been used to develop theoretical models of face recognition. Another topic will be the errors people make when seeing faces, and when a face may seem familiar but we do not know why. The last part of the chapter will divert from face recognition and explore when a face is familiar, and is associated with quite a bit of information, but there is no recall of the person's name.

Early research on everyday face recognition errors

One of the early studies to investigate everyday face recognition errors was a classic study by Young et al. (1985), although it should be noted that they were looking at identification using facial information and non-facial information, so in the strictest terms they were looking at identification errors. In order to investigate everyday errors in recognising faces they asked 22 participants to keep diaries of all the difficulties and errors they made when trying to identify people over an eight-week period. They were asked specifically to record the following information in their records:

1 **Type of incident** – giving a brief description of what happened.
2 **What information was available at the time**. They were given a checklist that included facial features, hair, clothing, name and voice; they were asked to cross off the sources of information that were not available and rank the other sources of information that helped the recognition.
3 **General details** – was it a famous person they had seen on TV? What were the viewing conditions like at the time?

4   **People involved** – for each person involved the diarist was asked to rate how well they knew them on a scale of 1 (unknown) to 5 (very well known).

5   **The way the incident ended** – were they able to identify them in the end or not?

6   **Person details available** – what details they were unable to recall, e.g. name, occupations, etc.

The findings from this study revealed that over the weeks the participants made many errors, resulting in over 900 incidents being recorded which were classified into different categories listed below. They are listed according to their prevalence, beginning with the most frequently occurring:

- **Person misidentified**. the most common error was mis-identifications of one person for another. In some incidents this was an unfamiliar person being mistakenly identified as being someone who was familiar, while in other incidents a familiar person was mistakenly thought to be another familiar person.

- **The person seemed familiar only**. In these cases, a person appeared to be familiar, but the participant was unable to recall any details about that person, such as their name or occupation. Often these incidents involved persons who were not highly familiar, although in some cases they did involve people who were highly familiar. For some incidents, it was a familiar person, but in an unexpected place, e.g. the participant was in the bank and a local shop keeper was in the queue. When a person seemed familiar, but no further information about the person could be recalled, some parti-cipants used a strategy where they would go through all the possible contexts in while they might know this person to aid their identification, e.g. is it a person from work, a neighbour etc. Sometimes using this searching strategy was successful and other times unsuccessful. In some cases, the person was identified, and other times the person was not and in some occurrences the participants realised that the person was in fact someone who was not known to them.

- **Difficulty in retrieving full details of the person**. In these incidents a person was recognised as being familiar and some information about them was recalled (for example their occupation), but the person's name was not recalled.
- **Person unrecognised**. One of the most common errors was a failure to recognise a familiar person. This is completely understandable when the person is not very familiar and the viewing conditions are poor; however, many of the incidents had good viewing conditions, and involved highly familiar people.
- **Decision problems**. For these occurrences a participant wasn't sure if it was a particular person or not. It could be that it looked like a specific individual, but the participant was not sure it was that person, or they thought it could be one of two people, but again couldn't be sure which one.

Young et al. (1985) came to the conclusion that these types of errors of face recognition demonstrated that when trying to identify a person there was a sequential access to different types of information that was stored in memory, and that the information would then be retrieved in a certain order. For example, first the face must be deemed to be familiar, before searching for information about the person; a person can then be identified (e.g. the shop keeper) despite other information not being recalled (e.g. their name). Interestingly, there were never any incidents reported whereby participants said they recognised a person, recalled their name (e.g. John Smith), but could not remember any details about them (e.g. their occupation, or how they knew them). Using the findings from their study Young et al. (1985) were able to develop a model of person recognition (see Figure 2.1).

In this model the representational systems create descriptions of the person we have just encountered (e.g. face, voice, build, etc.), which are used to activate the recognition units which decide how closely the descriptions match those of someone we already know; the recognition units can access the information in the person identity nodes that contain descriptions stored of people we know. According to Young et al. (1985) there is a person identity node for each person we know containing enough details about each individual so that we can identify

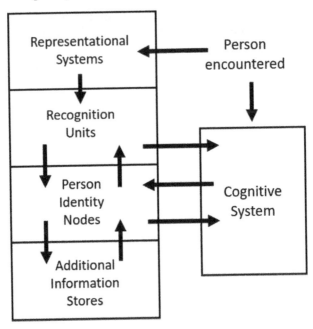

Figure 2.1 Young et al.'s model of person recognition.
Source: Young et al. (1985)

them. Names are stored separately in the additional information stores. The cognitive system is involved in the decision-making process and can feed back at any one stage to find more information about the person that is encountered. However, there might be instances when the cognitive system is unable to make an identification and face recognition 'may go wrong'.

Young et al. (1985) applied their model to explain the incidents that had been recorded by the participants. When a person was not recognised, they suggested this was because the descriptions (e.g. face, hair etc.) produced by the representational systems failed to activate the recognition units. When a person was misidentified, it was because they resembled a known person and the recognition units would be activated, suggesting that the person was known, and this was most likely to happen in a context in which the person would expect to be seen. When one familiar person was misidentified as being another, the recognition units would be activated but make contact with the wrong personal identity nodes, causing a misidentification. When a person was thought to be familiar only, the recognition units were activated, but there would be a block to the corresponding person identity nodes. When the person seemed familiar but there were problems in retrieving the full details, it was suggested that there was a block at the additional stores section of the model preventing access to their additional information, including a name. The cognitive system monitors the results of the recognition system and tries to prevent errors. It is thought to be crucial when there are decision problems and when we aren't sure if the person we are seeing is actually someone we know, or when we can't decide whether it's one person or another person.

Young et al.'s (1985) paper involved a novel study, collecting rich data from people recording their everyday experiences. However, one of the problems of using diary reports of face recognition errors as evidence is that diaries can be biased, because people only report errors that they are conscious of and that are easy to interpret, and they can also distort errors in ways that make them seem more obvious than they actually are (Young, 1988). Furthermore, diaries rely on an individual's memory for what they experienced and it can be that not all incidents were correctly recalled. One way to ensure that errors are correctly recorded is to conduct studies under laboratory conditions where there's no reporting of biases, because the errors can be systematically examined. Most of the research that has investigated face recognition errors has used lab-based experiments, where all the variables can be controlled.

At the time the Young et al. (1985) model of face recognition was ground-breaking; however, it has been critiqued as being over-simplified, although it should be noted that elements have persisted into subsequent models of face recognition, such as the classic Bruce and Young (1986) model of face recognition and the Burton et al. (1999) IAC model of face recognition. The Bruce and Young (1986) model in particular (see Figure 2.2) has become one of the most widely cited models of face recognition (Schweinberger & Burton, 2011). This model suggests face recognition involves serial processing and is very similar to the

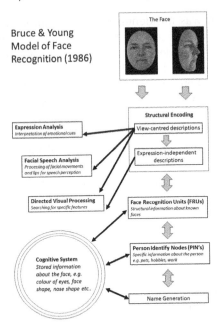

Figure 2.2 The Bruce and Young model of face recognition.
Source: Bruce and Young (1986)

earlier Young et al. (1985) model. Bruce and Young's (1986) model of face recognition also suggests that to correctly identify a face, all the stages need to be completed and a breakdown or block at any one of the stages will lead to an error or failure of face recognition.

According to Bruce and Young's (1986) model, face recognition and the perception of facial expression/emotions occur independently and in parallel. When a face is first seen, the recognition process begins with structural encoding, and a basic representation of the facial features including view centred descriptions of the face is created. This information can be used for expressional analysis to determine the emotional state of the person (e.g. whether they are smiling) and facial speech analysis (whether they are talking). Expression analysis and facial speech analysis occur in parallel to the face recognition processing and do not influence whether we recognise someone or not. This means we can surmise someone's expression regardless of whether we know them or not. In the directed visual processing stage, there is a search for anything to help recognition, such as whether the person is wearing glasses, and whether they have a beard or other distinctive feature that can aid identification. In the face recognition units (FRUs) there are images stored of familiar faces we know, one for each person, and the cognitive system tries to match the face that is currently being viewed with those stored in memory. If there is a match then the person identity nodes (PINs) can be activated and they store all the biographical information we have about people we know, for example what job does this person have? What hobbies? Do they have a dog? Or if it's a famous actor it might be which films or TV shows has this person starred in? The PINs can also be activated by other information, for example if we hear a familiar voice on the radio, while the FRUS can only be activated by the image of a person's face. Only once the PINs are activated can a name be generated. For example: 'That man with dark brown hair who was in several Marvel films, including *Iron Man*, oh, its Robert Downey Jr.' The cognitive system is involved in the decision making processes and ultimately decides if the person is who we think they are, or if we don't know them.

Young et al.'s (1985) diary study also supports the Bruce and Young (1986) model, when persons failed to fully recognise individuals and failed to retrieve any information about them, although they seemed familiar. The Bruce and Young model suggests the feelings of familiarity would mean the FRUS were activated, but in turn did not activate the PINs and therefore the semantic information about the person was not retrieved, including their name. In the diary study, often when face recognition failed in this way it was because the person was seen in a location they were not usually encountered in, and this is the topic of the next part of this chapter.

Seeing faces out of context: the 'butcher on the bus' phenomenon

Recently I was in my local supermarket and a middle-aged lady with an Irish accent came up to me and said 'hello' and then started making small talk. Her face was so familiar, and I knew I recognised her from somewhere, and she clearly knew me, but I couldn't for the life of me think where I knew her from. Was it from work? Was she one of my neighbours? I didn't feel I could ask who she was, or her name, as it was clear we knew each other, and we continued our conversation about the weather, and local news. Then she mentioned that her husband had been walking her dog Frankie as she had been unwell and then it all clicked into place. I had met this woman several times each week as we both walked our dogs in the same woods and had done so for several years, but because I was seeing her in another context – a supermarket rather than the woods, and without her dog – I did not recognise her. This is called the 'butcher on the bus' phenomenon: it's when you meet somebody out of the context of the usual setting where you most frequently encounter them, and because you don't have that contextual information you fail to identify who they are.

The most distinctive feature of the 'butcher on the bus' phenomenon is that usually when we see somebody who's familiar it's accompanied by the information of why we know that person is familiar. For example, it could be somebody from work, or somebody who drinks in the same pub we frequent, or someone who goes to the same gym. However, with the 'butcher on the bus' phenomenon we can have that sense of familiarity with no identifying information as to why that person is familiar, often because they are in a different location (i.e. a different context from where we would normally see them). Psychological research investigating the 'butcher on the bus' phenomenon is often used to illustrate the difference between familiarity and recognition memory. Familiarity is a subjective feeling that you have previously encountered a place, person or object, but you do not recall the details of when you had that experience. For example, you see a face that's familiar, you think you must know this person, but you can't think who the person is. In contrast, recognition is recognising a previously encountered place, object or person, along with the information of when you previously encountered it. For example when you see a person's face, you know it's familiar and you know exactly who that person is because you recognise them and you know their identity, and some information about them (e.g. they are my neighbour from two doors down). One of the first recorded incidences of familiarity and recognition was by William James, one of the founding fathers of psychology. Writing in 1893, James recalled that when he went to visit a friend he saw a painting, and thought he recognised the painting; he was sure he had seen it before, but couldn't remember where. It was only later on when he realised it was actually a copy of a painting that he himself owned and that was on his wall at home (cited in Brown, 2020).

The majority of the literature claims the term 'butcher on the bus' was first coined by Mandler (1980), who gave an example in his paper of seeing someone who was familiar on a bus and trying to figure out where he knew the person from, before coming to the conclusion it was the butcher from the supermarket. However, it has been suggested that he borrowed this illustration from an earlier researcher, Charles Osgood, who wrote about the problems of recognising people out of context in 1953 (cited in MacLeod, 2020). Regardless of who first came up with the term, the experience of not recognising someone because they are met out of context is a common phenomenon. In the study of Young et al. (1985), the 'butcher on the bus' phenomenon accounted for approximately 25% of all problems with person identification; most of the time they were successfully resolved, but it could take up to ten seconds for the person to correctly identify who it was, or in some cases they simply gave up. In another diary study by Bartlett, Strater and Fulton in 1990 (cited by Brown, 2020), they also found that the 'butcher on the bus' experience accounted for a quarter of all face recognition errors.

It seems the 'butcher on the bus' phenomenon is fairly common and most people have experienced it from time to time. Brown (2020) conducted a large survey of 359 respondents aged from 18 years of age all the way to 89 years of age investigating the 'butcher on the bus' phenomenon. When asked the question 'have you ever run into someone who looks familiar but you can't place where you know them from?', nearly every person (99%) in every age group agreed that this had happened to them at some time. Brown (2020) suggested that what is special about the 'butcher on the bus' experience is that when you come across someone who is familiar, it is very unusual to not have any idea about the context of why that person is familiar.

There have been several lab-based psychological studies that have investigated the 'butcher on the bus' phenomenon and the influence of changing the context in which faces are seen; this usually involves pairing an image of a face with another image of an object, or visual scene. The advantage of lab-based studies over diary studies is that they don't rely on participants to consciously remember and record their experiences, and they can control exactly what participants see, by presenting certain images and recording any responses (e.g. 'new' or 'old') to faces that were presented. Early studies investigating the effect of changes in context on face recognition found that people were more accurate at recognising faces if they were paired with the same face they that they had seen during the study phase, and less accurate if they were paired with a different face. So simply changing the face pair reduced the accuracy of remembering previously seen faces (Watkins et al., 1976). This can be applied to real-life encounters too, as sometimes we get used to seeing people along with other people, for example, work colleagues who we see with other work colleagues, or students who we see along with other students, and then when we see a person out of the normal group we are used to seeing them in, then we may be less likely to identify them, although they may seem familiar.

Other studies have taken a different approach to investigating how we recognise faces out of context by presenting faces on a specific background image during a study phase, and then changing the background images that the faces are presented on. Davies and Milne (1982) presented unfamiliar faces on various backgrounds during a study phase, and then during the test phase faces were presented either on the same background or a different background. They found that face recognition was more accurate for faces that were presented on the same backgrounds as they had first been encountered, and therefore that the context was useful for correctly identifying the faces.

Another method for investigating the 'butcher on the bus' phenomenon is to employ a classic memory paradigm called the remember/know procedure, devised by Tulving (1985). In this test participants are presented with a series of items (e.g. they could be faces, objects or words). Then after a delay they are presented with another series of items and asked to report whether they consciously 'remember' seeing the item previously, or just 'know' they have seen the item before. The remember response is the same as recognition mentioned earlier, while the know response is based on familiarity, the sense that an item or face has been seen before. The difference between remember decisions is that the person can remember details about the item, the 'how' and the 'when' they previously saw it, which requires a deeper level of processing and involves episodic memory, while with know decisions there is a feeling of familiarity, but not necessarily any other information, including the conscious recollection of when the information was presented and this involves semantic memory. In their study to investigate the butcher on the bus phenomenon Gruppuso et al. (2007) presented a series of photographs of faces in a study phase. Each face image was presented with a corresponding context photograph, for example a building, scenery, animals or sports. Participants were asked to rate on a scale of 1–6 (1 = very unlikely to 6 = very likely), whether the person, i.e. the face, would be associated with the context photo (see Figure 2.3 for an example). The aim was to promote a deeper form of semantic memory for each face and context photograph pair.

Then during a test phase, they were presented with faces that were paired with either the studied items, a different context item (switched), that had been presented previously with a different face, or new context item that had not been seen before. They were also presented with a new face that either had a previously seen context item, or a new context item. Participants were asked

Figure 2.3 Example of a face and context photograph.

to make judgements only about the faces, not the context items. For each face they had to decide if they had seen it before in the study phase, and secondly if they could 'remember' the face, that is remembered it along with the context photo, or if the face was just familiar but they weren't sure they could remember the context, they should select 'know'. The responses were analysed using *hits*, that is when a face was correctly recognised as having been seen before, and *false alarms* which is when a face was incorrectly claimed to have been seen before when it was in fact new. Participants were more likely to make a remember decision when the faces were tested with the same context image and more likely to make a know judgement when the face was paired with a switched, or with a new context image.

Gruppuso et al.'s (2007) findings support the 'butcher on the bus' phenomenon, as the faces were only thought to be familiar in the changed context picture, similar to seeing a person out of the usual context and being unable to fully identify who they are. Participants were more likely to make false alarms to faces (that is think they had seen a face before) if the faces were paired with a previously seen context image; this suggests that the familiarity of the context image was misattributed to seeing the face before. The misattribution of familiarity from the previously seen context image to a new previously unseen face is similar to unconscious transference, where familiarity is misattributed; this phenomenon will be explored in more detail in the next chapter. Gruppuso et al.'s (2007) work was replicated using a similar paradigm by Tunney et al. (2012). They found there were more remember decisions for faces paired with the same scene photographs, as compared to the switched or new context photographs.

A more recent approach to studying the effect of context on face recognition was taken by Laurence et al. (2021). They used a novel paradigm of presenting a familiar face in an unexpected context. In two experiments students were given surprise face recognition tasks, by being presented with an image of their lecturer at the end of unrelated experiments on learning faces at night. In the first experiment they were asked if they recognised anyone from the video and if they didn't, they were shown the video again. In the first showing of the video not one student recognised the lecturer and on the second viewing only four students out of the 42 who were familiar with the lecturer recognised her. In the second experiment, the same procedure was used, except on subsequent viewings the students were given a prompt, that one of the actors was a lecturer at their university. When viewing the video, 36 students out of 40 (66.7%) who were familiar with the lecturer recognised her this time. The findings from the first experiment suggest that when seeing a face out of context when you aren't expecting to see that face and it is in a context you wouldn't usually see it in (e.g. in the video of an experiment), then face recognition can be dramatically reduced. The second experiment shows that once a bit of context is given via a prompt, then this can increase the chances that a face is recognised.

Looking at the first research cited for the 'butcher on the bus' phenomenon in this chapter (Davies & Milne, 1982; Gruppuso et al., 2007), the Bruce and Young model explanation suggests you have this experience because the face recognition units (FRUs) are activated, but the second stage of the person identity nodes that store all the semantic identifying information about a person (e.g. they work in your local shop, or they are a student in your class) is not activated and therefore you have this sense of familiarity, but you can't place where you know the person from. Furthermore, because the person identity nodes are not activated then the name cannot be generated, and you can't remember what the person is called. The next section of this chapter diverges a little from face recognition per se by looking at naming faces, which is of course incredibly important for person identification.

Putting names to faces

Have you ever had the experience where you met someone you know, and you just can't remember their name? You might even remember the first letter of the name, and it feels like it is just out of reach, and you can't quite bring it into consciousness. This is a common phenomenon and doesn't happen just for people's names, and due to the corresponding feeling has been termed the tip of the tongue (TOT) state. This part of the chapter is going to look at the research on how we name faces and the TOT state for names.

It's all very well recognising a face as belonging to someone you know, but in many cases, you also need to remember what a person's name is, especially if you want to send them an email or look up their number in your phone. Some people, including me, can have difficulty in remembering people's names. I am often quite good at recognising faces and can remember quite a lot of information about those people, especially if they have a dog (are you sensing a theme here?), but I have real problems when it comes to remembering a person's name. Often my inability to remember someone's name happens at crucial times, for example just before I am about to introduce them to somebody. I also have this issue when I am trying to write an email to someone; I can usually bring the image of their face into my mind, recall lots of information about them, but for some reason I can't remember their name. I am not alone in my inability to recall people's names and surveys have revealed that failure to remember a person's name is fairly common and one of the most frustrating memory problems (Brédart & Vanootighem, 2021).

There has been a considerable amount of research which has revealed what many of us anecdotally know: that names can be more difficult to remember than faces. As Young et al. (1985) found in their diary study, participants could often remember a large amount of semantic information about an individual but were unable to remember that person's name. One study by McWeeny et al. (1987) investigated memory for names versus memory of other semantic information by presenting participants with faces and corresponding surnames and occupations. The participants were then presented with the faces again and asked to recall the surname and occupation associated with the faces. They found that semantic information about a person, i.e. their occupation, was more likely to be recalled as compared to a name. The advantage of semantic information was even found when the name and the occupation were the same word. For example, people were more likely to remember that someone was a baker than that their name is Mr Baker. This advantage for learning a person's occupation over their names was then replicated ten years later by Craigie and Hanley (1997), who presented faces paired with names and occupations and found that participants were more likely to recall names from a person's occupation than from their face.

Further research investigating the relationship between naming and face recognition has found that participants could judge a face as being familiar and retrieve that person's occupation, but still be unable to recall the person's name (Hanley & Cowell, 1988). Other research has found that it takes longer to name a face than to recall biographical information about the face (Scanlan & Johnston, 1997) or to make a yes/no decision about a person's occupation (Young et al., 1986). All the research findings mentioned so far give further support to the Bruce and Young (1986) model depicted in Figure 2.2. In this model the FRUs and the PINs that store the semantic information about a person need to be activated before a name can be recalled. However, not all the semantic information about a person needs to be recalled before retrieving their name; for example you may be able to name a famous actor without remembering every single film or TV show they have starred in.

Sometimes, when trying to name a familiar person, not only can biographical information about a person be retrieved, but occasionally the first letter of their name can also be retrieved. However, it seems the full name is just not accessible: the aforementioned TOT phenomenon (Brown & McNeill, 1966). One of the first studies to look at this in relation to naming found that when trying to retrieve the names of famous faces, participants first thought about the person's profession (they were an actor), then the last time they saw that person (they were in that film I watched last week), before then thinking about the first letter of the person's name or if the name sounded like another word (Yarmey, 1973). The findings suggested that names were retrieved using both semantic memory (the person's profession) and episodic (i.e. autobiographical) memory (remembering when the person was last seen).

In a more recent study, Brédart and Geurten (2020) investigated the TOT phenomenon for naming faces. In study one, participants were asked what strategies they used to help them retrieve a person's name. They were given a list of strategies and asked how often they used them, how easy the strategy was to use and how effective the strategy was in aiding retrieval. Participants reported that the most frequently and easily used and effective strategy, was searching for the context in which the person was usually encountered (e.g. at work, on TV, in the gym, etc.) as compared to trying to retrieve more biographical information about the person, or the first or last letters of their names, or names that sounded similar. In study two, participants were presented with the face of a famous person and asked to name them. If they couldn't name the person, but felt they might retrieve the name, they were asked to carry out a semantic search, to try and recall any biographical information, or a phonological search, such as the first or last sound of the person's name. Their findings revealed that people were more frequently able to retrieve semantic information about the famous face, as compared to phonological information, suggesting that phonological information may be more difficult to retrieve when trying to resolve naming retrieval failures.

All the evidence on naming thus far supports Burton and Bruce's (1992) assertion that names are stored separately from the biographical information we store about people, and that only once some semantic information about a person has been retrieved can the name be accessed. Evidence from neuroimaging studies and people who have suffered brain damage have revealed that there are different specific areas in the brain that are involved in storing biographic knowledge about familiar people (the right anterior temporal lobe, or rATL), and the retrieval of people's names (the left temporal pole, or LTP) (Brédart, 2017; Hanley, 2011). Studies with people who have brain damage, who are able to recall semantic information about familiar faces, but not familiar people's names, also support the theory that there are separate storage areas for names and faces (Busigny et al., 2015; Flude et al., 1989).

So far, all the evidence cited in this part of the chapter suggests that for us to remember a person's name we first need to remember some biographical information about them. In a review paper discussing the evidence for the Bruce and Young model, it was concluded that even 25 years later there was still evidence to support the claim that names could only be recalled once sematic information about a person was retrieved (Hanley, 2011). However, other research has found there are some instances when names can be accessed more easily than the retrieval of other semantic information about a person and the recognition of faces. This last part of the chapter will look at some more recent research investigating naming for faces.

Some researchers have suggested that the difficulty with retrieving people's names is a result of their uniqueness, unlike other properties about a person, such as their occupation, or their nationality, which may be shared by many other people (Brédart et al., 1995). Furthermore, we can often know people for several years and not frequently say their names, as we may use generic terms (like 'doctor', etc.). In their study investigating naming and biographical information, Brédart et al. (2005) compared naming versus either qualification status (Experiment 1) or nationality decision (Experiment 2), and found participants were quicker to name a face as belonging to a very familiar work colleague, than they were to make a semantic judgement (e.g. what is the qualification status or what is their nationality?) to that same face. However, their findings should be taken with caution, as they used small sample sizes and a small stimuli set for both experiments. Furthermore, they claimed for both studies that the semantic information was highly salient to the participants, e.g. academic qualifications and nationality, but this is based on anecdotal evidence rather than empirical research.

Another study also found an advantage of names over recognising faces using a novel paradigm in which both names and faces were tested using recognition. As described previously in this chapter, most studies investigating face recognition employ a paradigm whereby faces are presented for learning and then again for test and the task is to decide whether the faces are old or new. However, when investigating naming, participants are presented with names and then often asked to recall the names in test, so do not have any visual cues to aid memory retrieval. In their study, Burton et al. (2019) presented participants with 40 unfamiliar faces and names during a study phase and then 80 names and faces during a test phase and participants had to decide if the names and faces were old or new. Across three experiments they found an advantage of names over faces, suggesting that names are not more difficult to remember per se, contrary to previous research that compared recognition memory of faces with recall memory of names. They concluded that when names are present for familiar individuals they can be as easily recognised as faces, but that this still didn't explain why names were so difficult to retrieve from memory.

For those of you who, like me, might not be very good at recalling people's names, there are some strategies that can be applied to help remember them. First, one must pay attention to a person's name when they are introduced and if you don't catch it, ask them to repeat it. Another technique that can help to remember a person's name is to use retrieval practice, which is a strategy whereby the information is brought back to consciousness several times to aid learning. In the context of learning a person's name, this is when you first meet a person and obtain their name and then insert their name several times into the conversation. which should help to recall their names later (Morris et al., 2005). This advice is something that I should consider to improve my own social interactions and to remember people's names.

Conclusion

This chapter has looked at the everyday errors people make when trying to identify faces, whether it is not recognising someone that is known, seeing a person's face and sensing they look familiar, but not being able to place why, or recognising a person and remembering lots of details about them, but not being able to recall their name. Research has shown that all issues are fairly common as many people experience them from time to time, especially when an individual is encountered out of context, such as the 'butcher on the bus' phenomenon. Putting names to faces can also be problematic, as research has shown that often biographical information is more readily recalled than a person's name. However, everyday errors occur, they may be embarrassing or frustrating, but those lapses in memory usually do not have any serious consequences or make life-changing events occur. The next chapter will look at the more serious side of when face recognition goes wrong and when those errors can have life-changing consequences.

References

Brédart, S. (2017). The cognitive psychology and neuroscience of naming people. *Neuroscience and Biobehavioral Reviews*, 83(October), 145–154. https://doi.org/10.1016/j.neubiorev.2017.10.008.

Brédart, S., Brennen, T., Delchambre, M., McNeill, A., & Burton, A. M. (2005). Naming very familiar people: When retrieving names is faster than retrieving semantic biographical information. *British Journal of Psychology*, 96(2), 205–214. https://doi.org/10.1348/000712605X38378.

Brédart, S., & Geurten, M. (2020). Strategies to resolve recall failures for proper names: New data. *Memory and Cognition*, 48(8), 1417–1428. https://doi.org/10.3758/s13421-020-01057-x.

Brédart, S., Valentine, T., Calder, A., & Gassi, L. (1995). An interactive activation model of face naming. *The Quarterly Journal of Experimental Psychology Section A*, 48(2), 466–486. https://doi.org/10.1080/14640749508401400.

Brédart, S., & Vanootighem, V. (2021). Middle-aged people's perceptions of name recall failures. *Advances in Cognitive Psychology*, 17(4), 27–32. https://doi.org/10.5709/acp-0344-z.

Brown, A. S. (2020). The butcher on the bus experience. *Memory Quirks*, 224–247. https://doi.org/10.4324/9780429264498-17.

Brown, R., & McNeill, D. (1966). The 'tip of the tongue' phenomenon. *Journal of Verbal Learning and Verbal Behavior*, 5(4), 325–337. https://doi.org/10.1016/S0022-5371(66)80040-80043.

Bruce, V., & Young, A. (1986). Understanding face recognition. *British Journal of Psychology*, 77(3), 305–327. https://doi.org/10.1111/j.2044-8295.1986.tb02199.x.

Burton, A. M., & Bruce, V. (1992). I recognize your face, but I can't remember your name: A simple explanation? *British Journal of Psychology*, 83(1), 45–60.

Burton, A. M., Bruce, V., & Hancock, P. J. B. (1999). From pixels to people: A model of familiar face recognition. *Cognitive Science*, 23(1), 1–31. https://doi.org/10.1207/s15516709cog2301_1.

Burton, A. M., Jenkins, R., & Robertson, D. J. (2019). I recognise your name but I can't remember your face: An advantage for names in recognition memory. *Quarterly Journal of Experimental Psychology*, 72(7), 1847–1854. https://doi.org/10.1177/1747021818813081.

Busigny, T., de Boissezon, X., Puel, M., Nespoulous, J. L., & Barbeau, E. J. (2015). Proper name anomia with preserved lexical and semantic knowledge after left anterior temporal lesion: A two-way convergence defect. *Cortex*, 65, 1–18. https://doi.org/10.1016/j.cortex.2014.12.008.

Craigie, M., & Hanley, J. R. (1997). Putting faces to names. *British Journal of Psychology*, 88(1), 157–171. https://doi.org/10.1111/j.2044-8295. 1997.tb02626.x.

Davies, G., & Milne, A. (1982). Recognizing faces in and out of context. *Current Psychological Research*, 2(1–3),235–246. https://doi.org/10. 1007/BF03186766.

Flude, B. M., Ellis, A. W., & Kay, J. (1989). Face processing and name retrieval in an anomic aphasic: Names are stored separately from semantic information about familiar people. *Brain and Cognition*, 11(1), 60–72. https://doi.org/10.1016/0278-2626(89)90005–90005.

Gruppuso, V., Lindsay, D. S., & Masson, M. E. J. (2007). I'd know that face anywhere! *Psychonomic Bulletin and Review*, 14(6), 1085–1089. https://doi.org/10.3758/BF03193095.

Hanley, J. R. (2011). An appreciation of Bruce and Young's (1986) serial stage model of face naming after 25 years. *British Journal of Psychology*, 102(4), 915–930. https://doi.org/10.1111/j.2044-8295.2011.02032.x.

Hanley, J. R., & Cowell, E. S. (1988). The effects of different types of retrieval cues on the recall of names of famous faces. *Memory & Cognition*, 16(6), 545–555. https://doi.org/10.3758/BF03197056.

Laurence, S., Eyre, J., & Strathie, A. (2021). Recognising familiar faces out of context. *Perception*, 50(2), 174–177. https://doi.org/10.1177/0301006620984326.

MacLeod, C. M. (2020). Society for the history of psychology news. *History of Psychology*, 23(4), 383–387. https://doi.org/10.1037/h0101593.

Mandler, G. (1980). Recognizing: The judgment of previous occurrence. *Psychological Review*, 87(3), 252–271. https://doi.org/10.1037/0033-29 5X.87.3.252.

McWeeny, K. H., Young, A. W. A., Hay, D. C., & Ellis, A. W. (1987). Putting names to faces. *British Journal of Psychology*, 78(2), 143–149.

Morris, P. E., Fritz, C. O., Jackson, L., Nichol, E., & Roberts, E. (2005). Strategies for learning proper names: Expanding retrieval practice, meaning and imagery. *Applied Cognitive Psychology*, 19(6), 779–798.

Sauerland, M., & Sporer, S. L. (2008). The application of multiple lineups in a field study. *Psychology, Crime & Law*, 14(6), 549–564. https://doi.org/10.1080/10683160801972519.

Scanlan, L. C., & Johnston, R. A. (1997). I recognize your face but I can't remember your name: A group-up explanation. *The Quarterly Journal of Experimental Psychology Section A*, 50A(1), 183–198.

Schweinberger, S. R., & Burton, A. M. (2011). Person perception 25 years after Bruce and Young (1986): An introduction. *British Journal of Psychology*, 102(4), 695–703. https://doi.org/10.1111/j.2044-8295.2011.02070.x.

Tulving, E. (1985). Memory and consciousness. *Canadian Psychology/ Psychologie canadienne*, 26(1), 1–12.

Tunney, R. J., Mullett, T. L., Moross, C. J., & Gardner, A. (2012). Does the butcher-on-the-bus phenomenon require a dual-process explanation? A signal detection analysis. *Frontiers in Psychology*, 3, 208.

Watkins, M. J., Ho, E., & Endle, E. (1976). Context effects in recognition memory. *Journal of Verbal Learning and Verbal Behavior*, 15, 505–517. https://doi.org/10.1016/S0022-5371(72)80033-80031.

Yarmey, A. D. (1973). I recognize your face but I can't remember your name: Further evidence on the tip-of-the-tongue phenomenon. *Memory & Cognition*, 1(3), 287–290. https://doi.org/10.3758/BF03198110.

Young, A. W. (1988). *Face and mind*. Oxford University Press.

Young, A. W., Hay, D. C., & Ellis, A. W. (1985). The faces that launched a thousand slips: Everyday difficulties and errors in recognizing people. *British Journal of Psychology*, 76(4), 495–523. https://doi.org/10.1111/j.2044-8295.1985.tb01972.x.

Young, A. W., McWeeny, K. H., Ellis, A. W., & Hay, D. C. (1986). Naming and categorizing faces and written names. *Quarterly Journal of Experimental Psychology*, 38(2), 297–318.

3 Unconscious transference and misidentifications

Introduction

In the previous chapter we looked at everyday errors in face recognition, how important context can be when trying to identify someone's face, and how difficult it is to recognise a person if they are seen in an unusual context and not in the typical circumstances where they are most frequently encountered. This chapter focuses on more serious errors that can occur when trying to identify people, such as someone being wrongly identified as a perpetrator of a particular crime, while in fact they were seen near the time of the crime and were an innocent bystander at the crime scene, or they resembled the real culprit.

There have been many instances when innocent people have been wrongly arrested and convicted for crimes they did not commit, and this can happen when an eyewitnesse misidentifies an innocent person from a police lineup, and the person is convicted based upon that evidence (see https://innocenceproject.org for examples). One famous example that has been cited in the eyewitness literature several times is the case of an armed robbery at a train station. An innocent sailor was accused of the robbery and misidentified by a train station ticket clerk who picked him out of a lineup and claimed that he was the person who committed the robbery. However, it transpired that the sailor had irrefutable proof that he could not have been at the station at the time the robbery occurred. The feelings of familiarity arose because the sailor had been a customer and purchased train tickets several times previously, although the ticket clerk did not

DOI: 10.4324/9781003177128-3

remember this. So the sailor was familiar to the ticket clerk, as he had been seen in the context of the ticket office, but the clerk had mistakenly thought he was familiar as he had been the robber, rather than just another customer (Read et al., 1990). This type of mistaken identification has been termed unconscious transference, where one person's identity is transferred to another person's identity from the same context, setting or time (Glanville Williams, 1955, cited in Read et al., 1990).

Unconscious transference is thought to occur when the eyewitness of a crime misidentifies a familiar but innocent person from a lineup. This chapter will first look at some real-life cases where innocent people were mistakenly identified as being the culprits for a specific crime. Then it will examine some of psychological research that has investigated unconscious transference and how the use of certain police procedures may influence its occurrence, such as mugbook showup identification procedures and creating composite images for faces. The final part of the chapter will explore the use of social media by witnesses conducting their own investigations and how that might influence the subsequent eyewitness identification.

Real-life cases

There have been a few cases where unconscious transference has thought to have been responsible for innocent people being wrongly identified as perpetrators of crimes and in the box are two examples.

Real-life examples of unconscious transference

One well-cited example of unconscious transference occurred in 1975 when Professor Donald Thompson, an Australian psychologist and expert on eyewitness memory, was accused of rape. The night before he was arrested the victim had seen him on television, just prior to being raped. Seeing Professor Thompson on television made him familiar to the victim, but she confused the source of the familiarity with him being the rapist. Ironically, at the time he was on television Thompson was talking about errors in eyewitness testimony and offering practical suggestions on how to remember faces using his own face as an example. Thompson was arrested by the police, but as the show had aired live he had a solid alibi and the charges were dropped (Read et al., 1990).

A more recent and less straightforward case of unconscious transference is that of Khalid Baker (Mallett, 2020). In 2005, 18-year-old Khalid was at a party with some friends when a fight broke out on a top-floor landing between his group of friends and some other men. At some point during the fight Albert Snowball, from the other group of men, was pushed through a window, falling over five metres, and he later died in hospital. Some witnesses say that it was Khalid who was fighting with Snowball, and others said it was his friend LM. In his testimony LM admitted to pushing Albert away at the end of the fight and that he was the last one to touch Albert before he fell to his death. In court there were six eyewitnesses who gave testimony; three were Black (the same race as Khalid and his friends) and three were white. The three Black witnesses said that it was LM who was fighting with Albert and that Khalid was either being restrained or fighting with another person at the time. In contrast, the three white witnesses said it was Khalid who was fighting with Albert. No one saw him go through the window. Khalid was charged with his murder and although he has always claimed he was innocent he was sentenced to 17 years, while LM was acquitted.

Khalid's case involves not only unconscious transference, whereby the white eyewitnesses mistook Khalid for LM as being the person who pushed Albert, but also the fact that Khalid and his friends were a different race to half of the eyewitnesses. There is a phenomenon called the 'own-race bias', where people are better at recognising people of the same race as them and more likely to misidentify people who are of a different race to them; this will be explored further in Chapter 4. Taken together, unconscious transference and own-race bias appear to have acted together for Khalid to have been mistaken for LM and then charged with murder. Khalid was released in October 2018 and still maintains his innocence (for more details on this case see Mallett, 2020).

These are two examples of real-life cases where it seems that unconscious transference has been partly responsible for an innocent person being arrested for a crime they did not commit. What real-life cases can't explain is the mechanisms of how unconscious transference has occurred; for example does it occur at encoding when the innocent person is first seen or does unconscious transference occur at retrieval, when the innocent person is viewed in a lineup, and they produce feelings of familiarity, which are then misattributed by the witness to think they are the perpetrator. This is like the 'butcher on the bus' phenomenon as the face appears familiar, but the context in which the face was seen is not recalled, or misremembered; however, it can have much more serious consequences. The next section of this chapter will describe some of the psychological research that has been conducted to investigate how unconscious transference can occur and the theoretical explanation for it.

Psychological research investigating unconscious transference

One of the first studies to specifically try and investigate unconscious transference was conducted by Buckhout (1974), who showed students a mock crime of a professor being assaulted; then seven weeks later participants were asked to identify the perpetrator from a photo lineup that contained both the perpetrator and a bystander who was seen at the scene of the crime, but who wasn't involved in the assault. Only 40% of the participants correctly identified the perpetrator and 40% misidentified the bystander from the lineup. However, this study has been criticised as it failed to include a control group who saw the crime and were given the lineup, but not exposed to the innocent bystander (Ross et al., 1994b).

Another early study to investigate unconscious transference and misidentifications was by Loftus (1976). In this study participants were presented with an audio tape of a crime and shown yearbook photographs illustrating the characters in the story. Three days later participants were shown either a lineup that contained the perpetrator or an innocent bystander whose photo had been in the yearbook. When the perpetrator was present, just over 80% of participants made a correct identification; however, when the innocent bystander was present, 60% of participants falsely identified them. One of the criticisms of this study is that facial photographs were used to illustrate the characters in the story, but the participants did not have any contextual information available in the photographs (Ross et al., 1994b). As we saw from the last chapter, contextual information can be incredibly useful when trying to identify a person's face; as there was no contextual information to distinguish between the perpetrator and the bystander in the yearbook it may have been easy to confuse them.

A number of further studies have also replicated these findings. However, not all studies have found that bystanders are misidentified instead of perpetrators. Read et al. (1990) conducted five field study experiments. In the first two experiments retail clerks in shopping malls were approached by perpetrators; half were also able to observe a bystander in the shop at the same time. Either 20 mins or two hours after the interaction the retail clerks were interviewed, asked to describe the perpetrator and shown a six-person photo lineup. They found little evidence for unconscious transference, with a high correct identification rate for the perpetrator and very low false identification rates of the bystander. The few false identifications were thought to be the result of similarity in appearance between the bystander and the perpetrator. There was also little evidence of unconscious transference in the third experiment, which again used retail clerks as the participants and found a high correct identification rate for the perpetrator and very few false identification rates for the bystander. The fourth experiment used a slightly different paradigm and psychology undergraduate students were the participants; again there was little evidence of unconscious transference and very few participants identified the bystander. The fifth experiment employed undergraduate participants. There was a perpetrator, who was a technician who came to the classroom to repair the audio system and for half of the participants a bystander who either distributed papers to the class, or informed the class the lecturer would be late. All participants saw two lineups, first a TA lineup, then a TP lineup; lineups were also created so that they had either low similarity or high similarity in appearance to the perpetrator. There was evidence of unconscious transference when lineups were of low similarity, as they were more likely to choose the bystander. However, participants were more likely to choose the bystander than in the control condition, where they had not seen the bystander, suggesting that the bystander was chosen as he resembled the perpetrator more closely than any of the other foils.

Read and colleagues suggested that their results across the five different studies demonstrate that unconscious transference incidents in real criminal cases are most probably rare occurrences in real life and that certain conditions need to be met for unconscious transference to occur. They suggest unconscious transference can be explained in terms of the trace strength model of memory (Ross et al., 1994b). For example if the memory of the bystander and the perpetrator is strong and both have been seen for a long time, misidentification is unlikely because the witness should be able to distinguish one from another and this is what appears to have happened in most of Read et al.'s (1990) studies. If the bystander and the perpetrator are seen only for a short period of time and the memory trace is weak, then it's unlikely that the bystander will be identified because they may not be familiar to the witness. When the memory for the bystander and a perpetrator is moderate and of equal strength, then the witness should be able to recognise the bystander from a lineup but they may not have sufficient memory details to remember that it's the bystander and it is this familiarity that may result in unconscious transference and misidentification.

To understand why some studies had found an effect of unconscious bias while other had not, and to investigate the mechanisms behind unconscious bias, Ross and colleagues conducted four different experiments (Ross et al., 1994a). In their study they investigated three different theoretical approaches that have been developed to explain unconscious transference and the conflicting findings. They are outlined below.

Different theoretical explanations for unconscious processing

1   Automatic processing – claims the witness has no conscious recollection that they have previously encountered the bystander before and therefore when they see the bystander in a lineup and they appear familiar, they assume that the familiarity is due to the bystander being the perpetrator of the crime.

2   Deliberate source monitoring at retrieval – proposes the witness may consciously remember seeing the perpetrator and the bystander at the scene of the crime, and is aware they are different people, although they may look alike. However, their memories become confused upon retrieval when being presented with a lineup, where the witness mistakes the bystander for the perpetrator.

3   Conscious inference at encoding – suggests that eyewitnesses misidentify the bystander as they remember seeing the bystander and the perpetrator at the scene, but make the incorrect inference that they are the same person, as they have a similar appearance.

Ross and colleagues' studies were conducted using the eyewitness paradigm (Ross et al., 1994a). In all the experiments participants saw a film of a staged robbery, some saw only the perpetrator (control condition), while others saw the perpetrator and a bystander who was of a similar appearance to the perpetrator (transference condition). After watching the film, participants were asked context questions about 'who did what and where', and were shown one lineup that contained one of the following, the perpetrator, the bystander, the perpetrator and the bystander. The first experiment found that if participants saw the bystander, they were more likely to report he looked familiar, and were three times more likely than those in the control condition to falsely identify him from a lineup as being the perpetrator. About a third of the participants in this group also explicitly referred to him as the 'robber', or 'thief'. However, if the lineup contained both the bystander and the perpetrator, participants were more likely to correctly identify the perpetrator as compared to the bystander. Furthermore, when participants saw the bystander in the film, there were fewer correct identifications of the perpetrator, so the presence of bystander did impair recognition of the perpetrator. Their results appeared to support the conscious inference explanation of transference, although this was reduced when both men were in the same lineup.

In the second experiment Ross and colleagues tried to eliminate unconscious transference by informing participants that the thief and the bystander were two different people, prior to the lineup task, and then asking them to specifically identify the thief (Ross et al., 1994a). They found that this reduced the false identification rate for the bystander, as compared to the first experiment, but they only used lineups with the bystander. In the third experiment, participants were asked context questions such as 'Was the robber seen anywhere else?' and 'What was he doing?' either before or after seeing the lineup to investigate whether the conscious transference occurred at encoding or retrieval. Similarly, in the fourth experiment, participants were asked to stop the film as soon as they saw the same man a second time. The results from both of these experiments suggested that participants thought that the bystander and perpetrator were the same person and that conscious inference occurred at the encoding stage (watching the film), not retrieval stage of memory (responding to the lineup task).

Some more recent research has suggested an alternative explanation for unconscious transference related to conscious inference at encoding and that the process may relate to change blindness (Davis et al., 2008; Fitzgerald et al., 2016; Nelson et al., 2011). Change blindness occurs when an observer doesn't notice a change in the scene that they are viewing. There is a classic study by Simons and Levin (1998) where an experimenter asks a pedestrian for directions and while this is happening two confederates interrupt the dialogue walking between them carrying a door and the experimenter goes behind the door and is replaced by another person who continues talking to the pedestrian. If you haven't seen this already do have a look on YouTube for the 'Door' study. In their study they found that half the time participants did not notice that the person that they were talking to had changed identity during the conversation.

There are a few studies that have employed the eyewitness paradigm of showing participants a mock crime and then a lineup and adding a changed blindness element; for example, an innocent person walks through a door or from behind a stack of boxes and changes identity part-way through the film to become a perpetrator who then steals something. Participants are then shown either a lineup that contains the thief or the innocent person from the film and asked if they noticed any change. A number of these studies have reported that participants do not always notice a change, and those that do not notice that change are much more likely to identify an innocent person from a lineup (Davis et al., 2008; Fitzgerald et al., 2016; Nelson et al., 2011). It has been suggested that change blindness occurs because people fall for the illusion of continuity, whereby people fill in perceptual gaps based on typical observed events, i.e. a person does not usually change identity when they walk through a door or go behind a stack of boxes, therefore it is the same person.

Thus far this chapter has explored some of the real-world cases and psychological research that has investigated when an innocent bystander has been misidentified as being the perpetrator of a crime, where the police have not been able to control whether the witness has seen the innocent person. The next part of this chapter will explore research that has investigated whether certain police procedures can increase the chances through unconscious transference of an innocent person being identified, or reduce the likelihood that a perpetrator is identified.

The use of facial composites, mugshots and showups prior to lineup identifications

Sometimes, when a witness sees a crime and reports it to the police, the police may not have any idea who the suspect is if they do not find anyone near the scene of the crime and/or have any inside information. In cases like these, the police might interview the witness asking for a description of the perpetrator and get them to create a facial composite of the perpetrator and circulate it in the press in the hope that someone will recognise the suspect and inform the police of the person's identity.

The image on the left in Figure 3.1 is of Derry McCann; he was nicknamed the 'wedding day rapist'. In January 2012, in a park in London, a woman was raped and after the ordeal went to the police, where, with the help of a composite operator, an E-FIT facial composite (shown on the right of Figure 3.1) was created. McCann (the perpetrator) was married the following day to his pregnant girlfriend. When the officer on the case viewed the E-FIT, he said 'Bingo'. He had just been given details of Derry McCann as a potential suspect from his probation officer and this rape was almost identical to one committed in 2006. McCann was arrested, pleaded guilty and was sentenced to life in prison (Tony Barnes, personal communication, 2021).

In real-life cases, composites have helped find some perpetrators of horrific crimes. One example was a composite of a serial rapist in Manchester whose facial composite was shown on the TV programme *Crimewatch* and it was recognised by the man's brother, who informed the police of his identity (McLean, 2020). However, facial composites have also been publicly criticised for producing images that do not look like real people and they have received some ridicule in the media (Bell, 2016). Composites are usually employed at the beginning of a police investigation and then if a suspect is found they may be placed into a police lineup to see if the witness can identify them.

Psychological research investigating whether creating a composite before seeing a lineup can influence a person's memory has found mixed results. Some research has found that creating a

Figure 3.1 Derry McCann (the 'wedding day rapist') and an EFIT.

composite can damage a witness's memory, making them less likely to identify the perpetrator afterwards (Topp-Manriquez et al., 2016; Wells et al., 2005). This research suggested that creating the composite altered the witness's memory, or created a competing memory of the perpetrator's appearance, which then led to the witness being less likely to correctly identify the perpetrator from a lineup. However, these studies have been criticised, as the composite systems they used were feature-based systems, whereby a witness picks a set of features to create the face of the perpetrator (see Tanka & Simonyi, 2016 for a review of the literature on holistic processing). Therefore it could be that using feature-based composite systems where the face is broken down into a set of separate features impairs later face recognition of a perpetrator (Pike et al., 2019; Wells et al., 2005).

Not all research has found a detrimental effect for creating a facial composite prior to trying to identify a perpetrator from a lineup; several studies have even found a benefit for creating a composite prior to seeing a lineup (Davis et al., 2014; Meissner & Brigham, 2001). A meta-analysis examining 23 studies investigating whether constructing a composite affects a witness's lineup identification decision found that there were no significant negative effects of constructing a lineup prior to seeing a lineup (Tredoux et al., 2020). The paper also suggested that the newer systems, which are often holistic in nature, produced more accurate representations of target faces, while the older feature-based systems produced composites that did not bear as much of a likeness to the faces they were supposed to simulate. However there has been some research that has pitted featural (E-FIT) and holistic (EFIT-V) systems against each other, and found that neither system had a detrimental effect on a subsequent identification task (Pike et al., 2019).

The research investigating composite construction demonstrates that in some cases, if the composite created by the witness doesn't closely resemble the perpetrator they have seen, either due to the composite system or a poor memory of the perpetrator's face, then this can have a detrimental influence on identification. It could be in these instances the appearance of the composite interferes with the witness's memory for the actual culprit's appearance, so that when they are later presented with the culprit in a lineup he/she doesn't appear to be familiar.

However, the newer systems appear to create composites that are more realistic and don't appear to any negative effects on subsequent identification accuracy (Pike et al., 2019), which is good news for police investigations. Another procedure that police use when they have a witness to a crime, but no suspect in mind, is to present the witness with a book of mugshots (a mugbook), which is an album that has photographs of known criminals, to see if they can identify the perpetrator. The next part of the chapter will look at the influence of seeing mugshot images on the subsequent identification from a lineup.

In some criminal investigations, instead of creating a facial composite with an eyewitness, the witness might be asked by the police to look through a mugbook that contains images (mugshots) of known offenders to see if they recognise anyone. In the box is an example of real-life case when viewing a mugbook led to an innocent person being wrongfully imprisoned.

Real-life case of mugshot use and misidentification

In October 1985 in Virginia, USA a woman was raped in her home, but when interviewed by the police she said it was too dark to clearly see the perpetrator's face. However, her neighbours reported seeing a man called Walter Snyder outside his home across the road from the victim after the attack. The police questioned Snyder and took his photograph, and included it in a set of mugshots that were shown to the victim. Although she did not identify him as her attacker, she did look at his photograph for a while and said his eyebrows looked familiar.

Months later Snyder was asked to return to the police station and the woman was asked to identify him. When she saw him in reception, she became agitated and told the receptionist that he was the man who had raped her. The police say that Snyder confessed, and a pair of red shorts were found in his house that were similar to those worn by the perpetrator. Snyder was convicted and sentenced to 45 years in prison.

In 1992, Snyder's family, with support from the Innocence Project, sent the DNA from the vaginal swab taken at the time

for analysis and it was confirmed that Snyder was innocent. An
absolute pardon was granted in 1993 (Innocence Project, 2021).

This case illustrates the dangers of using a mugbook when a
witness is unsure of a perpetrator's appearance, as the images in
the mugbook can influence the real memory of a perpetrator's
appearance. In this case there was also the added issue of cross-
race identification. The victim was white, and Walter Snyder
was Black; as we will see in the next chapter, people are less
accurate at identifying faces that are a different race to them.
Research that has investigated the influence of seeing a mugbook prior to another form of identification (e.g. a lineup) has
employed 'a mugshot commitment design' (Deffenbacher et al.,
2006). In these studies participants see a target face (usually
from a mock crime video), and participants in the experimental
condition view a mugbook that doesn't contain the target face.
Then participants are shown a lineup that may or may not contain the target face, but will usually contain one of the faces
from the mugbook (innocent suspect). There are a number of
studies that have shown that when using this paradigm participants often choose an innocent person they have seen from the
mugbook at a level above chance (Dysart et al., 2001), and
some studies have found this can decrease the identification of
the perpetrator (Deffenbacher et al., 2006).

In their meta-analysis of 32 studies, Deffenbacher et al.
(2006) found that when participants saw a mugbook that did
not contain the previously seen perpetrator's face, they were
less likely to make an accurate identification from a lineup.
Furthermore, participants who viewed a target absent lineup
after seeing an innocent person in the mugbook were twice as
likely to make a false identification from a lineup compared to
those in a control condition who had not viewed a mugbook.
This type of error was called a 'transference error', similar to
the previously discussed process with misidentifying bystanders, and in these cases the participants mistake the innocent
person they have seen from the mugbook as being the perpetrator they have previously seen. This research suggests that
viewing mugbooks that don't contain a perpetrator can reduce

identification accuracy and increase the likelihood that an innocent person is misidentified. Even when the perpetrator was present in the mugbook, it did not statistically improve correct identifications.

Why do participants continue to misidentify the face of an innocent person they have seen in a mugshot, when they are later shown a lineup that contains the actual perpetrator? First, a witness may be reluctant to change their identification because they feel they need to be consistent with their testimony, a tendency that's referred to as the 'commitment effect' (Wells, 1984). Furthermore, when a witness misidentifies a bystander, or an innocent person from a mugbook, this might overwrite or alter the original memory of the observed perpetrator, so they are no longer as familiar as they once were (Ross et al., 1994b).

Showups

Another form of identification that can occur prior to a witness seeing a lineup is a police showup. This form of identification usually happens shortly after a person has witnessed a crime and they have given a description of the perpetrator to the police. Then if the police find someone near the crime scene matching the suspect's description, they might ask the witness whether the person they have apprehended is the individual they saw commit the crime. This is often used as a preliminary form of identification, and the witness may later see a lineup with the suspect along with other foils. The showup can be a single photo (like a mugshot), or a live person, which is also called a street identification. It has been suggested that using showups as a form of identification is inherently biasing (Behrman & Vayder, 1994).

There are a few advantages of using a showup and that is that they can be conducted quickly and therefore perpetrators doesn't have time to change their appearance. Also as memory declines over time, presenting a showup shortly after witnessing a crime can be a more reliable test for eyewitness memory (Neuschatz et al., 2016; Sjöberg, 2016). However, there are also several disadvantages of employing showups. They include the inability to administer them double blind, where both the lineup administrator and the witness do not know who the suspect is. It has been recommended by a number of researchers that lineups be administered double blind to prevent the lineup administer inadvertently influencing the witness's decision (Kovera & Evelo, 2020; Wells et al., 2020). By their very nature, showups, especially if they are live street identifications that occur shortly after a crime and in the vicinity, are administered single blind as the police officer will know who the suspect is. Also, there are no fillers in a showup, as there are in a lineup, so the suspect is not protected from a witness who may just guess. For example, in a lineup of six people, each person has a one in six chance of being selected, and if the witness chooses someone other than the suspect, the police know that the witness's memory might not be reliable. For a showup there is only one person, so even if the witness picks that person they could still be guessing. Research has also found that a witness might be more likely to choose from a showup whether the perpetrator is present or not, suggesting that there is more of a danger of an innocent person being identified from a showup (Neuschatz et al., 2016) and there have been several studies that have found their use can lead to misidentifications of innocent persons (Behrman & Vayder, 1994; Neuschatz et al., 2016; Steblay et al., 2003; Valentine et al., 2011).

There is evidence from real cases that showups can result in innocent people being convicted of crimes they have not committed. An analysis of court trials from 160 cases which were later exonerated from DNA evidence found that 33% involved misidentifications from showups (Garrett, 2011). These findings were also confirmed by meta-analyses comparing showups and lineups, which found that showups are more at risk of innocent persons being falsely identified as compared to lineups (Neuschatz et al., 2016) and the suspects are more likely to be picked from showups (Steblay et al., 2003). Davis et al. (2015) conducted field studies examining real police identification cases of showups, that were live street identifications followed by video lineups (the lineup method used in the UK). The street identifications in the UK usually involve either a drive-by with the witness in the car being driven around to see if they identify a suspect, or a planned confrontation, where the police have detained someone and they show them to the witness. They found that if a suspect was identified in the street identification and then seen again in a video lineup, they were identified 84% of the time from a lineup. Davis et al. (2015) suggest that witnesses who are shown a showup and then lineup, demonstrate a 'commitment effect' and that has also been found in previous studies (Dysart et al., 2001; Valentine et al., 2011) and that even if an innocent suspect is not chosen in the showup, if they are presented again in the lineup, they may appear familiar to the witness from the previous identification procedure and chosen in the second identification procedure due to the sense of familiarity, rather than being the perpetrator of the crime.

The previous section has revealed that some of the procedures that the police employ to try and find the identity of the perpetrator can in some cases lead to mistaken identification of innocent persons. The next section discusses an issue that the police have no control over and that is when victims of crime, witnesses and even well-intentioned citizens decide to conduct their own investigations after a crime using social media.

The use of social media, web sleuthing and misidentifications

One issue that has emerged over the last few years is 'web sleuthing', which is when witnesses, victims of crime or even other members of the public decide to conduct their own investigations often using social media platforms like Facebook, Twitter/X, Reddit and Instagram to try and find the perpetrators of a crime. Once the web sleuth has identified who they think the perpetrator is, they might then go to the police with this information and state that this is the person that committed the crime.

Hypothetical example

Imagine that you've gone out for the evening and you come back home to find that your house has been burgled and lots of items have been stolen. You call the police, who say they will come to your home, but in the meantime, you also remember that you have a video camera in your doorbell and you start looking at the footage. When looking at the footage from the video doorbell, you see two young men acting suspiciously outside your house. You decide to post a still from the video to your neighbourhood WhatsApp group, which consists of a group of people who live nearby, to ask if anyone saw anything. Within a few minutes someone from your WhatsApp group says they think that they recognise one of the men and give you the name Derek Tukey. You go on to Facebook and look up the name Derek Tukey and see that there is a profile of a young man who lives in your area and looks similar to one of the men in the video footage, and in addition in one of the photographs on his profile he's with another man who could be the other man from the doorbell video, and his name is Dean Whitehall. The police then turn up at your home and interview you about what has happened, and you provide them with the two names of the young men you think have burgled your home. The police are now obliged to go and question these men in relation to your burglary. The young men deny any wrongdoing; however, neither of them has a reliable alibi and they have in the past both been cautioned for smoking cannabis. They claim they were together at the local park, but with no one to corroborate their story they are arrested, and you are asked to go to the police station and view two video lineups. You identify both suspects from the video lineups and they are taken to court and convicted of burglary, although both still claim they are innocent.

A couple of months later the police conduct a raid on a property, and in the house they find several of the items that were stolen from your home, and it transpires the young men living in the house are the real culprits of your burglary and Derek and Dean were innocent all along.

This is a hypothetical example; however, it illustrates how easy it could be for members of the public to conduct their own investigations with good intentions; however, they could inadvertently be identifying innocent people. With the increase in home surveillance CCTV and the prevalence of social media, it has become easy for people to conduct their own investigations and there has been an increase in this type of reporting to the police. There have been several real-life cases where witnesses have taken to the internet in a bid to help solve crimes; one example is that after the Boston Marathon bombings, Reddit users conducted their own investigations using video footage and images from the incident and then publicly named several innocent suspects. This resulted in innocent people being prosecuted, none of whom were found to have had any involvement in the attacks by the FBI (Lee, 2013).

Some researchers have suggested that when a witness observes a crime and then looks at images on social media sites like Facebook and Instagram to find a perpetrator there can be a 'displacement effect' whereby the face of a person seen on Facebook can replace the face of a perpetrator, like copying and pasting one face onto another (McGorrery, 2015). This is similar to the idea of unconscious transference, when one person's identity is transferred to another person. Furthermore, searching for a perpetrator on sites like Facebook makes identifications unreliable as there are no safeguards in place as when viewing formal identification procedures, for example the unbiased instructions that 'the person may or may not be present' (McGorrery, 2016).

Although there is an increase in web sleuthing, there is still relatively little psychological research that has investigated whether it influences formal identification processes, leading to an increase in misidentifications. Two studies that investigated the influence of viewing Facebook-type websites to search for perpetrators of a mock crime had different findings (Elphick et al., 2021; Havard et al., 2021). In both studies participants viewed a film of a mock crime of a young man stealing a handbag and then after a delay one group viewed a mock social media site called 'Friendface' where they were asked if they could spot the thief among the different profiles. For half of the participants, the thief was present on the social media site, and for the other half the thief was not present, but there was a lookalike innocent suspect, while the control group did not view the social media site. Then after a week's delay the participant saw either a target present lineup that contained the thief, or a target absent lineup that contained the innocent suspect. Both studies predicted that exposure to an innocent lookalike might increase false identifications from the target absent lineups; however, neither study reported this finding. Elphick et al. (2021) found that when participants had seen the innocent lookalike suspect in the social media condition, they were less likely to correctly identify the thief in the target present lineup, suggesting that seeing the lookalike did alter the original memory of the thief, replicating the findings by Ross et al. (1994a). However, seeing the lookalike did not increase false identifications in the target absent lineup. In contrast, Havard et al. (2021) found no detrimental effect of seeing the innocent suspect on social media, and in fact seeing the thief in the social media condition increased the accuracy of target absent lineups, with high correct identification rates, replicating the findings of Read et al. (1990).

Other research investigating web sleuthing and the use of social media has found that if the perpetrator was seen on social media this could aid later identification; however, if an innocent foil was viewed on social media this would reduce subsequent identifications (Kleider-Offutt et al., 2022; Kruisselbrink et al., 2023). The findings from this research suggested that people had source monitoring errors, meaning that they could not remember whether the person they saw in a lineup was previously seen committing a crime or just seen on social media. These studies also suggest that when eyewitnesses take to viewing social media and web sleuthing this has the potential to lead to innocent people being misidentified.

Conclusion

This chapter has looked at a phenomenon known as unconscious transference and how it can influence misidentifications of faces. Research that has investigated the issue of whether bystanders can be mistakenly identified as perpetrators of crimes has found mixed results with some studies finding evidence to support misidentifications and unconscious transference (Ross et al., 1994b) and others not (Read et al., 1990). However, some researchers in psychology suggest these cases are rare (Professor Donald J. Read, personal communication, 4 June 2021). When it comes to creating a facial composite prior to a lineup identification, research has found that composites do not have a detrimental effect per se, unless the composite does not resemble the perpetrator. However, viewing mugbooks and showups prior to seeing a police lineup can lead to 'face recognition going wrong', which could lead to miscarriages of justice. One area that still needs more research is the influence of web sleuthing on identification procedures, as at the time of writing there are very few published studies that have investigated this phenomenon.

References

Behrman, B. W., & Vayder, L. T. (1994). Biasing influence of a police showup: Does the observation of a single suspect taint later identification? *Perception and Motor Skills*, 79, 1239–1248.

Bell, B. (2016). In e-fits of laughter: Farcical faces from the police. www.bbc.co.uk/news/uk-england-35422394.

Buckhout, R. (1974). Eyewitness testimony. *Scientific American*, 231(6), 23–31. https://doi.org/10.1038/scientificamerican1274-23.

Davis, D., Loftus, E. F., Vanous, S., & Cucciare, M. (2008). 'Unconscious transference' can be an instance of 'change blindness'. *Applied Cognitive Psychology*, 22(5), 605–623. https://doi.org/10.1002/acp.1395.

Davis, J. P., Gibson, S., & Solomon, C. (2014). The positive influence of creating a holistic facial composite on video line-up identification. *Applied Cognitive Psychology*, 28(5), 634–639. https://doi.org/10.1002/acp.3045.

Davis, J. P., Valentine, T., Memon, A., & Roberts, A. J. (2015). Identification on the street: a field comparison of police street identifications and video line-ups in England. *Psychology, Crime and Law*, 21(1), 9–27. https://doi.org/10.1080/1068316X.2014.915322.

Deffenbacher, K. A., Bornstein, B. H., & Penrod, S. D. (2006). Mugshot exposure effects: Retroactive interference, mugshot commitment, source confusion, and unconscious transference. *Law and Human Behavior*, 30(3), 287–307. https://doi.org/10.1007/s10979-006-9008-1.

Dysart, J. E., Lindsay, R. C. L., Hammond, R., & Dupuis, P. (2001). Mugshot exposure prior to lineup identification: Interference, transference, and commitment effects. *Journal of Applied Psychology*, 86(6), 1280–1284. https://doi.org/10.1037//0021-9010.86.6.1280.

Elphick, C., Philpot, R., Zhang, M., Stuart, A., Pike, G., Strathie, A., Havard, C., Walkington, Z., Frumkin, L. A., Levine, M., Price, B. A., Bandara, A. K., & Nuseibeh, B. (2021). Digital detectives: Websleuthing reduces eyewitness identification accuracy in police lineups. *Frontiers in Psychology*, 12. https://doi.org/10.3389/fpsyg.2021.640513.

Fitzgerald, R. J., Oriet, C., & Price, H. L. (2016). Change blindness and eyewitness identification: Effects on accuracy and confidence. *Legal and*

Criminological Psychology, 21(1), 189–201. https://doi.org/10.1111/lcrp. 12044.

Garrett, B. (2011). *Convicting the innocent: Where criminal prosecutions go wrong.* Harvard University Press.

Havard, C., Strathie, A., Pike, G., Walkington, Z., Ness, H., & Harrison, V. (2021). From witness to web sleuth: Does citizen enquiry on social media affect formal eyewitness identification procedures? *Journal of Police and Criminal Psychology, 0123456789.* https://doi.org/10.1007/s11896-021-09444-z.

Innocence Project. (2021). Walter Snyder. https://innocenceproject.org/cases/walter-snyder/.

Kleider-Offutt, H. M., Stevens, B. B., & Capodanno, M. (2022). He did it! Or did I just see him on Twitter? Social media influence on eyewitness identification. *Memory*, 30(4), 493–504. https://doi.org/10.1080/09658211.2021.1953080.

Kovera, M. B., & Evelo, A. J. (2020). Improving eyewitness-identification evidence through double-blind lineup administration. *Current Directions in Psychological Science*, 29(6), 563–568. https://doi.org/10.1177/0963721420969366.

Kruisselbrink, E. D., Fitzgerald, R. J., & Bernstein, D. M. (2023). The impact of viewing social media images on eyewitness identification. *Psychology, Public Policy, and Law*, 29(4), 457–470. https://doi.org/10.1037/law0000401.

Lee, D. (2013). Boston bombing: How internet detectives got it very wrong. www.bbc.co.uk/news/technology-22214511.

Loftus, E. F. (1976). Unconscious transference in eyewitness identification. *Law & Psychology Review*, 2, 93–98. https://psycnet.apa.org/record/1978-09799-001.

Mallett, X. (2020). *Reasonable doubt.* Pan Macmillan Australia.

McGorrery, P. (2015). The limited impact of Facebook and the displacement effect on the admissibility of identification evidence. *Criminal Law Journal*, 39(4), 208–217. http://eproxy.lib.hku.hk/login?url=http://search.ebscohost.com/login.aspx?direct=true&db=lpb&AN=109984958&site=ehost-live&scope=site.

McGorrery, P. (2016). 'But I was so sure it was him': how Facebook could be making eyewitness identifications unreliable. *Internet Law Bulletin*, 19(1), 255–258.

McLean, T. (2020). The evolution of police facial composites. www.bbc.co.uk/ideas/videos/do-police-sketches-actually-help-catch-criminals/p08dllt4.

Meissner, C. A., & Brigham, J. C. (2001). A meta-analysis of the verbal overshadowing effect in face identification. *Applied Cognitive Psychology*, 15(6), 603–616. https://doi.org/10.1002/acp.728.

Nelson, K. J., Laney, C., Fowler, N. B., Knowles, E. D., Davis, D., & Loftus, E. F. (2011). Change blindness can cause mistaken eyewitness identification. *Legal and Criminological Psychology*, 16(1), 62–74. https://doi.org/10.1348/135532509X482625.

Neuschatz, J. S., Wetmore, S. A., Key, K. N., Cash, D. K., Gronlund, S. D., & Goodsell, C. A. (2016). A comprehensive evaluation of show-ups. In M. K. Miller & B. H. Bornstein (Eds.), *Advance in psychology and law* (Issue June, pp. 43–69). Springer. https://doi.org/10.1007/978-3-319-29406-3_2.

Pike, G. E., Brace, N. A., Turner, J., Ness, H., & Vredeveldt, A. (2019). Advances in facial composite technology, utilizing holistic construction, do not lead to an increase in eyewitness misidentifications compared to older feature-based systems. *Frontiers in Psychology*, 10 (August). https://doi.org/10.3389/fpsyg.2019.01962.

Read, J. D., Tollestrup, P., Hammersley, R., McFadzen, E., & Christensen, A. (1990). The unconscious transference effect: Are innocent bystanders ever misidentified? *Applied Cognitive Psychology*, 4(1), 3–31. https://doi.org/10.1002/acp.2350040103.

Ross, D. F., Ceci, S. J., Dunning, D., & Toglia, M. P. (1994a). Unconscious transference and mistaken identity: When a witness misidentifies a familiar but innocent person. *Journal of Applied Psychology*, 79(6), 918–930. https://doi.org/10.1037/0021-9010.79.6.918.

Ross, D. F., Ceci, S. J., Dunning, D., & Toglia, M. P. (1994b). Unconscious transference and lineup identification: Toward a memory blending approach. In D. F. Ross, J. D. Read & M. P. Toglia (eds), *Adult eyewitness testimony* (pp. 80–100). Cambridge University Press. https://doi.org/10.1017/cbo9780511759192.005.

Simons, D. J., & Levin, D. T. (1998). Failure to detect changes to people during a real-world interaction. *Psychonomic Bulletin & Review*, 5(4), 644–649. https://doi.org/10.3758/bf03208840.

Sjöberg, M. P. (2016). The show-up identification procedure: A literature review. *Open Journal of Social Sciences*, 4(1), 86–95. https://doi.org/10.4236/jss.2016.41012

Steblay, N. K., Dysart, J. E., Fulero, S., & Lindsay, R. C. L. (2003). Eyewitness accuracy rates in police showup and lineup presentations: A meta-analytic comparison. *Law and Human Behavior*, 27(5), 523–540. https://doi.org/10.1023/A.

Tanaka, J. W., & Simonyi, D. (2016). The 'parts and wholes' of face recognition: A review of the literature. *Quarterly Journal of*

Experimental Psychology, 69(10), 1876–1889. https://doi.org/10.1080/ 17470218.2016.1146780

Topp-Manriquez, L. D., McQuiston, D., & Malpass, R. S. (2016). Facial composites and the misinformation effect: How composites distort memory. *Legal and Criminological Psychology*, 21(2), 372–389. https:// doi.org/10.1111/lcrp.12054.

Tredoux, C. G., Sporer, S. L., Vredeveldt, A., Kempen, K., & Nortje, A. (2020). Does constructing a facial composite affect eyewitness memory? A research synthesis and meta-analysis. *Journal of Experimental Criminology*. https://doi.org/10.1007/s11292-020-09432-z.

Valentine, T., Davis, J. P., Memon, A., & Roberts, A. (2011). Live show-ups and their influence on a subsequent video line-up. *Applied Cognitive Psychology*, 26(1), 1–23. https://doi.org/10.1002/acp.1796.

Wells, G. L. (1984). The psychology of lineup identifications. *Journal of Applied Social Psychology*, 14(2), 89–103. https://doi.org/10.1111/j. 1559-1816.1984.tb02223.x.

Wells, G. L., Charman, S. D., & Olson, E. A. (2005). Building face composites can harm lineup identification performance. *Journal of Experimental Psychology: Applied*, 11(3), 147–156. https://doi.org/10.1037/ 1076-898X.11.3.147.

Wells, G. L., Kovera, M. B., Douglass, A. B., Brewer, N., Meissner, C. A., & Wixted, J. T. (2020). Policy and procedure recommendations for the collection and preservation of eyewitness identification evidence. *Law and Human Behavior*, 44(1), 3–36. https://doi.org/10.1037/lhb0000359.

4   The influence of race

Introduction

The previous chapter looked at unconscious transference and when innocent people are misidentified as being the perpetrators of crime, and the real-life case example of Ronald Cotton, who was misidentified and wrongly convicted of a crime he did not commit. In Ronald's case and many other cases of misidentification, innocent suspects have come from a different racial background to the witness tasked with making the identification. This chapter is going to focus on the influence that a person's race has when it comes to trying to recognise or identify another person, and how race can lead to face recognition going wrong.

A wealth of psychological research dating back over 40 years has revealed that people are better at identifying faces that are the same race as they are and are less able to recognise faces that belong to a different race to them. This phenomenon has been called the cross-race effect, cross-race deficit and the own-race bias (ORB), the term that will be used throughout this chapter. This chapter will focus specifically on the ORB, and how it influences face recognition, identification from face matching tasks and eyewitness identification from police lineups. We will look at some real-life examples of people who have been wrongly identified because they were a different race to a person who had been a witness or victim of a crime. We will discuss some of the theoretical explanations that have developed to explain the mechanisms behind the own-race bias and how it can affect everyday life. To begin with this chapter will look at

DOI: 10.4324/9781003177128-4

the everyday issues that can occur when people try to recognise the faces of those who may come from a different racial group.

Note from the author: I acknowledge that many terms such as gender, race and ethnicity are socially constructed categories, differ across societies and cultures, and over time, and have no universally accepted meaning. Nevertheless, researchers have categorised individuals into groups such as Black, white, Asian, male, female, etc., based on their own notions of categories. Many of the terms used in this chapter and also in Chapter 5 will be standard terms that are used in psychological face recognition literature; however, they may not be terms that are used in other spheres of academic literature.

Everyday errors

Much of this chapter will focus on the more forensic elements of other-race misidentifications, such as innocent persons being falsely imprisoned due to misidentifications, or inaccuracies in matching a person to their identification, like their passport. There is however some evidence that the own-race bias can influence everyday identifications and social interactions and I have personally also fallen foul of the ORB too.

Personal anecdote

In 2009 BBC2 aired a fantastic HBO-created US crime drama show called *The Wire*. It had been shown earlier in the USA. It centred around a Baltimore police service and local drug gangs. There was a fantastic multi-racial cast of actors who were relatively unknown at the time, such as Idris Elba and Dominic West. My partner and I used to watch this show every week; it had fantastic plotlines and acting, however, I used to get confused between some of the characters and sometimes I was not able to follow who was who. For example, some weeks I couldn't understand how one character who I thought had died would suddenly appear again. Fortunately, my other half was able to explain that this character was in fact a completely different person. One common denominator was that the characters I would get confused about were Black; it was like I could not distinguish between the different Black characters. This was my own first-hand personal experience of the 'own-race bias'. I was easily able to differentiate between the characters that were the same race as me (white) and not as accurate at recognising faces that belonged to the characters who were a different race to me (Black). My tendency was to confuse two different characters as being the same person if they were Black, rather than think that the one person was a different person. When I think about it, how dangerous would it have been if I had been an eyewitness and asked to identify any of these characters from a lineup. I would certainly be likely to make a false identification.

My personal anecdote about my own experience of the own-race bias is embarrassing, and I did wonder whether I should include it in this book. I am like most people: we don't really like to admit when we have made mistakes that could have serious consequences in another context. There has been very little research that has investigated the impact of the ORB and its consequences for everyday social interactions, such as those people have with colleagues at work, or at a university or school, where it is important to recognise who someone is. There are some quite famous examples where people have misidentified other people, and the common denominators are white people making mistakes identifying Black people. In July 2020, two white US senators, Marco Rubio and Dan Sullivan, took to social media to mourn the death of Representative John Lewis, who was a well respected figure of the civil rights movement. However, both senators posted the photograph of another Black representative, Elijah E. Cummings, who had died the previous year, to their social media and Facebook accounts. One of the senators even posted a photograph of himself shaking hands with the wrong person! As you can imagine social media was very quick to criticise the senators for posting photos of the wrong Black man (Morales, 2020). These mistakes have not been exclusive to US politicians; in the UK, two female Black MPs, Florence Eshalomi and Abena Oppong-Asare, reported on occasions that some their white colleagues in Westminster have confused them for one another (Proctor, 2020).

Although there have been lots of personal anecdotes of people who have been victims of the own-race bias and have been misidentified in everyday interactions, there has until recently been very little psychological research that has investigated this phenomenon. One study by McKone et al. (2021) surveyed Asian international students who had moved to Australia as adults to study and investigated how the ORB affected everyday social interactions. They found that the international students often had problems recognising white people and that white people often had problems recognising them, which affected their ability to socialise with white people. Furthermore, the majority of international students (81%) had experienced being confused for another Asian student by a white figure of authority (e.g. university lecturer, tutor and/or workplace boss), suggesting this was a common occurrence.

These anecdotes and the findings from research suggest that when it comes to trying to identify people of a different race, the faces 'all look the same'. However, there is some research that suggests the opposite is also true: people may wrongly identify two images of the same other-race person as two different people. In a study using a face sorting task that you read about in Chapter 1 (Andrews et al., 2015; Jenkins et al., 2011) a group of Asian and Caucasian students were presented with a set of Asian and Caucasian faces, and they had to sort them into piles for each identity. The set of faces was made up of two Caucasian identities, for which there were 20 different images, and two Chinese identities, again with 20 images for each, and they had to sort them into a pile for each identity. Participants sorted the faces into more piles when they were other-race faces as compared to own-race faces, which suggested that the same identities of other-race faces looked like different people (Laurence et al., 2016).

Making mistakes when trying to recognise people who may belong to a different race can be embarrassing for both the person who is misidentified, and the person who made the mistake. In relation to everyday errors, these often do not have serious consequences; however, when it comes to misidentifications in a forensic context, the ramifications of misidentification of innocent suspects can be serious, especially when there is the potential for incarceration and even the death penalty. The next section will explore the issue of eyewitness misidentifications where race has been a factor.

Eyewitness misidentification

Eyewitness identification can be persuasive evidence in court, especially when a witness appears to be confident in their identification of an assailant. However, research has shown that eyewitness identification is prone to error and a survey with real police lineups found that suspects were only chosen around 40% of the time from lineups (Memon et al., 2011). Even if a suspect is chosen from a lineup, it does not necessarily mean they are guilty; they could have been in the wrong place at the wrong time and look similar to the actual assailant. Mistaken eyewitness identifications are one of the main causes of wrongful convictions, which to date have contributed to approximately 70% of 375 convictions overturned by subsequent DNA evidence in the US. Of those cases of misidentification nearly 35% involved cross-race identification where the suspect and the witness were from different racial backgrounds. The Innocence Project found that for the majority of cross-race mistaken identifications, the witnesses were white, while the suspects were Black or Latino (data from https://innocenceproject.org). This finding demonstrates the serious ramifications that the own-race bias has on the criminal justice system, as wrongful convictions do not only mean an innocent person is imprisoned, but a guilty person may still be at large in the community (see box for real-life examples of wrongful convictions).

Real-life examples of misidentification

In 1982 a young white woman was brutally attacked by a Black man who had approached her on a bicycle. During the attack he told the victim that she wasn't special as he had been with a white girl before. The local police instantly singled out Marvin Anderson, not because he had any police record, but because he was known to have a white girlfriend. In fact, because Marvin did not have a criminal record the police did not have any mugshots of him, and when they went to the victim to see if she could identify her attacker from a photographic lineup, they used a colour photo taken from Marvin's work ID card and placed this in a lineup along with six other monochrome photographs. The victim was then shown a live lineup and Marvin was the only person who had been shown in the photo lineup. The victim identified Marvin as her assailant, although it was discovered later that the actual perpetrator was present in the photo array. Marvin's mother, girlfriend and all his neighbours said he was innocent, and according to Marvin everyone in the local community knew the real perpetrator was John Otis Lincoln. However, the court convicted him of two accounts of rape, sodomy, robbery and abduction. He was sentenced to 210 years, and spent 15 years in prison and 10 years on parole. It wasn't until 2002 that Marvin was eventually exonerated, when DNA evidence demonstrated that it was John Otis Lincoln who had been the real perpetrator, and not Marvin (Garrett, 2011).

In 1983, Habib Wahir Abdal, then known as Vincent Jenkins, was convicted of raping Leslie A. Werner, a young white woman, in a nature reserve in Buffalo, New York. Even though she had been blindfolded, Leslie's initial description of her assailant was a Black man who was between 5 foot 8 and 5 foot 10, with a space between his front teeth and wearing a hooded jacket. Four and a half months later Habib, who did not fit the description in any way, was arrested and questioned about the rape. Leslie was informed by police that Habib was the suspect; however, she initially failed to identify him as her assailant. After viewing a photo that was four years old, Leslie eventually identified Habib from a showup (where a single suspect is presented). On 6 June 1983 Adal was convicted by a jury and sentenced to prison for twenty years to life. Then in September 1999, after serving 16 years in prison for a crime he did not commit, Habib was exonerated through DNA evidence (data from https://innocenceproject.org). This is typical of several cases of mistaken identity in which it has later been found that the suspect was wrongfully convicted; in many of these cases, the suspect is from a different racial group to the victim.

Marvin and Habib haven't been alone in their experiences of being wrongly identified; as you will remember from reading about Ronald Cotton in Chapter 1, the Innocent Project found that 58% of people who were wrongfully convicted were Black. In both cases, being a different race to the victims of the crimes had some influence over being identified. A considerable amount of psychological research has also found that people are generally better at recognising the faces of people who are the same race as them, and much more likely to misidentify someone, or make a false identification of a person who is of a different race (Havard et al., 2017; Meissner & Brigham, 2001b). As you will have read from the previous chapter, also employing multiple identification procedures of being shown a photograph and then a showup containing the same individual will also have influenced the likelihood that both were misidentified. In Habib's case it was a photograph followed by a showup and in Marvin's case a biased photo array, as his photograph was the only colour one, followed by a lineup.

Psychological research has also confirmed the ORB using eyewitness identification paradigms. In these studies participants are shown either a live or video of a mock crime and then a lineup that either contains the previously seen perpetrator or a similar-looking innocent suspect. Findings from this research have revealed that when a person witnesses someone committing a crime who is a different race to them, and then they are shown a lineup that contains that perpetrator, they are much more likely to misidentify a foil, or filler member from the lineup, and are less likely to correctly identify the actual perpetrator. If they are shown a lineup where the perpetrator is not present and replaced by an innocent suspect, they are much more likely to make a misidentification and choose someone, rather than correctly say that the culprit is not there. In contrast, when a witness sees a culprit who is the same race as them they are much more likely to correctly identify that culprit if they are present in a lineup, or correctly say they aren't present if they are absent from a lineup (Havard et al., 2017, 2019; Jackiw et al., 2008). An example of this type of study was conducted by Havard et al. (2017) in the UK. In the study they showed groups of children two identical mock crimes, both depicting a young man who goes into an office and steals a laptop, mobile phone and a wallet. The only difference was that one film had a white thief and the other film had an Asian thief. After a delay of two or three days the children (individually) saw two lineups, one for the white thief and one for the Asian thief. The study found that white children showed an ORB and were much more accurate at identifying the white thief than the Asian thief, and were likely to misidentify an innocent Asian male from a lineup as compared to an innocent white male. In contrast the Asian children showed no ORB and were as accurate at identifying both thieves. I will explain why there was not an ORB in all children later on in the chapter, when we look at the explanations for the ORB.

As well as showing an ORB in identifying people from a lineup, an ORB has also been demonstrated in lineup construction, whereby those constructing the lineup are more selective when creating a lineup that has same race faces, and more likely to make a biased lineup for other-race faces (Brigham & Ready, 1985). Another form of bias in lineup construction that has been investigated in relation to the ORB involved small variations in the and background of the lineup images (Havard et al., 2019, 2023). Over several different experiments white and Black participants were shown Black and white target faces for five seconds and then there was a two-second delay before they saw a ten-face lineup (array) of the same race as the target face (see Figure 4.1). Participants had to decide whether the face they had just seen was one of the face in the lineup, or if the target face was not present in the lineup. The array either had all the backgrounds for each face exactly the same colour, or there were slight variations in the colours. Half of the arrays had the face that had been previously shown (target present) and half did not have the face that had been previously seen (target absent). The study found that the white participants were more accurate with faces that were the same race as them (white) and less accurate with faces that were of a different race (Black), while Black participants were in some cases more accurate with Black faces, but in other circumstances as accurate with white faces as they were Black faces. The main finding across all the studies was that when faces were presented on target absent arrays (where the target face wasn't present), and all the backgrounds were slightly

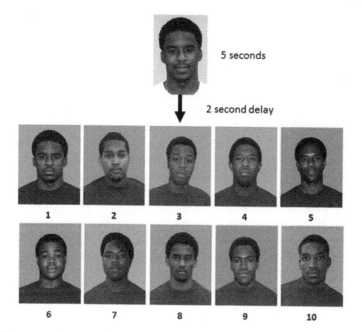

Figure 4.1 Do you think the target face is present in the array? If so, which number is he? Answer at the end of the chapter.
Source: From Havard, et al. (2023)

different shades of green or grey this increased the false choosing rate (i.e. innocent faces that hadn't been seen before were more likely to be chosen), and this was especially the case if the faces were Black.

This research and also real-life examples of misidentifications suggest that when it comes to creating lineups they should be created by people who are the same ethnicity as the suspect, as they might create less biased lineups (Wells & Olson, 2001). Also that when the lineups are created the backgrounds are all uniform and exactly the same colour and hue (Havard et al., 2019, 2023).

Face recognition and matching tasks

Psychological research investigating the ORB using face recognition tasks can be traced back to the 1960s and 1970s, where

Black and white participants in US were asked to recognise Black and white faces. The results often found evidence for the ORB, but especially so for the white participants trying to recognise Black faces (Cross et al., 1971; Malpass & Kravitz, 1969). Since the twenty-first-century research exploring the ORB has employed a variety of different populations around the world; such as Asians looking at Caucasian faces in the UK, China and Australia (Havard, 2021; Hayward et al., 2017; Wan et al., 2017), and Caucasians and African American faces viewing Caucasian and African American faces in the UK and USA (Havard et al., 2019; Meissner et al., 2005), Caucasians and Egyptians looking at Egyptian and Caucasian faces in the UK and Egypt (Kokje et al., 2018; Megreya et al., 2011) and research in multiracial societies such as Malaysia where a number of different racial groups (e.g. Chinese, Indian, Caucasian, Malaysian) reside a variety of people from different ethnic backgrounds (Wong et al., 2020). Much of the face recognition research has duplicated findings from eyewitness research, confirming that people are more likely to make false positives (falsely recognising an unknown face from someone who is of a different race), and also false negatives (failing to recognise a previously seen face if it belongs to someone who is of a different race) (Hancock & Rhodes, 2008; Meissner et al., 2008; Singh et al., 2021; Wong et al., 2020).

The ORB has also been replicated in face matching tasks where people are shown two photographs side by side and they must decide if they are the same person or two different people, similar to the task at passport control, where the passport officer must determine whether a traveller matches the photograph on their identification documents. Studies have found that people are much more accurate at matching faces that are the same race as them, and much more likely to make an error when matching faces that are a different race (Havard, 2021; Kokje et al., 2018; Megreya et al., 2011; Meissner et al., 2013). In one study, Caucasian and Egyptian participants were presented with Caucasian and Egyptian faces for a matching task. The results found not only were people better at matching faces that were the same race as them and less accurate with faces of a different race, but that matching was more accurate for matched pairs, two images of the same identity, as compared to mismatched pairs, where the images belong to two different people (Kokje et al., 2018). Meissner et al. (2013) also replicated the ORB where they presented Mexican American (own-race) and African American (other-race) target faces along with passport photographs to Mexican American participants and found greater accuracy for own-race pairings. Another race-matching study with Chinese and white participants found that not only was matching more accurate for own-race faces, but when the external features were removed (e.g. hair) this reduced matching more for other-race faces as compared to own-race faces (Havard, 2021).

As matching studies have demonstrated, the ORB is present when there is little memory component and the task involves face perception; this suggests that this phenomenon occurs at encoding. However, there are theories that propose that the way faces are stored in memory may also influence the ORB (Chiroro & Valentine, 1995). The next section will discuss the theoretical explanations that have arisen to try and understand the mechanisms for the ORB.

Theoretical explanations for own-race bias

As a result of the research that has investigated the own-race bias several theories have developed to explain why people are more accurate at identifying faces that are the same race as them. This section will now explore the main explanations that have arisen to explain the ORB, including the contact hypothesis, motivation and general face recognition ability.

Interracial contact

The contact hypothesis suggests that through the high level of contact that individuals have naturally with people who are the same race as them, they develop a perceptual expertise for recognising own-race faces, while less contact with other-race people results in poorer processing of other-race faces, i.e. people struggle to recognise people from races with which they have less frequent interactions (Chiroro & Valentine, 1995; Meissner & Brigham, 2001a; Singh et al., 2021). According to the contact hypothesis, the more experience that one has with a different racial group the more accurate one should be at identifying members of that particular group (Brigham & Malpass, 1985; Wong et al., 2020).

There are several studies that have investigated this theory and they have found mixed results. As you read earlier, the eye-witness study I ran with white and Asian children found a relationship between the level of contact that the children had with other-race individuals correlated with their correct identification of other-race targets. The Asian children had higher rates of inter-racial contact with whites and therefore showed no ORB, while the white children had little contact with Asians and they demonstrated an ORB in their responses (Havard et al., 2017). This finding replicates other studies that have found a relationship between interracial contact and the ORB (Corenblum & Miessner, 2006; Hancock & Rhodes, 2008).

Psychological research has not consistently found a relationship between levels of interracial contact and other-race recognition accuracy. In their study Wong et al. (2020) conducted a face recognition experiment in Malaysia with Malaysian, Chinese, Indian and Caucasian participants, who were asked to recognise Malaysian, Chinese, Indian and Caucasian faces, so all participants were recognising both same-race and other-race faces. Their results found no support for the contact hypothesis, as there were no correlations between self-reported contact with other races and performance on the recognition task, despite their participants living in a multi-racial society.

One of the reasons that some studies may have found a relationship while others have not might be the way that the interracial contact is measured. The majority of research investigating the ORB and the influence of interracial contact on face recognition most commonly measures interracial contact using a self-report questionnaire and there are a few different ones that have been developed over the years. The interracial contact questionnaire used by Hancock and Rhodes (2008) presented participants with a number of statements (e.g. 'I know lots of Chinese people', 'I socialize with Chinese people', etc.) and asked them to decide on a scale of 1 (for very strongly disagree) to 6 (for very strongly agree) for each statement. In their paper they found that there was reduced ORB for those who had higher levels of contact. Similarly, Walker and Hewstone (2006) asked participants to rate statements on 1–5 scales, but split up the statements into social contact (e.g. 'I spend time with Asian people', 'I often go round to the house of Asian people') and individuating experience (e.g. 'I have looked after my Asian friend when someone was causing them trouble', 'An Asian person has looked after me when I was feeling sad'). The individuating contact was to investigate the quality of contact and close personal contact individuals have with people from a different race, and it was found to reduce the ORB, and this has been replicated by further research investigating face matching (Havard, 2021). However as mentioned earlier, Wong and colleagues found no relationship between self-reported levels of contact and a reduction in the own-race bias, suggesting that either the contact measures used were not effective at assessing the levels of contact people had with other-race individuals, or as they suggested levels of contact only account for a small part of the ORB (Wong et al., 2020). Wong and colleagues used a questionnaire similar to the social contact questionnaire that does not assess individuating experiences and other research has confirmed that the social aspect of the contact questionnaire doesn't always predict the ORB. They also suggested that interracial contact measures should include not only current measures of contact, but also past contact as there is some suggestion that having interracial contact may need to occur in childhood to be effective at reducing the ORB.

In a study that investigated the effect of experience on the ORB, Zhou and colleagues compared face recognition of East Asians who were born and raised in Canada to those who had immigrated to Canada at different ages, from infancy to adulthood (Zhou et al., 2019). They found that those who were born in Canada showed no ORB, and that the length of stay in Canada correlated to the extent of the ORB, with those who arrived as adults showing the most impairments in recognising other-race faces. They concluded that the ORB was malleable and that early experience with other-race faces plays a role in the ORB. Estudillo et al. (2020) also support the idea of early expertise and the ORB. They found that Malaysian Indians showed no ORB when viewing Chinese faces (one of the predominant racial groups in

Malaysia), but did show reduced recognition accuracy when viewing white faces. This finding again lends more support to the idea that early experience and interracial contact are important factors in the ORB.

The notion of perceptual expertise suggests that cross race face recognition is a skill that can be improved with practise and the more time people spend with individuals of different races they will learn how to individuate members of different racial groups as a result the own-race bias should be reduced. However, it may be the case that there is a critical window for cross-race contact during childhood which results in a larger reduction in ORB as compared to contact in adulthood. One study explored the influence of age and duration of interracial contact on face recognition for other-race faces and found that to reduce the ORB interracial contact had to be before 12 years of age, and once in adulthood even after several years of social contact there was no reduction in the ORB (McKone et al., 2019).

There have been two meta-analyses that have examined the influence of contact and the own-race bias. and both reported a relationship between the levels of contact and the reduction in the ORB (Meissner & Brigham, 2001b; Singh et al., 2021). Although both studies found the relationship between self-report measures of contact and the ORB were relatively weak suggesting that self-report measures may underestimate the true relationship between levels of contact and the ORB, furthermore contact earlier in life seemed to be more effective for reducing the ORB.

The fact the ORB appears to only be reduced with contact from childhood up to the age of 12 years old might explain why many studies have failed to find a relationship between self-report questionnaires of interracial contact and accuracy for recognising other-race faces, as most self-report questionnaires are set in the present and do not ask about childhood experience, which it seems is the most important aspect to reduce the ORB.

Multidimensional face space

Another theory, that is also related in the contact hypothesis for the ORB, comes from the face space model, which focusses on how faces are stored in memory (Chiroro & Valentine, 1995;

Valentine, 2001; Valentine et al., 2016). This model suggests faces are stored in a multidimensional space, and the dimensions of the space represent different physical properties of the face (e.g. face shape, eyes, nose length, etc.) with the centre being an exemplar face combining the features of the most commonly encountered faces.

According to this model, own-race faces that are more frequently encountered, are stored near the centre of the space and spread out over the dimensions in relation to features that are useful for within group differentiations, depending on the race of face (e.g. for white face this could be eye colour, nose shape, hair colour and texture), while other-race faces, that are encountered less frequently, are stored further away from the centre in a cluster on the periphery and according to dimensions that are specific to that outgroup (e.g. skin tone). There is some research evidence that has supported the face space theory for the ORB (Abudarham & Yovel, 2016; Byatt & Rhodes, 2004; Corenblum & Meissner, 2006); however, it still isn't clear what exactly the dimensions are and how interracial contact can reduce the own-race bias in this model.

Motivation

An alternative explanation relates to social processes and the idea that we categorise people as being either from an ingroup (own race) or outgroup (different race). When meeting an ingroup member, we typically look for features to differentiate one person from another. However, if we categorise someone as being from an outgroup, we do not process their faces in the same way and instead look at more category specific features (e.g. brown or white skin) that are less effective at differentiating individuals (Levin, 1996, 2000). One effect of categorisation is that it can make faces that belong to the same category (e.g. race) as looking more similar to one another, leading to weaker recognition (Wilson et al., 2016).

The related categorization-individuation model (Hugenberg et al., 2010; Wilson et al., 2016) suggests that the ORB is due to the social factors of categorising faces into outgroup and ingroup, where there is greater motivation to individuate faces from an ingroup, that is look for the differentiating features, while for an outgroup face there is less motivation to differentiate outgroup faces from one another. This model suggests that it is possible to reduce the ORB if the correct motivation is applied and those viewing faces of outgroup members are asked to specifically try to look at features that individuate faces from one another. There is some evidence to support this model. Hugenberg et al. (2007) conducted a face recognition test with white and Black faces employing white participants. During the learning phase of the experiment some participants received additional instructions that informed them about the ORB and asked them to specifically look at what differentiated one face from another when it was a face that was of a different race. When it came to the recognition phase, those in the control group showed the typical ORB and were more accurate with own race faces; however, those who had had the additional instructions appeared to show no ORB.

There has been mixed support for the use of individuating instructions to reduce the ORB. Bornstein et al., (2013) tried to replicate Hugenberg and colleagues' study using the exact same instructions; however, they found that the ORB was not reduced, although the instructions did reduce overall the false alarm rates by making participants more conservative in their responses to new faces. Wan and colleagues also found no advantage of individuation instructions across five separate experiments, using white and East Asian faces and white and East Asian participants (Wan et al., 2015). They suggested that the social motivation model and categorization-individuation model are only relevant to particular cultural settings where people from a high social economic status (typically US whites) are looking at the faces of lower social status groups (typically US Blacks). They suggest that in other cultures where there is less distinction between social economic status and race, that lack of experience (i.e., inter-racial contact) is the main cause for the ORB.

General face recognition ability

An alternative theory to explain the ORB relates to people's ability to generally recognise faces and faces that are the same race as them. As you will read later in this book there are some people who have extraordinary abilities for recognising faces and have been called 'super recognisers' (Chapter 11), and there are other people who have a clinical deficit called prosopagnosia (Chapter 9) and cannot recognise the face of their family, friends and sometimes their own face in the mirror. The majority of people's face recognition abilities will be somewhere in the middle; however, there are individual differences in people's ability to recognise faces with some individuals who are naturally better at recognising faces, and others that are worse at recognising faces, but not to a clinical deficit level (Bindemann et al., 2012; Megreya & Burton, 2006).

There is some evidence that a person's general face recognition ability when viewing own-race faces can influence their ability to recognise other-race faces. In the face-matching task described earlier by Kokje and colleagues with white and Egyptian faces, performance on the same-race faces correlated to performance on the other-race faces, i.e. those who were more accurate with own-race faces were also more accurate with other-race faces, and the reverse pattern was found for those who were less accurate with own-race faces. In another study looking at recognition of own-race and other-race faces with Caucasian and Chinese participants, it was found that people who performed poorly recognising own-race faces were even less accurate at other-race faces, and some were so poor at other-race face recognition that they could be classified as having other-race face blindness (Wan et al., 2017). The study suggested that the ORB was due to a person's underlying face recognition ability, and also a lack of interracial contact. Another study investigated the influence of face processing ability and interracial contact, by comparing performance on face recognition and face matching tasks (Correll et al., 2021). The study found that those more accurate on the face recognition task using memory showed a reduced ORB, while those who performed more accurately on the matching task only showed a reduced ORB if they also had higher rates of interracial contact. Other research has also found a correlation between accuracy at identifying own-race faces and also those from another race (Havard et al., 2023). These studies suggest that both underlying face recognition ability and interracial contact are an important aspects of the ORB. It could be that the ORB develops as a combination of general face recognition ability and the lack of interracial contact and many previous studies that have investigated the ORB have not measured individuals' underlying general face recognition ability with own-race faces.

More evidence of the influence on underlying face recognition ability and its effect on the ORB comes from research with super recognisers, who have extraordinary face recognition ability There is some evidence that super recognisers, although outperforming other individuals on face recognition tasks with other-race faces, still perform more poorly with other-race faces as compared to own-race faces (Bate et al., 2019). Using a battery of face recognition and face matching tasks, Robertson et al., (2020) found that higher accuracy on for own-race faces was also correlated to higher performance on other-race faces. Furthermore, a group of super recognisers outperformed the rest of the participants (typical recognisers) on both own-race and other-race face identification tasks, although they still demonstrated an ORB.

However, not all research has supported the idea that general face recognition ability influences the ORB. In a large-scale study of over 800 participants in seven different countries, there was no clear relationship between individual face recognition ability and levels of contact, measured by the social contact questionnaire and the ORB. Nearly all the participants did reveal an ORB and many had very low level of contact with other-race individuals (Childs et al., 2021). This research suggests that we still have some way to go to fully understand the mechanisms behind the ORB. For example, many of the face recognition tests researchers use to test people's face recognition ability use artificially created stimuli such as the Cambridge Face Memory Test (Duchaine & Nakayama, 2006), which will be discussed in more detail later in this book. Also measures of interracial contact such as the Social Contact questionnaire (Walker & Hewstone, 2006) don't always seem to adequately measure contact, especially past contact, which seems to be important in reducing the ORB.

Conclusion

This chapter looked at the well-researched phenomenon of the own-race bias and when face recognition goes 'wrong' because someone is trying to identify someone who is a different race than they are. The effects of the ORB are far-reaching. When it comes to eyewitness misidentifications, wrongful convictions can have serious ramifications for the criminal justice process. Also, errors in matching passports could lead to people being let across borders illegally. The ORB also influences everyday interactions for those who live in countries where they are no longer the most commonly seen race. Further research still needs to be undertaken to fully understand mechanisms underlying the ORB, although interracial contact, motivation and general face recognition ability appear to be involved in some capacity. It could be that the best way to prevent misidentifications due to the ORB at passport control and for other situations that involve face identification is to recruit a more ethnically diverse group of people to these roles, and also those that naturally have a higher-than-average ability at face recognition.

(Answer to Figure 4.1: the correct answer is no. 9)

References

Abudarham, N., & Yovel, G. (2016). Reverse engineering the face space: Discovering the critical features for face identification. *Journal of Vision*, 16(3), 1–18. https://doi.org/10.1167/16.3.40.

Andrews, S., Jenkins, R., Cursiter, H., & Burton, A. M. (2015). Telling faces together: Learning new faces through exposure to multiple instances. *Quarterly Journal of Experimental Psychology*, 68(10), 2041–2050. https://doi.org/10.1080/17470218.2014.1003949.

Bate, S., Bennetts, R., Hasshim, N., Portch, E., Murray, E., Burns, E., & Dudfield, G. (2019). The limits of super recognition: An other-ethnicity effect in individuals with extraordinary face recognition skills. *Journal of Experimental Psychology: Human Perception and Performance*, 45(3), 363–377. https://doi.org/10.1037/xhp0000607.

Bindemann, M., Avetisyan, M., & Rakow, T. (2012). Who can recognize unfamiliar faces? Individual differences and observer consistency in person identification. *Journal of Experimental Psychology. Applied*, 18 (3), 277–291. https://doi.org/10.1037/a0029635.

Bornstein, B. H., Laub, C. E., Meissner, C. A., & Susa, K. J. (2013). The cross-race effect: Resistant to instructions. *Journal of Criminology*, 2013, 1–6. https://doi.org/10.1155/2013/745836.

Brigham, J. C., & Malpass, R. S. (1985). The role of experience and contact in the recognition of faces of own- and other-race persons.

Journal of Social Issues, 41(3), 139–155. https://doi.org/10.1111/J.1540-4560.1985.TB01133.X.

Brigham, J. C., & Ready, D. J. (1985). Own-race bias in lineup construction. *Law and Human Behavior*, 9(4), 415–424. https://doi.org/10.1007/BF01044480.

Byatt, G., & Rhodes, G. (2004). Identification of own-race and other-race faces: Implications for the representation of race in face space. *Psychonomic Bulletin and Review*, 11(4), 735–741. https://doi.org/10.3758/BF03196628.

Childs, M. J., Jones, A., Thwaites, P., Zdravković, S., Thorley, C., Suzuki, A., Shen, R., Ding, Q., Burns, E., Xu, H., & Tree, J. J. (2021). Do individual differences in face recognition ability moderate the other ethnicity effect? *Journal of Experimental Psychology. Human Perception and Performance*, 47(7), 893–907. https://doi.org/10.1037/xhp0000762.

Chiroro, P., & Valentine, T. (1995). An Investigation of the contact hypothesis of the own-race bias in face recognition. *The Quarterly Journal of Experimental Psychology Section A*, 48(4), 879–894. https://doi.org/10.1080/14640749508401421.

Corenblum, B., & Meissner, C. A. (2006). Recognition of faces of ingroup and outgroup children and adults. *Journal of Experimental Child Psychology*, 93(3), 187–206. https://doi.org/10.1016/j.jecp.2005.09.001.

Correll, J., Ma, D. S., & Davis, J. P. (2021). Perceptual tuning through contact? Contact interacts with perceptual (not memory-based) face-processing ability to predict cross-race recognition. *Journal of Experimental Social Psychology*, 92(January), 104058. https://doi.org/10.1016/j.jesp.2020.104058.

Cross, J. F., Cross, J., & Daly, J. (1971). Sex, race, age and beauty as factors in recognition of faces. *Perception*, 10(6), 393–396.

Duchaine, B., & Nakayama, K. (2006). The Cambridge Face Memory Test: Results for neurologically intact individuals and an investigation of its validity using inverted face stimuli and prosopagnosic participants. *Neuropsychologia*, 44(4), 576–585. https://doi.org/10.1016/j.neuropsychologia.2005.07.001.

Estudillo, A. J., Lee, J. K. W., Mennie, N., & Burns, E. (2020). No evidence of other-race effect for Chinese faces in Malaysian non-Chinese population. *Applied Cognitive Psychology*, 34(1), 270–276. https://doi.org/10.1002/acp.3609.

Garrett, B. (2011). *Convicting the innocent: Where criminal prosecutions go wrong* (pp. 45–83). Harvard University Press.

Hancock, K. J., & Rhodes, G. (2008). Contact, configural coding and the other-race effect in face recognition. *British Journal of Psychology*, 99(1), 45–56. https://doi.org/10.1348/000712607X199981.

Havard, C. (2021). The importance of internal and external features in matching own and other race faces. *Perception*, 50(10). https://doi.org/10.1177/03010066211043464.

Havard, C., Memon, A., & Humphries, J. E. (2017). The own-race bias in child and adolescent witnesses. *International Journal of Police Science and Management*, 19(4). https://doi.org/10.1177/1461355717731579.

Havard, C., Richter, S., & Thirkettle, M. (2019). Effects of changes in background colour on the identification of own- and other-race faces. *I-Perception*, 10(2). https://doi.org/10.1177/2041669519843539.

Havard, C., Breese, E., Thirkettle, M., Kask, K., Leol, K. L., & Mädamürk, K. (2023). A background of bias: Subtle changes in lineup backgrounds increase the own race bias. *Journal of Police and Criminal Psychology*, 0123456789. https://doi.org/10.1007/s11896-023-09578-2

Hayward, W. G., Favelle, S. K., Oxner, M., Chu, M. H., & Lam, S. M. (2017). The other-race effect in face learning: Using naturalistic images to investigate face ethnicity effects in a learning paradigm. *Quarterly Journal of Experimental Psychology*, 70(5), 890–896. https://doi.org/10.1080/17470218.2016.1146781.

Horry, R., & Wright, D. B. (2008). I know your face but not where I saw you: Context memory is impaired for other-race faces. *Psychonomic Bulletin and Review*, 15(3), 610–614. https://doi.org/10.3758/PBR.15.3.610.

Hugenberg, K., Miller, J., & Claypool, H. M. (2007). Categorization and individuation in the cross-race recognition deficit: Toward a solution to an insidious problem. *Journal of Experimental Social Psychology*, 43 (2), 334–340. https://doi.org/10.1016/j.jesp.2006.02.010.

Hugenberg, K., Young, S. G., Bernstein, M. J., & Sacco, D. F. (2010). The categorization-individuation model: An integrative account of the other-race recognition deficit. *Psychological Review*, 117(4), 1168–1187. https://doi.org/10.1037/a0020463.

Jackiw, L. B., Arbuthnott, K. D., Pfeifer, J. E., Marcon, J. L., & Meissner, C. A. (2008). Examining the cross-race effect in lineup identification using Caucasian and First Nations samples. *Canadian Journal of Behavioural Science*, 40(1), 52–57.

Jenkins, R., White, D., Van Montfort, X., & Mike Burton, A. (2011). Variability in photos of the same face. *Cognition*, 121(3), 313–323. https://doi.org/10.1016/j.cognition.2011.08.001.

Kokje, E., Bindemann, M., & Megreya, A. M. (2018). Cross-race correlations in the abilities to match unfamiliar faces. *Acta Psychologica*, 185 (January), 13–21. https://doi.org/10.1016/j.actpsy.2018.01.006.

Laurence, S., Zhou, X., & Mondloch, C. J. (2016). The flip side of the other-race coin: They all look different to me. *British Journal of Psychology*, 107(2), 374–388. https://doi.org/10.1111/bjop.12147.

Lebrecht, S., Pierce, L. J., Tarr, M. J., & Tanaka, J. W. (2009). Perceptual other-race training reduces implicit racial bias. *PLoS ONE*, 4(1). https://doi.org/10.1371/journal.pone.0004215.

Levin, D. T. (1996). Classifying faces by race: The structure of face categories. *Journal of Experimental Psychology: Learning Memory and Cognition*, 22(6), 1364–1382. https://doi.org/10.1037/0278-7393.22.6.1364.

Levin, D. T. (2000). Race as a visual feature: Using visual search and perceptual discrimination tasks to understand face categories and the cross-race recognition deficit. *Journal of Experimental Psychology: General*, 129(4), 559–574. https://doi.org/10.1037/0096-3445.129.4.559.

Malpass, R. S., & Kravitz, J. (1969). Recognition for faces of own and other race. *Journal of Personality and Social Psychology*, 13(4), 330–334. https://doi.org/10.1037/h0028434.

McKone, E., Dawel, A., Robbins, R. A., Shou, Y., Chen, N., & Crookes, K. (2021). Why the other-race effect matters: Poor recognition of other-race faces impacts everyday social interactions. *British Journal of Psychology*, 1–23. https://doi.org/10.1111/bjop.12508.

McKone, E., Wan, L., Pidcock, M., Crookes, K., Reynolds, K., Dawel, A., Kidd, E., & Fiorentini, C. (2019). A critical period for faces: Other-race face recognition is improved by childhood but not adult social contact. *Scientific Reports*, 9(1). https://doi.org/10.1038/s41598-019-49202-0.

Megreya, A. M., & Burton, A. M. (2006). Unfamiliar faces are not faces: Evidence from a matching task. *Memory & Cognition*, 34(4), 865–876.

Megreya, A. M., White, D., & Burton, A. M. (2011). The other-race effect does not rely on memory: Evidence from a matching task. *Quarterly Journal of Experimental Psychology*, 64(8), 1473–1483. https://doi.org/10.1080/17470218.2011.575228.

Meissner, C. A., & Brigham, J. C. (2001a). A meta-analysis of the verbal overshadowing effect in face identification. *Applied Cognitive Psychology*, 15(6), 603–616. https://doi.org/10.1002/acp.728.

Meissner, C. A., & Brigham, J. C. (2001b). Thirty years of investigating the own-race bias in memory for faces: A meta-analytic review. *Psychology, Public Policy, and Law*, 7(1), 3–35. https://doi.org/10.1037//1076-8971.7.1.3.

Meissner, C. A., Brigham, J. C., & Butz, D. A. (2005). Memory for own- and other-race faces: A dual-process approach. *Applied Cognitive Psychology*, 19(5), 545–567. https://doi.org/10.1002/acp.1097.

Meissner, C. A., Sporer, S. L., & Susa, K. J. (2008). A theoretical review and meta-analysis of the description-identification relationship in memory for faces. *European Journal of Cognitive Psychology*, 20(3), 414–455. https://doi.org/10.1080/09541440701728581.

Meissner, C. A., Susa, K. J., & Ross, A. B. (2013). Can I see your passport please? Perceptual discrimination of own- and other-race faces. *Visual Cognition*, 21(9–10),1287–1305. https://doi.org/10.1080/13506285. 2013.832451.

Memon, A., Havard, C., Clifford, B., Gabbert, F., & Watt, M. (2011). A field evaluation of the VIPER system: a new technique for eliciting eyewitness identification evidence. *Psychology, Crime & Law*, 17(8), 711–729. https://doi.org/10.1080/10683160903524333

Morales, C. (2020). 2 Republican senators post photos of Elijah Cummings in John Lewis tributes. *The New York Times*, 18 July. www.nytimes. com/2020/07/18/us/marco-rubio-elijah-cummings-john-lewis.html.

Proctor, K. (2020). Black MPs tell of being confused with other politicians. *The Guardian*, 12 January. www.theguardian.com/politics/ 2020/jan/12/black-mps-tell-of-being-confused-with-other-politicians.

Robertson, D. J., Black, J., Chamberlain, B., Megreya, A. M., & Davis, J. P. (2020). Super-Recognisers show an advantage for other race face identification. *Applied Cognitive Psychology*, 34(1), 205–216. https:// doi.org/10.1002/acp.3608.

Singh, B., Mellinger, C., Earls, H. A., Tran, J., Bardsley, B., & Correll, J. (2021). Does cross-race contact improve cross-race face perception? A meta-analysis of the cross-race deficit and contact. *Personality and Social Psychology Bulletin*, 48(6). https://doi.org/10.1177/01461672211024463.

Slone, A. E., Brigham, J. C., & Meissner, C. A. (2000). Social and cognitive factors affecting the own-race bias in whites. *Basic and Applied Social Psychology*, 22(2), 71–84. https://doi.org/10.1207/ S15324834BASP2202_1.

Valentine, T. (2001). Face-space models of face recognition. *Computational, Geometric, and Process Perspectives on Facial Cognition: Contexts and Challenges*, July, 83–113. http://ivizlab.sfu.ca/arya/Pap ers/Others/Facespace Models.pdf

Valentine, T., Lewis, M. B., & Hills, P. J. (2016). Face-space: A unifying concept in face recognition research. *Quarterly Journal of Experimental Psychology*, 69(10), 1996–2019. https://doi.org/10.1080/ 17470218.2014.990392

Walker, P. M., & Hewstone, M. (2006). A perceptual discrimination investigation of the own-race effect and intergroup experience. *Applied Cognitive Psychology*, 20(4), 461–475. https://doi.org/10.1002/acp.1191.

Wan, L., Crookes, K., Dawel, A., Pidcock, M., Hall, A., & McKone, E. (2017). Face-blind for other-race faces: Individual differences in other-race recognition impairments. *Journal of Experimental Psychology: General*, 146(1), 102–122. https://doi.org/10.1037/xge0000249.

Wan, L., Crookes, K., Reynolds, K. J., Irons, J. L., & McKone, E. (2015). A cultural setting where the other-race effect on face recognition has no social-motivational component and derives entirely from lifetime perceptual experience. *Cognition*, 144(10), 91–115. https://doi.org/10.1016/j.cognition.2015.07.011.

Wells, G. L., & Olson, E. A. (2001). The other-race effect in eyewitness identification: What do we do about it? *Psychology, Public Policy, and Law*, 7(1), 230–246. https://doi.org/10.1037/1076-8971.7.1.230.

Wilson, J. P., Bernstein, M. J., &, & Hugenberg, K. (2016). A synthetic perspective on the own-race bias in eyewitness identification. In B. H. Bornstein & M. K. Miller (eds), *Advances in psychology and law, volume 2* (pp. 241–270). Springer.

Wong, H. K., Stephen, I. D., & Keeble, D. R. T. (2020). The own-race bias for face recognition in a multiracial society. *Frontiers in Psychology*, 11(6 March). https://doi.org/10.3389/fpsyg.2020.00208.

Zhou, X., Elshiekh, A., & Moulson, M. C. (2019). Lifetime perceptual experience shapes face memory for own- and other-race faces. *Visual Cognition*, 27(9–10), 687–700. https://doi.org/10.1080/13506285.2019.1638478.

5 The influence of gender

Introduction

The own-race bias is one of several biases found in face recognition, and there is also much less researched bias known as the own-sex or own-gender bias, which suggests that people are more accurate at recognising faces that are the same sex/gender as them. There has also been some evidence from psychological research that there are differences in face recognition according to a person's gender/sex, with women, on average, being more accurate at recognising faces than men. This chapter will focus on the own-sex bias and the influence of a person's sex on their ability to recognise faces, and whether women make better eye-witnesses than men. It will also explore some of the possible mechanisms for sex differences in face recognition and whether sexual orientation should also be taken into consideration.

Categorising gender

When you meet someone new one of the first thing you notice is the person's race and their gender. As you read in the last chapter, this can be important in whether we can recognise that face later. A person's race is one of the first things we automatically categorise when we see a face, along with their gender. Psychological research also provides evidence that sex or gender categorisation occurs quickly and often very accurately (Bruce et al., 1993; Burton et al., 1993). We seem to need to categorise a person by their gender, even if it is a person we do not plan to

DOI: 10.4324/9781003177128-5

interact with and often do this automatically until there is ambiguity over a person's gender. For example, my grandmother, who in her last years was very hard of hearing, often used to say very loudly upon seeing a stranger out and about, '*Is that a man or a woman?*', even though she had no intention of talking to that person. Like the rest of us, she still felt she needed to know the gender of a stranger to be able to categorise them.

Author's note

Before examining the literature that has investigated the influence of gender/sex differences in face recognition, it is important to make a clarification about this research. The psychological research that has looked at whether there are differences in face recognition according to sex or gender has focused on the binary categorisation of sex, rather than gender identification. As a result, at the time of writing this book, research has only focused on male and female participants trying to recognise male and female faces. There is currently no face recognition research that has investigated the influence of gender with nonbinary participants, or those who identify as a different gender to the biological sex they were assigned at birth. Throughout the face recognition literature, gender and sex have been terms that have been used interchangeably; however, in reality the research has only focused on sex and not gender identification.

Sex differences in face recognition

In the last chapter we looked at the influence of race and how it affected face recognition. One of the underlying mechanisms behind the own-race bias was a person's underlying ability to recognise own-race faces, with individual differences accounting for how well people can recognise faces. One of the individual differences that has been found to influence face recognition is a person's sex. There are a large number of studies that have found, on average, females out-perform males on face recognition tasks (Herlitz & Lovén, 2013; Herlitz & Rehnman, 2008; Lewin & Herlitz, 2002; Lovén et al., 2011; Petersen & Leue, 2021;

Rehnman & Herlitz, 2006, 2007). Studies have found that males are less likely to correctly recognise a previously seen face as compared to females, but they are also more likely to incorrectly say a new face has been previously seen, and therefore more likely to make a misidentification or false positive as compared to females (Guillem & Mograss, 2005). So according to this research face recognition is more likely to 'go wrong' when males are making the face recognition decision as compared to females.

There are several suggestions as to why females outperform males on face recognition tasks. The perceptual expertise model is supported by research which discovered infant girls pay more attention to faces than infant boys (Connellan et al., 2000) and that women are better at recognising facial expressions (Gregorić, et al., 2014; Wingenbach et al., 2018). From an early age, female infants make more eye contact than boys, giving them greater exposure to faces from early childhood (Leeb & Rejskind, 2004). Another reason for females' advantage over males for face recognition may be due to females being better at perceiving, recognising and interpreting facial expressions (Wingenbach et al., 2018). There is also evidence that females process faces faster and more efficiently than males (McBain et al., 2009; Megreya et al., 2011; Sommer et al., 2013). Furthermore, females' superior face recognition skills could be related to outperforming males on a number of other episodic memory tasks that involve personal experiences (Asperholm et al., 2019).

In their meta-analysis, Herlitz and Lovén (2013) found that on average females remembered more faces as compared to males and that they remembered more female faces as compared to male faces. Furthermore, females were only more accurate than males with female faces, and when it came to recognising male faces there were no differences in accuracy. Interestingly, when experiments used only male faces, females were more accurate than males on those faces, but when studies used both male and female faces, females were only more accurate than males with the female faces. Herlitz and Lovén (2013) suggested females may focus more on female faces at the expense of male faces, similar to the ingroup/outgroup bias that has also been used to explain the own-race bias (Hugenberg et al., 2013; Sporer, 2001). They suggest that when only male faces are presented females' general advantage of face processing and episodic memory leads to higher face recognition; however, when both male and female faces are presented, more cognitive resources (e.g. attention) are spent on the ingroup (female faces) at the expense of the male faces that have been categorised as belonging to an outgroup.

So far most of the research has suggested that males are worse at face recognition than females; however, there have been a few studies that have shown that has not always been the case. One study found that males could remember more faces than females in a face recognition task, but this was only the case when the faces had been seen for very short periods of time (e.g. less than 1 second); once the length of exposure was increased there were no differences in the number of faces remembered by males or females. However, when females saw only female faces and males saw only male faces, females still remembered more faces than males (Hansen et al., 2021). One of the criticisms of this study is that it used the exact same images from study to test, so it could be argued that this was an image recognition task rather than face recognition task (Burton, 2013).

Another study that aimed to investigate whether it was possible to find a face recognition task where males might outperform females used the faces of children's toys as test stimuli (Ryan & Gauthier, 2016). The study presented Barbie doll faces and Transformer figure faces for a recognition task, and the findings revealed that males were more accurate with Transformer faces, and females with Barbie faces. Interestingly, there were no gender differences with human faces in this study. Ryan and Gauthier (2016) suggested that the role of experience has a part to play in females' advantage in recognising faces. In their study they suggest that males' greater self-reported experience with Transformer faces was the underlying reason for the increase in accuracy; however, they also point out that recognising Transformer faces may be more akin to object recognition rather than face recognition. Furthermore, females had greater self-reported experience with Barbies than men, resulting in increased accuracy for these faces, which were more like human faces.

In a study examining the role of experience in face recognition, the influence of a person's hometown population density was also considered in addition to the effect of a person's gender.

Individuals who came from hometowns with smaller populations were poorer at unfamiliar face recognition tasks as compared to participants from higher density population towns (Balas & Saville, 2017). It was suggested those who grow up in places with small populations will see fewer faces while growing up, and therefore have limited exposure to a variety of faces and fewer opportunities to learn different types of faces. In their study, Sunday et al. (2019) presented male and female participants with a battery of face recognition tasks, and found that females from small hometowns outperformed males from small hometowns; however, when it came to participants from large hometowns there were no differences as a function of gender. These findings appear to show there are multiple factors that can influence face recognition, and that hometown density along with gender can influence how well we are able to recognise unfamiliar faces.

Sex differences in face matching and perception

As you will have read in previous chapters, another way to verify someone's identity is to see two different images of that same person, and try and determine if they are the same person or two different people. Some research found differences in matching accuracy as a function of the viewer's sex. Megreya, Bindemann and Havard (2011) presented pairs of male and female faces either as whole faces, with internal features masked (eyes, nose and mouth), or the external features masked (hair and face shape), and participants had to decide if they were the same person or two different people. For whole faces, they found female participants were more accurate than males at determining that two faces were two different persons (mismatch), regardless of the sex of the faces. Furthermore, females showed an own-sex advantage for faces that were the same identity (match), while males showed no bias. When it came to matching faces that had either the internal or external features removed, female participants demonstrated an own-sex advantage on trials where the two faces were the same person (match), and were more accurate than males on mismatch trials where the two faces were different people.

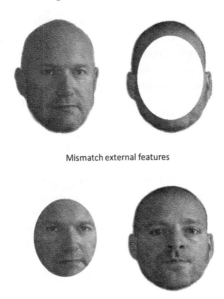

Mismatch external features

Mismatch internal features

Figure 5.1 Example of face matching task.

What Megreya et al. (2011) revealed is that the own-gender bias is not only related to females having superior encoding and memory for own-sex faces, but this phenomenon also occurs at the perception stage. They did find the sex differences in their matching task were not as large as other studies have found, suggesting that memory also has a part to play in sex differences in face recognition and the own-sex bias.

McBain et al. (2009) investigated gender differences in face perception using two different experiments. The first experiment utilised an unusual paradigm where participants had to detect if an upright or inverted (upside down) face or upright tree was present in a line drawing. Across shorter and longer presentation times females consistently outperformed males at detecting both upright and inverted faces, but there were no differences when it came to trees. In their second experiment participants were presented with a target face and then a face pair and had to decide which of the pair was the originally presented with the target face. Replicating experiment 1, females out-performed males, and were more accurate at detecting previously presented faces. McBain and colleagues claim that their findings demonstrate that there is a female advantage not only for the memory of faces, but also the perception and detection of faces.

Sommer et al. (2013) used a different method to investigate gender differences by reanalysing the datasets from several previously conducted studies that had employed a variety of face memory (e.g. face recognition, eyewitness experiments) and face perception tasks (e.g. face matching), along with a series of other measures of general cognition. None of the previous studies had explicitly looked at gender differences in their findings. Across both the face memory and face perception tasks female participants had superior performance, especially as the age groups got older as male participants' ability declined with age. Age is another factor that can influence face recognition and will be explored in the next chapter (Chapter 6).

The studies described in this section have demonstrated that females not only out-perform men on face recognition tasks that require memory, but females are more accurate at face perception tasks, e.g. face matching and deciding if a pair of acesfaces are the same person or not; all of these tasks do not require any memory component. Although women appear to be on average more accurate on face processing and recognition tasks as compared to men, it does appear the sex of the faces they are presented with can also influence performance and this is explored in the next section of this chapter.

Own-sex bias

As you read earlier, there are biases where individuals are better at recognising some faces over others, and one of those biases appears to be related to the gender or sex of the faces being viewing and the person viewing them. The own-gender bias, also known as the cross-sex effect, or own-sex bias, the term that I will use throughout the rest of this chapter, suggests that we have a better memory for faces that are the same sex as us (Sporer, 2001). The own-sex bias (OSB) phenomenon has not received as much research as the own-race bias, and this is thought to be because sex differences in face recognition studies were generally not analysed (Sporer, 2001). It's only over the last 20 years or so that there has been more research that has investigated the OSB and why it may occur.

Although it has been suggested that there is an OSB for both males and females (Herlitz & Lovén, 2013), there have been very few studies that found a full cross-over bias where both males and females are more accurate at recognising same-sex faces (Wright & Sladden, 2003). Using a typical face recognition study, Wright and Sladden (2003) presented photographs of male and female faces, with and without hair, that had been mounted on cards for a face recognition task. They found a strong sex bias, with both male and female participants being more accurate in recognising same sex faces, especially when those faces had hair as opposed to having the hair removed. This finding, along with Megreya et al. (2011) finding suggests that hair is important for recognising faces, especially those that are the same sex. However, it should be noted that Wright and Sladden's (2003) study used the exact same photographs in the study phase to the test phase and so may be more of an image recognition task rather than a face recognition task.

Although Wright and Sladden (2003) found an OSB for both men and women, the majority of research from psychological studies does not support this assertion, although there is evidence that there is an OSB for females recognising female faces. Lewin and Herlitz (2002) conducted a standard face recognition task of viewing male and females target faces during a learning phase and then male and female faces, half of which had been previously seen in a test phase. When it came to recognising previously seen male faces there were no differences between the accuracy for the male and female participants; however, females were significantly more accurate than males for female faces.

Herlitz and Lovén (2013) conducted a meta-analysis that looked at 43 different studies of sex differences in face recognition, with male and female participants of different ages. They found that woman and girls remembered more faces than men and boys. For the majority of studies, women and girls demonstrated an own-sex advantage by remembering more female than male faces, but this was not found consistently with men and boys recognising male faces. The female advantage was small though and not as large as the own-race bias, although it was persistent even when recognising other-race faces (Herlitz & Lovén, 2013).

The own-sex bias may have been masked in some face recognition research as there are several hundred studies that have used the Cambridge Face Memory Test (CFMT) developed by Duchaine and Nakayama (2006), which is a face recognition test to assess for prosopagnosia, or face blindness, which will be discussed later in this book (Chapter 9.) In the CFMT, participants are presented with a series of male faces specifically to try and prevent the own-gender bias that had previously been reported in other studies (Duchaine & Nakayama, 2006). The long version was developed, the CFMT+, specifically to investigate people who had superior face recognition ability, and this will be discussed later in the book (Chapter 11). More recently, Arrington et al. (2022) developed a new test for face recognition, the Female Cambridge Face Memory Test–Long Form (F-CFMT+). The F-CFMT+ was specifically designed so that the own-gender bias could be investigated using a test that was equivalent to the male version. At this time of writing, the FCFMT+ is a relatively new recognition test and therefore there has been limited research published using this test to investigate the own-gender bias. One study found no gender bias in using either the F-CFMT+ or CFMT+ (Scherf et al., 2017). One criticism of all the Cambridge face recognition tests is that hair is cropped out of the face images, and as you read earlier, research shows that hair is important for face recognition (Megreya et al., 2011; Wright & Sladden, 2003). Also, all the images are very uniform, showing little variation in lighting and natural ambiance.

Why do only women demonstrate an own-sex bias?

What are the mechanisms underlying the OSB in females? Why is it that only females show an OSB and males do not? Like most phenomena in psychology, there are several different theoretical explanations for the OSB. One explanation that has also been used to explain the own-race bias described in the previous chapter and early in this chapter is own-group bias (OGB). This theory suggests when we see a new person, we categorise them as either being from the same group as us, or being from a different group to us, and depending on how we categorise the person will influence how well we process their faces. For people we deem to be from the same group as us (ingroup) we will use more attentional resources, processing their faces at an individual level resulting in deeper encoding, and a more accurate memory. If we categorise someone as coming from a different group to us (outgroup), we use fewer attentional resources, and process their face on a shallower category level. For this shallow processing, we look at facial features that are common for that category of group, and not features that are useful to discriminate individuals from one another, resulting in the faces being more difficult to tell apart (Fuller et al., 2021). There is some evidence to support this theory as research has shown that own-group bias can be manipulated using various types of ingroup/outgroup categories such as football teams (Fuller et al., 2021) and political leanings (Harrison et al., 2020). In these studies, faces are presented which belong to both ingroup and outgroups, and the findings have revealed that people are better at recognising those categorised as ingroup (e.g. same football team supporters) rather than being from the outgroup (supporters of a different football team). However, the relationship between the own-group bias and the own-sex bias still isn't clear, but it does appear that people have to feel some affiliation with an ingroup, in order to belong (van Bavel & Cunningham, 2012).

Psychological research has not given universal support for the ingroup/outgroup theory, thus far, there is not sufficient evidence that males demonstrate and OSB when viewing same sex faces, as the phenomenon has only been found in females. It has been proposed that the OSB is not just related to ingroup/outgroup processes but has roots in perceptual learning from an early age. As early caregivers are often female (e.g. mothers), infants will have more experience with female faces than those of males. There is some evidence that infants can discriminate between female faces before they can discriminate between male faces and prefer looking at female faces as compared to male faces (Herlitz & Lovén, 2013). This, added to the evidence that female infants make more eye contact and look longer at faces than male infants, could be responsible for the more accurate processing of female faces (Connellan et al., 2000). It could be a combination of the greater exposure of female faces from a young age and infant girls' propensity to look more at faces than males, has created an early perceptual advantage for females to recognise faces, especially female faces, over males.

To explicitly test the underlying mechanisms for the OSB in women, Lovén et al. (2011) designed several experiments looking at how attention would influence the OSB. They surmised that if the ingroup/outgroup model was responsible for the OSB then females would use more attentional resources to process ingroup faces (females) and less for outgroup (male) faces when encoding faces. If this were the case, then dividing the viewer's attention by asking them to do an additional task when looking at faces should reduce the advantage for females' face recognition, as they should not be able to use as many attention resources to encode the faces. Across three experiments using the divided attention task they found a reduced performance on the face recognition tasks. However, an own-sex bias was still demonstrated by females who recognised more female faces than male faces. Male participants did not demonstrate an OSB and did not perform as accurately as the females in the study. The findings from these experiments appear to establish that the OSB in women remains regardless of attentional resources, suggesting that it is not due to attentional resources that underlie the ingroup/outgroup model, but more likely due to a perceptual expertise that has developed in childhood (Lovén et al., 2011).

Another study investigated the influence of attention and the own-sex bias using two different face identification tasks found conflicting results to the Lovén et al. (2011) study. Palmer, Brewer and Horry (2013) conducted face recognition and eyewitness identification experiments, whereby participants saw faces in full attention conditions and also in a divided attention condition where they were asked to complete an additional task. Their findings were at odds with Lovén et al. (2011), who found that for both experiments dividing attention reduced the accuracy of female faces, so that there was no longer an own-sex bias demonstrated by females for that condition. The own-sex bias did remain for the full attention condition. They suggest that the differences in findings between their study and that of Lovén and colleagues could be due to differences in the divided attention task, and that their attention task was stronger and therefore disrupted the recognition of females faces (Palmer et al., 2013).

Mishra et al. (2019) have taken a slightly different approach and propose that socio-cultural factors are responsible for the own-sex bias demonstrated in some face recognition studies. They suggest that one of the reasons for females' superior face recognition for unfamiliar female faces is a result of gender inequalities, and in societies where there is more gender equality then the OSB should be reduced. Using an experiment where they presented famous faces of American celebrities to participants from countries with lower gender equality than the USA (Pakistan, India, Brazil, Egypt, Indonesia) and those with higher gender equality than the USA (Sweden, Denmark, Norway, Finland, Netherlands), there were some interesting findings that were quite different to previous studies using unfamiliar faces. Female and male participants from the USA showed no differences in overall recognition, but there was a male OSB, with male participants recognising more male celebrity faces as compared to females. Female participants were more accurate with female celebrities than male participants were. They suggest the OSB demonstrated with this sample is due to males being more likely to be in positions of power as compared to females in the USA, resulting in males attending more to male celebrity faces as compared to female celebrity faces. The findings from participants from the more gender equal countries showed similar results to the USA, with no differences in accuracy as a function of gender, and males were more accurate for male celebrities than female celebrities, but there were no differences for the female celebrities. For the countries with low gender equality, the results were the same as the USA, with no overall differences in accuracy between female and male participants, but males were more accurate with male celebrities as compared to female celebrities. Overall, their results suggest that there was a small influence of socio-cultural gender equality on the results; however, there are a number of issues with this study, namely that the stimuli used were faces of American celebrities which may be more famous in some countries as compared to others, and may rely on access to internet and television etc. to become familiar.

There are also some gender issues in relation to using American celebrities, especially Hollywood actors, where male actors are much more likely to star in films and have leading roles as compared to women, and therefore their faces will have more exposure in comparison to celebrity women's faces (McKinney, 2015). As Mishra and colleagues suggest, there does appear to be some interaction between culture, gender and face recognition; however, it may be a complex relationship (Mishra et al., 2019).

As mentioned earlier in the chapter, another explanation for the own-gender bias in females relates to perceptual expertise and females' interest in looking at female faces from an early age. As a result of seeing more female faces from an early age (e.g. caregivers) and a propensity to look at faces more than male infants (Connellan et al., 2000), this has led to a perceptual expertise for female faces. To test the perceptual expertise hypothesis, Man and Hills (2016) conducted a face recognition study using an eye tracker, where they could see what parts of a face people looked at when viewing the face and for how long. Using a typical face recognition paradigm, the findings revealed an OSB for females, but not males viewing own-sex faces. The eye-tracking data found that the participants viewed the faces in different ways depending on whether they were the same sex or a different sex. Females looked at the eyes of own-sex faces for longer than male faces, and more fixations on the noses of male faces, demonstrating that own-sex and other-sex faces are processed in different ways. They suggest that their findings reveal there is greater motivation to process own-sex faces and that greater exposure to female faces during childhood has led women to have an own-sex bias.

How does gender influence eyewitness identification?

As you will have read in this chapter, there is a substantial amount of evidence to support the idea that females are more accurate at remembering unfamiliar faces compared to males, especially when it comes to female faces, although there is also evidence they are also more accurate with male faces. Evidence from face recognition studies suggests that if female eyewitnesses see someone commit a crime they should be more accurate at identifying perpetrators from a lineup as compared to male eye-witnesses. PC Tony Barnes has over 11 years' experience of making E-FIT facial composites for the Metropolitan Police using descriptions from over 2,000 witnesses and claims that women have more accurate memories for crimes and make better eye-witnesses as they pay more attention to faces (Simpson, 2021). However, there has been relatively little psychological research that has investigated the OSB using eyewitness paradigms compared to face recognition paradigms.

The few studies that have used eyewitness paradigms where a mock crime is shown to a group of participants and then they are asked to try to remember details of the event and identify the perpetrator from a lineup have not found consistent results. Areh (2011) showed a large group of participants a mock crime of a violent robbery and concluded that females are more reliable as eyewitnesses. The results found the female participants gave more accurate person descriptions, whereas males were more accurate at describing the overall event and were more confident in their answers. Longstaff and Belz (2020) showed a group of participants a video of a stranger that was either male or female, and found that females were much more accurate at remembering details about the stranger as compared to the males, regardless of whether the stranger was male or female. In a further study it seems as though the own-sex bias also influenced eyewitness descriptions as males gave more accurate descriptions of a male perpetrator and females gave more accurate descriptions of a female perpetrator (Areh & Walsh, 2020). Unfortunately, none of these studies used an iden-tification task, so it wasn't clear if the increase in accurate reported information led to an increase in correct identifications.

There are a few studies that have examined lineup identification using an eyewitness task; however, whether women are more accurate at identifying previously seen person from lineups, wasn't consistently found. Furthermore, some eyewitness studies have found a gender bias while others report no bias at all. Two studies conducted in the 1990s found that when groups of male and female students were shown lineups of a previously seen assailant that was either male or female, both males and females showed an own-gender bias and were more accurate at identifying someone who was the same gender (Shaw & Skolnick, 1999, 1994).

Another study that was not looking directly at the influence of gender, compared the information recalled and lineup identifications of surveillance detectives, uniformed police and civilians after viewing a mock crime. The results found there were no significant differences in the information recalled, or lineup identifications in relation to the gender of the participants; however, the majority of males were from the police group and the majority of females were from the civilian group (Vredeveldt et al., 2017).

In another study, Fazlić et al. (2020) showed a group of male and female participants a mock crime of a robbery with a male perpetrator and found no differences in the identification accuracy of male and females who took part. They concluded that gender had no influence on eyewitness identification, as the correct identification rates were the same for each group. However, there are some issues with this study that also related to other eyewitness paradigms and that is that as participants only contribute one data point (i.e. their response to a lineup), a large number of participants are required for each study to ensure that there is enough statistical power. Fazlić and colleagues employed a relatively small sample of participants in their study, and therefore it could be said that they did not have enough power to find any effects. Also, as participants only saw one male perpetrator in their mock crime, if there was a gender advantage for females this was not the case for a male perpetrator. There is another general criticism of eyewitness studies and that is they tend to only use one perpetrator and a lineup of a few faces, unlike face recognition studies that use a larger number of faces, and therefore it could be that the small number of faces used in an experiment may not be representative, meaning that results from these studies cannot be generalised (Wright & Sladden, 2003).

Sexual orientation

The majority of research described in this chapter has looked at the influence of a person's gender upon their face recognition ability, without recording their sexuality. One issue that has received relatively little research is whether a person's sexuality influences face recognition and the own-sex bias. It has been suggested that lesbians may show a stronger OSB as they may be more motivated to look at women's faces as compared to het-erosexual women. Similarly, gay men may be more motivated to look at male faces as compared to heterosexual men, and may demonstrate an OSB (Steffens et al., 2013).

Hills et al. (2018) conducted a typical recognition study using a sample of both homosexual and heterosexual partici-pants, presented with male and female faces. Their findings revealed that both male and female homosexual participants demonstrated an OSB; however, heterosexual participants of both sexes did not demonstrate an OSB. They suggest that homosexual individuals are more motivated to process own-sex faces as compared to other-sex faces, which results in the OSB. This is a really interesting point; however, it does not explain the overwhelming data supporting an own-sex bias found in female participants by a large number of previous studies, as it is unlikely that all the female participants in pre-vious research were lesbians.

Employing another typical face recognition study, Brewster et al. (2011) presented male and female faces to a group of homo-sexual and heterosexual males and female participants. In their study they found that heterosexual women out-performed het-erosexual males; however, homosexual males were more accu-rate than heterosexual males and homosexual females. However, they did not split the data to look at differences in recognition accuracy as a function of the sex of the faces, which could be because they used a small number of stimuli (five male and five female faces) for the learning phase. One of the criticisms of some of the research that has investigated sexual orientation and face recognition is that they have used small often opportunity samples and therefore it is not clear if the individuals who have taken part are representative of the general population.

In an attempt to gain a larger, more representative sample, Steffens et al. (2013) conducted an online study with over a thousand participants, nearly half of whom were homosexual. Using a face recognition task with male and female faces, they found that heterosexual females and lesbians demonstrated an OSB, as did homosexual males. Interestingly, heterosexual males showed an advantage for recognising female faces over male faces. Steffens et al. (2013) suggest that their findings support the perceptual expertise hypothesis for the OSB, and that sexual orientation is an important factor when investigating any effects related to participant gender, especially when it involves face recognition.

Conclusion

This chapter has looked at whether gender and sex influence face recognition. A wealth of research appears to show that on average females are more accurate than males on both face memory tasks (e. g. recognition) and also face perception tasks (e.g. detection and matching). However much of the research has found that one of the reasons that females are more accurate on face processing tasks is due to an advantage with female faces, resulting in an own-sex bias. The own-sex bias appears to be more prevalent in females, and there has been less support for the own-sex bias in males. There are several explanations for the own-sex bias in females, including the ingroup/outgroup model and the perceptual expertise account. More recently research has also looked at a person's hometown and whether its population density can influence face recognition, as well as a person's sexual orientation. Thus far there is no overarching theory that can fully explain the own-sex bias found in women but not men, and it could be due to several interacting factors. This is still an area that warrants more research from face recognition researchers, especially in relation to gender identification, as all research conducted thus far has used binary sex to categorise participants.

References

Areh, I. (2011). Gender-related differences in eyewitness testimony. *Personality and Individual Differences*, 50(5), 559–563. https://doi.org/10.1016/j.paid.2010.11.027.

Areh, I., & Walsh, D. (2020). Own-gender bias may affect eyewitness accuracy of perpetrators' personal descriptions. *Journal of Criminal Investigation and Criminology*, 71(4), 247–256.

Arrington, M., Elbich, D., Dai, J., Duchaine, B., & Scherf, K. S. (2022). Introducing the female Cambridge Face Memory Test–Long Form (F-CFMT+). *Behavior Research Methods*, 54, 3071–3084. https://doi.org/10.3758/s13428-022-01805-8.

Asperholm, M., Högman, N., Rafi, J., & Herlitz, A. (2019). What did you do yesterday? A meta-analysis of sex differences in episodic memory. *Psychological Bulletin*, 145(8), 785–821. https://doi.org/10.1037/bul0000197.

Balas, B., & Saville, A. (2017). Hometown size affects the processing of naturalistic face variability. *Vision Research*, 141, 228–236. https://doi.org/10.1016/j.visres.2016.12.005.

Brewster, P. W. H., Mullin, C. R., Dobrin, R. A., & Steeves, J. K. E. (2011). Sex differences in face processing are mediated by handedness and sexual orientation. *Laterality*, 16(2), 188–200. https://doi.org/10.1080/13576500903503759.

Bruce, V., Burton, A. M., Hanna, E., Healey, P., Mason, O., Coombes, A., Fright, R., & Linney, A. (1993). Sex discrimination: how do we tell the difference between male and female faces? *Perception*, 22(2), 131–152. https://doi.org/10.1068/p220131.

Burton, A. M. (2013). Why has research in face recognition progressed so slowly? The importance of variability. *Quarterly Journal of Experimental Psychology*, 66(8), 1467–1485. https://doi.org/10.1080/17470218.2013.800125.

Burton, A. M., Bruce, V., & Dench, N. (1993). What's the difference between men and women? Evidence from facial measurement. *Perception*, 22(2), 153–176. https://doi.org/10.1068/P220153.

Connellan, J., Baron-Cohen, S., Wheelwright, S., Batki, A., & Ahluwalia, J. (2000). Sex differences in human neonatal social perception. *Infant Behavior and Development*, 23(1), 113–118. https://doi.org/10.1016/S0163-6383(00)00032-00031.

Duchaine, B., & Nakayama, K. (2006). The Cambridge Face Memory Test: Results for neurologically intact individuals and an investigation of its validity using inverted face stimuli and prosopagnosic participants. *Neuropsychologia*, 44(4), 576–585. https://doi.org/10.1016/j.neuropsychologia.2005.07.001.

Ellis, H., Shepherd, J., & Bruce, A. (1973). The effects of age and sex upon adolescents' recognition of faces. *Journal of Genetic Psychology*, 123(1), 173–174. https://doi.org/10.1080/00221325.1973.10533202.

Fazlić, A., Deljkić, I., & Bull, R. (2020). Gender effects regarding eyewitness identification performance. *Kriminalističke Teme*, 20(5), 31–42. https://doi.org/10.51235/kt.2020.20.5.31.

Fuller, E. A., Majolo, B., Flack, T. R., & Ritchie, K. L. (2021). The importance of out-group characteristics for the own-group face memory bias. *Visual Cognition*, 29(4), 263–276. https://doi.org/10.1080/13506285.2021.1905125.

Gregorić, B., Barbir, L., Ćelić, A. (2014). Recognition of facial expressions in men and women. Recognition of emotions from human faces in men and women. *Medicina Fluminensis*, 50(4), 454–461. www. scopus.com/inward/record.uri?eid=2-s2.0-84911871566&partnerID= 40&md5=cefb1038df23f09c161578b50dcabb63.

Guillem, F., & Mograss, M. (2005). Gender differences in memory processing: Evidence from event-related potentials to faces. *Brain and Cognition*, 57(1), 84–92. https://doi.org/10.1016/j.bandc.2004.08.026.

Hansen, T., Zaichkowsky, J., & de Jong, A. (2021). Are women always better able to recognize faces? The unveiling role of exposure time. *PLoS ONE*, 16(10 October), 1–16. https://doi.org/10.1371/journal.pone.0257741.

Harrison, V., Hole, G., & Habibi, R. (2020). Are you in or are you out? The importance of group saliency in own-group biases in face recognition. *Perception*, 49(6), 672–687. https://doi.org/10.1177/0301006620918100.

Herlitz, A., & Lovén, J. (2013). Sex differences and the own-gender bias in face recognition: A meta-analytic review. *Visual Cognition*, 21(9–10),1306–1336. https://doi.org/10.1080/13506285.2013.823140.

Herlitz, A., & Rehnman, J. (2008). Sex differences in episodic memory. *Current Directions in Psychological Science*, 17(1), 52–56. https://doi.org/10.1111/j.1467-8721.2008.00547.x.

Hills, P. J., Pake, J. M., Dempsey, J. R., & Lewis, M. B. (2018). Exploring the contribution of motivation and experience in the postpubescent own-gender bias in face recognition. *Journal of Experimental Psychology: Human Perception and Performance*, 44(9), 1426–1446. https://doi.org/10.1037/XHP0000533.

Hugenberg, K., Wilson, J. P., See, P. E., & Young, S. G. (2013). Towards a synthetic model of own group biases in face memory. *Visual Cognition*, 21(9–10), 1392–1417. https://doi.org/10.1080/13506285.2013.821429.

Leeb, R.T., Rejskind, F. G. (2004). Here's looking at you, kid! A longitudinal study of perceived gender differences in mutual gaze behavior in young infants. *Sex Roles 5*, 50(October), 1–4. https://doi.org/10.1023/B.

Lewin, C., & Herlitz, A. (2002). Sex differences in face recognition: Women's faces make the difference. *Brain and Cognition*, 50(1), 121–128. https://doi.org/10.1016/S0278-2626(02)16–17.

Longstaff, M. G., & Belz, G. K. (2020). Sex differences in eyewitness memory: Females are more accurate than males for details related to people and less accurate for details surrounding them, and feel more anxious and threatened in a neutral but potentially threatening context. *Personality and Individual Differences*, 164(April). https://doi.org/10.1016/j.paid.2020.110093.

Lovén, J., Herlitz, A., & Rehnman, J. (2011). Women's own-gender bias in face recognition memory: The role of attention at encoding. *Experimental Psychology*, 58(4), 333–340. https://doi.org/10.1027/1618-3169/a000100.

Man, T. W., & Hills, P. J. (2016). Eye-tracking the own-gender bias Eye-tracking the own-gender bias in face recognition: Other-gender faces are viewed differently to own-gender faces 2 -. *Visual Cognition*, 24(9–10), 447–458.

McBain, R., Norton, D., & Chen, Y. (2009). Females excel at basic face perception. *Acta Psychologica*, 130(2), 168–173. https://doi.org/10.1016/j.actpsy.2008.12.005.

McKinney, K. (2015). Hollywood's devastating gender divide, explained. www.vox.com/2015/1/26/7874295/gender-hollywood.

Megreya, A. M., Bindemann, M., & Havard, C. (2011). Sex differences in unfamiliar face identification: evidence from matching tasks. *Acta Psychologica*, 137(1), 83–89. https://doi.org/10.1016/j.actpsy.2011.03.003.

Mishra, M. V., Likitlersuang, J., B Wilmer, J., Cohan, S., Germine, L., & DeGutis, J. M. (2019). Gender differences in familiar face recognition and the influence of sociocultural gender inequality. *Scientific Reports*, 9(1), 1–12. https://doi.org/10.1038/s41598-019-54074-5.

Palmer, M. A., Brewer, N., & Horry, R. (2013). Understanding gender bias in face recognition: Effects of divided attention at encoding. *Acta Psychologica*, 142(3), 362–369. https://doi.org/10.1016/j.actpsy.2013.01.009.

Petersen, L. A., & Leue, A. (2021). Extraordinary face recognition performance in laboratory and online testing. *Applied Cognitive Psychology*, 35(3), 579–589. https://doi.org/10.1002/acp.3805.

Rehnman, J., & Herlitz, A. (2006). Higher face recognition ability in girls: Magnified by own-sex and own-ethnicity bias. *Memory*, 14(3), 289–296. https://doi.org/10.1080/09658210500233581.

Rehnman, J., & Herlitz, A. (2007). Women remember more faces than men do. *Acta Psychologica*, 124(3), 344–355. https://doi.org/10.1016/j.actpsy.2006.04.004.

Ryan, K. F., & Gauthier, I. (2016). Gender differences in recognition of toy faces suggest a contribution of experience. *Vision Research*, 129, 69–76. https://doi.org/10.1016/j.visres.2016.10.003.

Scherf, K. S., Elbich, D. B., & Motta-Mena, N. V. (2017). Investigating the influence of biological sex on the behavioral and neural basis of face recognition. *ENeuro*, 4(3). https://doi.org/10.1523/ENEURO.0104-17.2017.

Shaw, J. I., & Skolnick, P. (1999). Weapon focus and gender differences in eyewitness accuracy: Arousal versus salience. *Journal of Applied Social Psychology*, 29(11), 2328–2341. https://doi.org/10.1111/j.1559-1816.1999.tb00113.x.

Shaw, & Skolnick. (1994). Sex differences, weapon focus, and eyewitness reliability. *The Journal of Social Psychology*, 134(4), 413–420.

Simpson, J. (2021). Why women make better witnesses. *The Times*, 25 January. www.thetimes.co.uk/article/why-women-make-better-witnesses-wl0zjrvms.

Sommer, W., Hildebrandt, A., Kunina-Habenicht, O., Schacht, A., & Wilhelm, O. (2013). Sex differences in face cognition. *Acta Psychologica*, 142(1), 62–73. https://doi.org/10.1016/j.actpsy.2012.11.001.

Sporer, S. L. (2001). Recognizing faces of other ethnic groups: An integration of theories. *Psychology, Public Policy, and Law*, 7(1), 36–97. https://doi.org/10.1037/1076-8971.7.1.36.

Steffens, M. C., Landmann, S., & Mecklenbräuker, S. (2013). Participant sexual orientation matters: New evidence on the gender bias in face recognition. *Experimental Psychology*, 60(5), 362–367. https://doi.org/10.1027/1618-3169/a000209.

Sunday, M. A., Patel, P. A., Dodd, M. D., & Gauthier, I. (2019). Gender and hometown population density interact to predict face recognition ability. *Vision Research*, 163(June), 14–23. https://doi.org/10.1016/j.visres.2019.08.006.

van Bavel, J. J., & Cunningham, W. A. (2012). A social identity approach to person memory: Group membership, collective identification, and social role shape attention and memory. *Personality and Social Psychology Bulletin*, 38(12), 1566–1578. https://doi.org/10.1177/0146167212455829.

Vredeveldt, A., Knol, J. W., & van Koppen, P. J. (2017). Observing offenders: Incident reports by surveillance detectives, uniformed police, and civilians. *Legal and Criminological Psychology*, 22(1), 150–163. https://doi.org/10.1111/lcrp.12087.

Wingenbach, T. S. H., Ashwin, C., & Brosnan, M. (2018). Sex differences in facial emotion recognition across varying expression intensity levels from videos. https://doi.org/10.1371/journal.pone.0190634.

Wright, D. B., & Sladden, B. (2003). An own gender bias and the importance of hair in face recognition. *Acta Psychologica*, 114(1), 101–114. https://doi.org/10.1016/S0001-6918(03)00052-0

6 The influence of age

Introduction

As you've probably realised now you have got to this chapter of the book, the ability to recognise faces is extremely important for a variety of tasks, including social interactions and also in security settings. In previous chapters you read about how race and sex could influence face recognition, and this chapter is going to focus on whether age influences face recognition. It will explore research that has investigated whether a person's age makes face recognition more error prone. It will also ask whether the age of the eyewitness influences identification from a police lineup and whether children are less reliable than adults at recognising faces.

Many cognitive abilities develop throughout the lifespan, for example raw speed in processing information peaks around 18 or 19 years of age before immediately declining, while working memory appears to peak at around 25 years of age and begins to decline after 35 years of age. Other cognitive abilities mature later on, for example emotion recognition peaks at around 40 years and vocabulary continues to improve into later adulthood (Hartshorne & Germine, 2016). Face recognition is another cognitive ability that follows a lifespan trajectory and is influenced by a person's age. This chapter will look at research that has explored how face recognition and eyewitness identification ability changes over the lifespan and then focus on research that has investigated how children, adults and older adults perform on face recognition and eyewitness identification tasks. As with other biases, such as the own-race and own-sex bias, research

DOI: 10.4324/9781003177128-6

has also revealed an own-age bias, and some of this research will also be explored. Finally, the chapter will look at how we recognise faces as they age across the lifespan.

Face recognition and eyewitness identification across the lifespan

Face recognition, like many other cognitive functions, such as attention and memory, is an ability that can develop over time, but also appears to decline with age. This section is going to look at face recognition across the lifespan, starting with childhood through to old age. There have been a few large-scale studies, meta-analyses and reviews that have investigated face recognition across the lifespan, whether there is an optimum age for face recognition abilities and when this ability then goes into decline. Germine et al. (2011) undertook a large-scale study with over 60,000 participants aged from 10 up to 70 years of age to investigate face recognition ability across the lifespan. They conducted three face recognition experiments, and found that face recognition ability increases steeply from 10 years up to 20 years and then gradually continues to increase until the early 30s, and then gradually starts to decline until 70 years of age. They suggest that the data from their studies demonstrates that face recognition ability peaks at just after 30 years of age.

Another study that investigated whether face recognition improved during young adulthood was conducted by Susilo et al. (2013) using the Cambridge Face Memory Test (CFMT; Duchaine & Nakayama, 2006) with a group of over 2,000 participants aged 18–33 years of age. As described in the previous chapters, in the CFMT participants are presented with target faces that they are shown one at a time during a study phase, and then during a test phase they are shown a series of face triplets in a different viewpoint and they have to decide if any of the three faces are ones they have seen before (see Figure 6.1 for an example). Susilo et al. (2013) found that face recognition ability gradually improved from 18 to 33 years of age and proposed that face recognition ability has a late maturation. They suggest that the underlying mechanism for the late maturation of face recognition ability could be due to the quantity of faces people are exposed to in

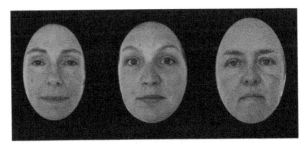

Figure 6.1 Example of CFMT-like stimuli. Which face is the target face?
Answer at the end of the chapter.

daily life, for example when people are in their 20s and early 30s they are more likely to leave home and start careers etc. and meet and interact with more new people.

Researchers have also looked at whether there are age effects for eyewitness identification, where a participant usually only sees one target face and has to try and identify them from a lineup of several faces. Ryan Fitzgerald and Heather Price conducted a meta-analysis looking at the data of over 20,000 participants across 91 eyewitness studies (Fitzgerald & Price, 2015). Participants ranged from as young as 3 years of age up to 77 years old. Their results revealed that when it came to making a correct identification from a target present lineup, young adults were more accurate as compared to children and older adults, although older children were more accurate than younger children. When it came to correctly saying the culprit wasn't present in a target absent lineup, young adults were also more likely to correctly reject the lineup, as compared to children and older adults. Fitzgerald and Price (2015) concluded that young adults' identifications were the most reliable, compared to other age groups. When it comes to making a decision for target absent lineups it appears that children and older adults are more compelled to choose someone from a lineup, even when they might not recognise anyone; however, the reasons for this false identification may come from different underlying mechanisms, which will be discussed later in this chapter.

Megreya and Bindemann (2015) investigated whether there were differences in face matching ability as a function of a person's age and conducted two different experiments. In the first experiment they used the 1 in 10 face matching task (Bruce et al., 1999) where a participant is presented with an array that has one face at the top and then 10 faces in two rows below that are numbered. They had over 300 participants that ranged in age from 7 years to 65 years of age. They found when it came to correctly identifying a target face that was present in an array, matching accuracy increased from ages 7 to 16 years of age, but there were no differences in those aged 16, 19 and 35 years of ages. Face matching accuracy then decreased from 35 years to 65 years of age. However, when the target was absent from an array (the correct decision was to say 'the target wasn't there'), accuracy increased from 7–10 years, but then remained stable until 35 years before starting to decline. This suggested that discriminating between different faces appears to mature faster than determining that two different images of the same person are the same identity.

In the second experiment by Megreya and Bindemann (2015), 200 participants (aged 7–65 years of age) had the more simple task of being presented with two faces and having to decide if they were the same person or two different people. The results revealed that for this task all participants were more accurate than they were with the 1 in 10 face matching task. Furthermore, there was an improvement in performance from ages 7 up until 19 years, but then a decrease in performance at 65 years of age. Unfortunately, Megreya and Bindemann did not employ a middle age group between 19 years and 65 years for their second experiment and so we cannot ascertain at what age the decrease in matching performance begins, only that at 65 years it is lower than at 19 years of age.

Megreya and Bindemann's experiments demonstrated an improvement in face matching as participants' age increased from childhood into young adulthood; however, compared to previous studies using face recognition tasks, face matching performance appeared to reach adult-like levels at a younger age. This could be due to the nature of different paradigms and that face matching does not rely on memory as it is a perceptual task. When there is no memory component, and a simple two-item face matching task children can perform accurately from a young age. The next section of this chapter will focus specifically on the research that has investigated children's face recognition ability.

There are few general criticisms that can be made of the studies that have taken a lifespan approach to face recognition, eyewitness identification and face matching. Often studies comparing different age groups have employed specific stimuli, usually with young adult white male target faces (Fitzgerald & Price, 2015; Germine et al., 2011; Megreya & Bindemann, 2015; Susilo et al., 2013), and therefore don't account for the own-age bias (discussed later in this chapter), and any other group is put at a disadvantage as compared to the young white adults in the studies. As is often the case in many psychology studies, including face recognition research, the group of young adults who are often the participants in the research are undergraduate psychology students and have been termed WEIRD as they are usually from Westernised, educated, industrialised, rich, democratic societies that are home to 12% of the world's population (Henrich et al., 2010). It could therefore be argued how representative this group is for cognitive abilities and if they should be used as a comparison group with children and older adults.

Children

Over the last 40 years children's face recognition and eyewitness ability has been widely researched within psychology. A number of face recognition studies report that children up until adolescence are not as accurate as adults at correctly recognising faces (Carey et al., 1980; de Heering et al., 2012; Havard, 2017), although some research also suggests that this could be even later, around 16 years of age (Grill-Spector et al., 2008; Itier & Taylor, 2004). There are two main explanations for children's poorer performance on face recognition tasks. One theory proposes, that there is a specialised deficit in face processing, and that children have not developed the specific skills needed for adult face recognition, such as holistic processing. The other theory suggests that there is a general cognitive deficit, i.e. children have less mature perceptual, attentional and memory abilities, compared to adults that can affect face recognition. However, some researchers do not agree that children necessarily have poorer face recognition abilities as compared to adults, and of the methods (e.g. experimental paradigms designed for adults) used in past research that has put children at a disadvantage as compared to adult participants. For example, Elinor McKone et al. (2012) conducted a critical examination of the research of children's face recognition ability and concluded that adult-like face recognition processes were present at an early age (3–4 years) and could be fully mature by 5 years of age.

Studies that have used eyewitness paradigms to investigate children's ability to make an identification from a police lineup have found that when it comes to correctly identifying a previously seen culprit from a target present lineup then children can sometimes be as accurate as adults; however, they are much more likely to make a false identification and choose an innocent person from a target absent lineup as compared to adults (Havard, 2013). This false choosing is thought to be because when presented with a lineup by an adult, children feel a social pressure to choose someone, even though they may not recognise any of the faces. They may feel that they need to make a positive response, rather than say 'No, I don't think the person is there' or 'I don't know' or 'I don't recognise anyone'. To allow children to give in to the compulsion or social pressure to choose or make a non-positive response, studies have included an alternative response that children can select without making a false identification. Research has included a silhouette of a head called either 'wildcard' or 'mystery man' (see Figure 6.2 for an example) who is placed in the lineup and can be chosen by the child witness when no one is recognised and this has helped to

Figure 6.2 Example of the Mystery Man study.
Source: Havard and Memon (2012)

reduce this false identification rate (Havard & Memon, 2012; Karageorge & Zajac, 2011).

It is interesting that in some cases children can perform as accurately as adults on eyewitness identification tasks, especially when recognising previously seen faces. There are some differences between face recognition and eyewitness experiments, as you will have read about in Chapter 1. Face recognition studies use multiple trials during a study phase (e.g. 20 or more faces), that are usually presented for short time periods, then during the test phase there are often twice as many faces presented and the task is to decide which faces are old and which are new. Whereas for eyewitness studies usually only 1 or 2 targets are presented for later identification. It could be that through boredom of being presented with multiple trials, children pay less attention to the faces during face recognition tasks than they do to eyewitness tasks, resulting in different accuracy rates (Havard, 2017). Furthermore, evidence from real eyewitness decisions made by children has found that children made more suspect identifications as compared to adults. It should be noted that there was no corresponding conviction data from this research and so it isn't known whether all suspects were in fact guilty (Memon et al., 2011).

Another explanation for why children might perform more poorly on face recognition tasks as compared to adults is that most research has used experiments that were designed for adults, often using young adult faces as stimuli, rather than children's faces. As you will read later in this chapter there appears to be some evidence that we are often better at recognising faces that are the same age as we are, compared to those belonging to a different age group. Furthermore, in the majority of research the other group of participants that children are compared to is young adults and most face recognition and eyewitness identification tasks use young adults as targets therefore young adults are identifying same age faces, whereas children are trying to identify or recognise other age faces.

One of the most commonly used face recognition tests is the CFMT mentioned above, and there has been a version adapted for children with a slightly different type of methodology to make it easier for children; however, this new test still uses adult faces and not children's faces (Croydon et al., 2014). Therefore children are at a disadvantage if the to be remembered faces are adult faces and not child faces (Havard, 2017). There has been another adaptation of the CFMT using children's faces, which does help with reducing the own-age bias (Dalrymple et al., 2014). Another issue that may influence face recognition research with children using tasks like the CFMT, including the one designed for children, and other similar face recognition tests is that faces are often cropped to remove hair and the face shape, or the features are slightly moved around, and therefore the faces are often not very natural looking faces, which can be problematic for research (Burton, 2013). This along with the own-age bias has put children at a disadvantage in psychological research investigating face identification and may have resulted in an underestimation of children's abilities (Havard, 2017). As McKone et al. (2012) points out, if children were really less accurate than adults at recognising faces then they would struggle to learn new faces when starting school, but that has not been reported to be the case.

Older adults

Eyewitness and face recognition research has also found that older adults (over 60 years of age), like children, also do not perform as well on face identification tasks as compared to young adults, aged 18–30 years of age. One of the most important applied aspects of face identification is when witnesses are asked to identify a previously seen culprit from a lineup. In the UK the population is getting older and by 2050 it has been predicted that over 25% of the population will be aged over 65 years of age, making research with older adult witnesses more important. A number of studies have already compared older adult and younger adults' identification accuracy from police lineups (Martschuk & Sporer, 2018). Some of this research has found that often older adults are less accurate at correctly identifying a previously seen culprit from a police lineup (Havard & Memon, 2009; Wilcock & Bull, 2005); however, some research has found that older adults can be as accurate as young adults when correctly previously seen culprits (Memon et al., 2003; Memon & Gabbert, 2003; Memon & Hope, 2002). When presented with target absent lineups older adults appear to be more likely to choose someone as compared to younger adults and thereby make a false identification (Erickson et al., 2016; Fitzgerald & Price, 2015; Havard & Memon, 2009; Martschuk & Sporer, 2018; Memon & Gabbert, 2003; Wilcock & Bull, 2005). There have been several suggestions for why older adults might be more inclined to choose from a lineup as compared to younger adults. There is a natural cognitive decline as adults age, with general poorer memory function which could influence face recognition memory. Some researchers have suggested that older adults do not remember the non-biased instruction before viewing a lineup that says 'the person may or may not be there', and therefore they assume that a culprit is present and they need to choose someone (Wilcock & Bull, 2005).

Research has also investigated how accurate older adults are compared to young adults, using face recognition paradigms. Martschuk and Sporer (2018) conducted a meta-analysis of 19 face recognition studies with 79 comparisons employing young and older adult participants, viewing young and older adult faces. Their analyses revealed that when it came to correctly recognising previously seen faces, younger adults were more accurate than older adults for young target faces, while the reverse was found for older faces, where older adults were more accurate. For faces that had not been previously seen, young adults were more accurate for young adult faces as compared to older adult faces.

However older adults were more likely to incorrectly say a new face had been previously presented, regardless of the age of the face. The increased choosing rate for previously unseen faces replicates the findings from eyewitness literature and suggests that older adults are more likely to choose in general and might base their decisions on feelings of general familiarity.

Through the natural ageing process memory usually begins to decline after 65 years of age, and therefore it would not be surprising if older adults are able to remember fewer faces correctly compared to younger adults. Many of the studies that have investigated older adults' memory for faces have used young adult target faces, and the group older adults have been compared to are younger adults. In a similar vein to the research with children, it seems from the outset that studies using these methodologies are putting older adults at a disadvantage as compared to younger adults as they are being tasked to recognise faces that are outside their own age group.

The own-age bias

As you will have read in the previous chapters there are cognitive biases when it comes to recognising faces. On the whole people tend to be more accurate at recognising and remembering faces that belong to individuals who are similar to them, such as the same race and the same sex. Perhaps it won't surprise you to learn that people can also be more accurate with faces that are the same age as them. A survey of just over 1,000 police lineup decisions made by real witnesses in England found that as the age difference between a suspect and an eyewitness increased, witnesses were less likely to identify suspects (Horry et al., 2012). There has also been experimental research that has found that people are better at recognising others that are of a similar age, suggesting an own-age bias (OAB) in face recognition, although this has not been unanimously supported. What is different about the OAB and other biases such as the own-sex bias or own-race bias is that age changes throughout a person's life, unlike race and sex, which are generally fixed (although people can decide to change their gender).

Many of the theories used to try and understand the OAB have been borrowed or adapted from the own-race bias (ORB) literature. One of the explanations first used to explain the ORB involves perceptual expertise and that through contact with certain groups we become experts at recognising the faces of those we have more social contact with. There is some evidence to support the perceptual expertise or contact hypothesis for the OAB, as research has found that primary school teachers who had worked for a minimum of one year did not demonstrate an OAB when trying to recognise child and adult faces (Harrison & Hole, 2009). The reduction in OAB was replicated with pre-school teachers who were more accurate with children's faces (Macchi Cassia et al., 2012). These findings suggest that the OAB can be reduced by contact with those of a different age, even if that contact isn't until adulthood. Furthermore, it could also be that children and older adults are more likely to interact with individuals who are of different ages, such as parents, teachers and adult children, or grandchildren. In contrast, research that has looked at the ORB has found that contact with people from another race had to be from an early age for it to be effective at reducing the ORB (Zhou et al., 2019). These contrasting findings seem to suggest the OAB might be more flexible that the ORB and that through contact even in adulthood the OAB can be reduced whereas this does not seem to necessarily be the case for the ORB.

A further explanation for OAB again borrowed from the ORB literature relates to ingroup/outgroup processes (Sporer, 2001), and the categorization-individuation model suggests when we meet someone we categorise them as either belonging to an ingroup or an outgroup. Faces that are categorised as belonging to an ingroup, are processed on an individual level using deeper processing of the different facial features, whereas faces categorised as belonging to an outgroup, are processed on a superficial categorical level (Hugenberg et al., 2010). According to this approach, if properly motivated to process faces on an individual level, rather than a category level, this should reduce the OAB. There has been some support for the categorization-individuation model, although less support than using instructions that help to individuate faces from another age actually reduces the own-age bias (Craig & Thorne, 2019). Support for the social relevance component for the own-age bias has been found in a study that not only investigated the own-age bias in face recognition, but whether people were more likely to remember the name of someone who was the same age as them. A study by Strickland-Hughes et al. (2020) found that both older and younger adults were more likely to recall names that had been paired with own-age faces.

Although some researchers have suggested that the OAB is driven by similar mechanisms to the ORB, other researchers have suggested that the OAB may have different mechanisms (Wiese et al., 2013). Some of the evidence for this comes from the finding that often the ORB effect is driven by higher false alarms for other-race faces as compared to own-race faces (Meissner & Brigham, 2001), while the OAB appears to be driven by both hits and false alarms in young adults, whereas older adults showed an OAB in hits, but not false alarms (Rhodes and Anastasi, 2012). Another difference between the OAB and the ORB is that the OAB appears to manifest in childhood, and although it is not always present in preschool children, it is usually present by 5 years of age (Wiese et al., 2013). In contrast the ORB has been found in infants as young as 3–6 months of age and then has been found to be fairly consistent from 9 months of age, suggesting that there might be different mechanisms underlying the two biases (Hills & Mahabeer, 2017).

Although there doesn't appear to be a consensus on the mechanisms of the OAB, like other biases in face recognition, there is most probably an interaction between multiple factors. These factors could include not just the social contact one has with individuals of different ages, but also the quality of that contact. Another factor could be the motivations to recognise faces of different ages and whether other tasks are being undertaken while might take up cognitive resources. One area that needs more research in relation to the OAB is whether a person's underlying face recognition ability also influences their ability to recognise other-age faces.

Ageing faces

As we grow older our faces change. They become less symmetrical, our skin pigment changes, and after the age of 30 years the body starts to lose collagen, leading to wrinkle formation. There are not only biological factors that affect our faces as we age, but also lifestyles choices we make that can influence how we age and how our faces may end up ageing, for example, smoking, diet, drug use and alcohol consumption. As you read in the last section, people are often more accurate at recognising faces that are the same age as them, but what about recognising the faces of people who are familiar but who have aged?

Anecdotal experience

At Easter in 2022 I went up to a village in the Scottish Highlands with my family and some friends and we rented a cottage. I had lived in this village, but had moved away nearly 30 years ago. Once we had settled into our holiday cottage a lady appeared to check everything was OK. I was chatting to her for quite some time before I realised that I knew her. In fact, we had both worked together over 30 years ago in the same kitchen for nearly two years! It took both of us a while to recognise one another as we had both aged and looked quite different to how we did over 30 years ago. I am pretty sure I would not have recognised her if I had just walked past her in the street – it took talking to her for several minutes and then realising she was familiar before I finally recognised her as the person I used to work with all those years ago!

There is still relatively little research that has investigated how we recognise familiar faces that have aged. For example, we can often recognise a photograph of a celebrity such as Paul McCartney over a number of different images, with changes in hairstyles and as his face has changed through ageing across the decades. Some research has turned to computer simulations to try and understand the mechanisms for recognising faces that are encountered across the lifespan, and they suggest that in order for faces to be correctly recognised there need to be several encounters across a person's lifespan to keep hold of a usable stored representation of that person's face (Mileva et al., 2020).

Research with human participants also supports the idea that we have an internal representation of people that we know and that this gets updated as they age and we see them at different points throughout their life (Laurence et al., 2022). If newly learnt faces are seen at a particular age then recognition of those faces when they are older is greatly reduced (Longmore et al., 2017). Also, the longer the age gap between seeing the faces, the less likely they are to be recognised (Sexton et al., 2024). Coming back to my anecdotal example, perhaps if I had seen the lady I used to work with at a few intervals over the 30 years from us working together I would have more easily recognised her; as I hadn't seen her for 30 years it took quite a bit of time and talking to one another before we were able to recognise one another.

Being able to recognise someone after not seeing them for long periods has some real-world implications, especially when it comes to missing persons who may have disappeared for many years and yet the police and their families are still looking for them. Children's faces change more over a shorter period of time as compared to adults' faces, and therefore can be more difficult to recognise if they haven't been seen for many years. Perhaps the

Figure 6.3 Example of faces of the same person from ages 3 to 50 years of age.

most famous case in the UK of a missing person is the case of Madeine McCann, who disappeared in Portugal on 3 May 2007 aged 3, but at the time of writing would be 18 years old. Figure 6.2 shows how my own face has aged from the age of 3 years to middle age. As you can see my face has changed significantly and I wonder if anyone who didn't personally know me would recognise that it was the same person over different time points?

Various organisations involved in searching for missing people now use specialist age progression software, or forensic artists to age-progress the faces of missing of people who have been missing for many years. These images are then given to the media to show the public what the missing persons might look like today and increase the likelihood of someone recognising them. This is especially relevant for children, whose faces can change a lot from childhood to adulthood. There has been research that has investigated the effectiveness of using age-progressed faces for identification, and it was found to be no more effective than using out-of-date photographs (Charman & Carol, 2012; Lampinen et al., 2012). These studies used human participants, but there has also been research using face recognition technology which also has been found to struggle to recognise the identity of persons who had appeared to age by five or more years compared to the original source image that was learned by the algorithm (Sparkes, 2022). The topic of face recognition technology will be covered in more detail in the next chapter.

Conclusion

Age is a factor that can influence whether a face is accurately recognised. According to the psychological research, face recognition is more likely to go wrong when the person trying to recognise the face is a child or an older adult (over 65 years of age). However, it is still debatable whether this deficit in face recognition ability is due to the person's age or another factor such as the faces they are trying to identify, or social pressure to make decisions, such as choosing a face even though none are recognised. Face recognition ability appears to peak around 30 years of age and then begins to decline again. Furthermore, face recognition is more likely to go wrong if the individual trying to recognise a specific face belongs to a different age to the person they are trying to identify, and the errors appear to grow the wider the gap between the recogniser and the face to be recognised. Face recognition is also more likely to go wrong if the person trying to identify the face hasn't seen the individual for many years, and face recognition technology also appears to struggle with faces that have aged.

(Answer to Figure 6.1: the correct answer is the third face.)

References

Bartlett, J. C., & Memon, A. (2007). Eyewitness memory in young and older adults. In R. Lindsay, R. Ross, D. Read, & M. P. Toglia (eds), *Handbook of eyewitness psychology: Memory for people, vol. 2* (pp. 309–338). Lawrence Erlbaum and Associates.

Bruce, V., Henderson, Z., Greenwood, K., Hancock, P. J. B., Burton, A. M., & Miller, P. (1999). Verification of face identities from images captured on video. *Journal of Experimental Psychology: Applied*, 5(4), 339–360. https://doi.org/10.1037/1076-898X.5.4.339.

Burton, A. M. (2013). Why has research in face recognition progressed so slowly? The importance of variability. *Quarterly Journal of Experimental Psychology*, 66(8), 1467–1485. https://doi.org/10.1080/17470218.2013.800125.

Carey, S., Diamond, R., & Woods, B. (1980). Development of face recognition: A maturational component? *Developmental Psychology*, 16(4), 257–269. https://doi.org/10.1037/0012-1649.16.4.257.

Charman, S. D., & Carol, R. N. (2012). Age-progressed images may harm recognition of missing children by increasing the number of plausible targets. *Journal of Applied Research in Memory and Cognition*, 1(3), 171–178. https://doi.org/10.1016/j.jarmac.2012.07.008.

Craig, B. M., & Thorne, E. M. (2019). Social categorization and individuation in the own-age bias. *British Journal of Psychology*, 110(4), 635–651. https://doi.org/10.1111/bjop.12376.

Croydon, A., Pimperton, H., Ewing, L., Duchaine, B. C., & Pellicano, E. (2014). The Cambridge Face Memory Test for Children (CFMT-C): A new tool for measuring face recognition skills in childhood. *Neuropsychologia*, 62(1), 60–67. https://doi.org/10.1016/j.neuropsychologia.2014.07.008.

Dalrymple, K. A., Garrido, L., & Duchaine, B. (2014). Dissociation between face perception and face memory in adults, but not children, with developmental prosopagnosia. *Developmental Cognitive Neuroscience*, 10(August), 10–20. https://doi.org/10.1016/j.dcn.2014.07.003.

de Heering, A., Rossion, B., & Maurer, D. (2012). Developmental changes in face recognition during childhood: Evidence from upright and inverted faces. *Cognitive Development*, 27(1), 17–27. https://doi.org/10.1016/j.cogdev.2011.07.001.

Duchaine, B., & Nakayama, K. (2006). The Cambridge Face Memory Test: Results for neurologically intact individuals and an investigation of its validity using inverted face stimuli and prosopagnosic participants. *Neuropsychologia*, 44(4), 576–585. https://doi.org/10.1016/j.neuropsychologia.2005.07.001.

Erickson, W. B., Lampinen, J. M., & Moore, K. N. (2016). Eyewitness identifications by older and younger adults: A meta-analysis and discussion. *Journal of Police and Criminal Psychology*, 31(2), 108–121. https://doi.org/10.1007/s11896-015-9176-3.

Fitzgerald, R. J., & Price, H. L. (2015). Eyewitness identification across the life Span: A meta-analysis of age differences. *Psychological Bulletin*, 141(6), 1228–1265. https://doi.org/10.1037/bul0000013.

Germine, L. T., Duchaine, B., & Nakayama, K. (2011). Where cognitive development and aging meet: Face learning ability peaks after age 30. *Cognition*, 118(2), 201–210. https://doi.org/10.1016/j.cognition.2010.11.002.

Grill-Spector, K., Golarai, G., & Gabrieli, J. (2008). Developmental neuroimaging of the human ventral visual cortex. *Trends in Cognitive Sciences*, 12(4), 152–161. https://doi.org/10.1016/j.tics.2008.01.009. Developmental.

Harrison, V., & Hole, G. J. (2009). Evidence for a contact-based explanation of the own-age bias in face recognition. *Psychonomic Bulletin and Review*, 16(2), 264–269. https://doi.org/10.3758/PBR.16.2.264.

Hartshorne, J. K., & Germine, L. T. (2016). When does cognitive functioning peak? The asynchronous rise and fall of different cognitive abilities across the lifespan. *Psychological Science*, 26(4), 433–443. https://doi.org/10.1177/0956797614567339.

Havard, C. (2013). Are children less reliable at making visual identifications than adults? A review. *Psychology, Crime & Law*, 1–17. https://doi.org/10.1080/1068316X.2013.793334.

Havard, C. (2017). Children's face identification ability. In M. Bindemann & A. M. Megreya (eds), *Face processing: Systems, disorders and cultural differences* (pp. 255–271). Nova Science Publishing.

Havard, C. & Memon, A. (2009). The influence of face age on identification from a video line-up: a comparison between older and younger adults. *Memory (Hove, England)*, 17(8), 847–859. https://doi.org/10.1080/09658210903277318.

Havard, C. & Memon, A. (2012). The mystery man can help reduce false identification for child witnesses: Evidence from video line-ups. *Applied Cognitive Psychology*, 27(1), 50–59. https://doi.org/10.1002/acp.2870.

Henrich, J., Heine, S. J., & Norenzayan, A. (2010). The weirdest people in the world? *Behavioral and Brain Sciences*, 33(2–3),61–83. https://doi.org/10.1017/S0140525X0999152X.

Hills, P. J. & Mahabeer, A. (2017). The own-group biases in face recognition: One theory to explain them all. In M. Bindemann & A. Megreya (eds), *Face processing: Systems, disorders and cultural differences* (pp. 337–364). Nova Science Publishing.

Horry, R., Memon, A., Wright, D. B., & Milne, R. (2012). Predictors of eyewitness identification decisions from video lineups in England: a field study. *Law and Human Behavior*, 36(4), 257–265. https://doi.org/10.1037/h0093959.

Hugenberg, K., Young, S. G., Bernstein, M. J., & Sacco, D. F. (2010). The Categorization-Individuation Model: An Integrative Account of the Other-Race Recognition Deficit. *Psychological Review*, 117(4), 1168–1187. https://doi.org/10.1037/a0020463.

Itier, R. J., & Taylor, M. J. (2004). Face inversion and contrast-reversal effects across development: In contrast to the expertise theory. *Developmental Science*, 7(2), 246–260. https://doi.org/10.1111/j.1467-7687.2004.00342.x.

Karageorge, A., & Zajac, R. (2011). Exploring the effects of age and delay on children's person identifications: verbal descriptions, lineup performance, and the influence of wildcards. *British Journal of Psychology*, 102(2), 161–183. https://doi.org/10.1348/000712610X507902.

Lampinen, J., Arnal, J. D., Adams, J., Courtney, K., & Hicks, J. L. (2012). Forensic age progression and the search for missing children. *Psychology, Crime & Law*, 18(4), 405–415. https://doi.org/10.1080/1068316X.2010.499873.

Laurence, S., Baker, K. A., Proietti, V. M., & Mondloch, C. J. (2022). What happens to our representation of identity as familiar faces age? Evidence from priming and identity aftereffects. *British Journal of Psychology*, February, 1–19. https://doi.org/10.1111/bjop.12560.

Longmore, C. A., Santos, I. M., Silva, C. F., Hall, A., Faloyin, D., & Little, E. (2017). Image dependency in the recognition of newly learnt faces. *Quarterly Journal of Experimental Psychology*, 70(5), 863–873. https://doi.org/10.1080/17470218.2016.1236825.

Macchi Cassia, V., Pisacane, A., & Gava, L. (2012). No own-age bias in 3-year-old children: More evidence for the role of early experience in building face-processing biases. *Journal of Experimental Child Psychology*, 113(3), 372–382. https://doi.org/10.1016/j.jecp.2012.06.014.

Martschuk, N., & Sporer, S. L. (2018). Memory for faces in old age: A meta-analysis. *Psychology and Aging*, 33(6), 904–923. https://doi.org/10.1037/pag0000282.

McKone, E., Crookes, K., Jeffery, L., & Dilks, D. D. (2012). A critical review of the development of face recognition: Experience is less important than previously believed. *Cognitive Neuropsychology*, 29 (1–2), 174–212. https://doi.org/10.1080/02643294.2012.660138.

Megreya, A. M., & Bindemann, M. (2015). Developmental improvement and age-related decline in unfamiliar face matching. *Perception*, 44 (1), 5–22. https://doi.org/10.1068/p7825.

Meissner, C. A., & Brigham, J. C. (2001). Thirty years of investigating the own-race bias in memory for faces: A meta-analytic review. *Psychology, Public Policy, and Law*, 7(1), 3–35. https://doi.org/10.1037//1076-8971.7.1.3.

Memon, A., Bartlett, J., Rose, R., & Gray, C. (2003). The aging eyewitness: Effects of age on face, delay, and source-memory ability. *Sciences-New York*, 58(6), 43–50.

Memon, A., & Gabbert, F. (2003). Improving the identification accuracy of senior witnesses: Do prelineup questions and sequential testing help? *Journal of Applied Psychology*, 88(2), 341–347. https://doi.org/10.1037/0021-9010.88.2.341.

Memon, A., Havard, C., Clifford, B., Gabbert, F., & Watt, M. (2011). A field evaluation of the VIPER system: a new technique for eliciting eyewitness identification evidence. *Psychology, Crime & Law*, 17(8), 711–729. https://doi.org/10.1080/10683160903524333.

Memon, A., & Hope, L. (2002). Eyewitness recognition errors: The effects of mugshot viewing and choosing in young and old adults. *Memory & Cognition*, 30(8), 1219–1227.

Mileva, M., Young, A. W., Jenkins, R., & Burton, A. M. (2020). Facial identity across the lifespan. *Cognitive Psychology*, 116(December), 101260. https://doi.org/10.1016/j.cogpsych.2019.101260.

Rhodes, M. G., & Anastasi, J. S. (2012). The own-age bias in face recognition: A meta-analytic and theoretical review. *Psychological Bulletin*, 138(1), 146–174. https://doi.org/10.1037/a0025750.

Sexton, L., Mileva, M., Hole, G., Strathie, A., & Laurence, S. (2024). Recognizing newly learned faces across changes in age. *Visual Cognition*, 31(8), 617–632. https://doi.org/10.1080/13506285.2024.2315813.

Sparkes, M. (2022). Face recognition struggles to recognise us after five years of ageing. *New Scientist*, 24 August. www.newscientist.com/a

rticle/2334375-face-recognition-struggles-to-recognise-us-after-fi
ve-years-of-ageing.

Sporer, S. L. (2001). The cross-race effect: Beyond recognition of faces in the laboratory. *Psychology, Public Policy, and Law, 7*(1), 170–200. https://doi.org/10.1037/1076-8971.7.1.170.

Strickland-Hughes, C. M., Dillon, K. E., West, R. L., & Ebner, N. C. (2020). Own-age bias in face-name associations: Evidence from memory and visual attention in younger and older adults. *Cognition,* 200(March), 104253. https://doi.org/10.1016/j.cognition.2020.104253.

Susilo, T., Germine, L., & Duchaine, B. (2013). Face recognition ability matures late: Evidence from individual differences in young adults. *Journal of Experimental Psychology: Human Perception and Performance, 39*(5), 1212–1217. https://doi.org/10.1037/a0033469.

Wiese, H., Komes, J., & Schweinberger, S. R. (2013). Ageing faces in ageing minds: A review on the own-age bias in face recognition. *Visual Cognition,* 21(9–10), 1337–1363. https://doi.org/10.1080/13506285.2013.823139.

Wilcock, R. A., & Bull, R. (2005). Aiding the performance of older eye-witnesses: Enhanced non-biased line-up instructions and line-up presentation. *Psychiatry, Psychology and Law, 12*(1), 129–140.

Wilcock, R., Bull, R., Vrij, a, & Wilcock, R. (2007). Are old witnesses always poorer witnesses? Identification accuracy, context reinstatement, own-age bias. *Psychology, Crime & Law, 13*(3), 305–316. https://doi.org/10.1080/10683160600822212.

Yarmey, a. D., Yarmey, M. J., & Yarmey, a. L. (1996). Accuracy of eye-witness identifications in showups and lineups. *Law and Human Behavior,* 20(4), 459–477. https://doi.org/10.1007/BF01498981.

Zhou, X., Elshiekh, A., & Moulson, M. C. (2019). Lifetime perceptual experience shapes face memory for own- and other-race faces. *Visual Cognition,* 27(9–10), 687–700. https://doi.org/10.1080/13506285.2019.1638478.

7 Machine errors in face recognition

Introduction

Automatic face recognition (AFR) technology has become more widespread for the variety of different situations where identity verification is required. For example, AFR can be used for unlocking a phone or laptop instead of a password, for real-time facial monitoring in public places for law enforcement and security, and to identify culprits caught on CCTV from police databases. AFR systems have also been installed in supermarkets and other retail stores to try and identify suspected shoplifters and prevent thefts. Many airports now have automatic ePassport gates or automated passport control where the gate captures a live image of the traveller's face and scans their passport and to verify that they are the same person (see Figure 7.1). Next time you are at passport control, see how many people go through these automatic gates trouble-free and notice how many people try several times and then end up having to go to the passport gate where a human carries out the passport check. What you will notice is that the automatic passport gates do not correctly work 100% of the time. My personal experience is that in one year alone I was twice allowed to go through the ePassport gate, and it was able to verify my identity, but on one other occasion it didn't work and after three attempts I had to go through the non-automated channel where a human looked at my passport for verification. What this demonstrates is that AFR algorithms are not always reliable for verifying identity and often a human is required to intervene and make a decision, and this will be discussed in more detail later in the chapter.

DOI: 10.4324/9781003177128-7

Figure 7.1 Example of ePassport gates.

Face recognition is one of the most widely researched areas in computer vision, with thousands of studies being carried out and published (Alturki et al., 2022). As more research is being undertaken to improve the technology AFR algorithms are becoming more accurate as newer systems are developed. When undertaking the research for this chapter I entered the search term 'automatic face recognition' into Google Scholar and the search returned over 9000 entries, with over 400 articles since 2022 alone. As there is already a huge volume of research of AFR that is constantly updating it became apparent that if the chapter were to focus too much on the computer science and psychological research investigating the accuracy of different AFR systems, the chapter would be out of date very quickly. It therefore made more sense to focus on some of the applied issues of employing AFR technology, the types of errors we know AFR can produce and the ethical implications of using this technology.

A very brief history of face recognition technology

The development of automatic face recognition software can be traced back to the 1960s and 1970s, where computers were used to try and match the distance between areas of one face (e.g. eyes, nose, mouth, etc.) to another face, to determine if they were the same identity. In 1980s the Eigenface technique was developed and it used more complex analyses, based not solely on the geometry of different facial points, but also the relationship between the pixels in the image and using linear algebra (Payal & Goyani, 2020). In the 1990s researchers continued to develop algorithms to identify human faces in real time, in the hope of bringing the software to the commercial market. It wasn't until the attacks of 11 September 2001 that the US federal government heavily invested in face recognition technology, giving grants to create databases and to improve AFR accuracy (Benedict, 2022). In 2010 the social media platform Facebook introduced its face recognition algorithm that automatically tagged photos of people's faces with their names, meaning that people were then associated with any information they shared on the platform. Facebook passed on its users' personal data to a consulting firm called Cambridge Analytica, which is no longer operating. Then in 2018, the Information Commissioner's Office, the UK's data protection watchdog, fined Facebook £500,000 for its role in the scandal and Facebook dropped its face recognition system (Shaieles, 2021). Meanwhile in 2014, the FBI launched its new Next Generation Identification (NGI) system which combined both fingerprints and face images to create a large database to be used for identification in criminal cases (Snyder, 2018), and which is still being used in 2023.

Current state-of-the-art face recognition algorithms are more complex, and use deep convolutional neural networks (DCNNs), with multiple levels of processing. DCNNs have been compared to how primates process visual information in the brain, so faces can be recognised from different viewpoints and under different lighting. DCNNs can be more accurate than older systems; however, for them to be effective they need to be trained on a large number (millions) of faces, and importantly not just one image but multiple images for each identity (e.g. different viewpoints, and lighting) (Noyes & Hill, 2021).

Implementing automatic face recognition technology

There are several benefits to using automatic face recognition (AFR) systems, one being that algorithms can process many images of faces much more quickly than the human eye (Noyes & Hill, 2021). There are several ways in which AFR systems are used to verify a person's identity (see Figure 7.2 for some examples). One way is to decide whether two images are the same person or two different people; this is a one-to-one matching process and used by a variety of different systems such as ePassport gates and banking apps on a mobile phone that may ask the owner to verify their identity when certain transactions are made, by matching a live image of the person making the transaction using the phone's camera with an image already stored in the app. Another way ARF systems are used is when there is one image of a person and the system searches though its database to

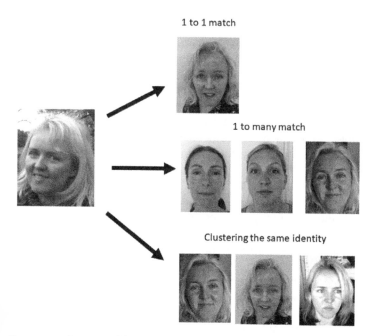

Figure 7.2 The uses of face recognition technology.

try and find an identity match to the image, this is a one-to-many matching process (Buolamwini et al., 2020). This is often used by the police when trying to identify an offender from video footage, for example a thief at a robbery, and the police search their dataset to see if the individual is a known offender. Another way AFR algorithms can also be employed is for clustering; this is to determine whether several images, often from different sources and locations, are the same person. For example, the police may be investigating a number of very similar crimes and have CCTV footage of the suspects involved who look similar to one another. The AFR algorithm can be employed to try and determine whether the different images are the same person (Noyes & Hill, 2021). Whichever AFR process is used, the end result is that software will come up with some estimated probability that there is an identity match (e.g. 90% probability of a match) and then the human operator will have to decide if they think the algorithm's probability is indicative that the images are the same identity.

Although there are some benefits to using AFR algorithms as the can examine many more images faster than humans, they can also make errors just like humans. There are two errors that an AFR algorithm can make and both types of error can have serious consequences if the operator of the software is not aware of them. There is a false positive, or false acceptance, where the algorithm suggests that two or more different images are the same person, when they are in fact different people. This can have serious consequences for individuals who have been mis-identified by the police for committing crimes they are innocent of, and this will be described in more detail later in the chapter. There is also a false negative, or false rejection, which is where the algorithm fails to match images of the same identity, such as when the ePassport gate doesn't work even though the person is carrying a legitimate passport, or the face recognition technology fails to recognise a known criminal whose image already exists in the database. This can also have serious consequences such as in the case of the Boston Marathon bombings in 2013, when the two culprits were not recognised via the CCTV footage prior to the incident despite both being on the police's database. Many of the failures of AFR systems can have very serious outcomes, especially if they do not prevent terrorist attacks, or innocent persons are arrested for crimes they did not commit. There have also been less serious failures of AFR systems that have caught the public's attention, which are described in the box.

When automatic face recognition goes wrong publicly

There have been several high-profile failures of face recognition technology, some of which have serious consequences, while others have just caused embarrassment. In 2017 two big mobile phone companies installed software in their phones that allowed a user to unlock their phone by looking at it. When Craig Federighi from Apple tried to demonstrate the new iPhone X's Face ID feature during its live launch, it failed to work, and he had to resort to using a backup phone that did recognise his face. Another phone-related face recognition failure that year was that Samsung Galaxy S8 users found that they could use a selfie from another phone to fool the face recognition technology and unlock the phone. Although both types of failure of face recognition technology were embarrassing to the phone companies, they did not have serious ramifications for anyone's lives; after all, even with the Samsung case there is always the failsafe of using a passcode to unlock the phone.

Humans and machines

As you read earlier, AFR algorithms do not provide 100% reliable decisions; however, they can often have high levels of accuracy. In the UK, the Data Protection Act states that any decision made by an algorithm must be checked by a human, and this is another potential source of error. A human might be asked to judge a number of possible matches to a given target image (White et al., 2015), or make a decision based on a similarity score produced by an AFR algorithm (Phillips et al., 2018). A number of studies have found that humans can be influenced by the prior judgements of an AFR system, which can lead to greater accuracy when the algorithm has correctly identified an individual; however, it can reduce accuracy if the algorithm has made an incorrect decision, such as saying two images of two different people are the same person, or suggesting that two images of the same person are two different people. This section will explore some of the research that has investigated how AFR decisions can influence human decision making for face recognition.

To investigate the influence of AFR responses on human face matching performance, Fysh and Bindemann (2018) presented pairs of faces that were either two images of the same identity (match) or two different people (mismatch) that were labelled either 'same' 'different' or 'unresolved'. For most of the trials the information was consistent with the face pair; however, for some pairs the label provided inconsistent information. Their findings revealed that even when participants were told that the information might not be totally reliable, it influenced the decisions, with consistent information increasing accuracy and inconsistent information reducing accuracy. Fysh and Bindemann (2018) suggest their findings demonstrate that humans may not be reliable to serve as an additional verification at border control when electronic passport gates have made incorrect decisions, for example when an imposter is labelled as an identity match. Howard, Rabbitt and Sirotin (2020) conducted a similar study where participants were presented with face pairs along with a fictitious ARF response about whether the pair was match or mismatch. For half the pairs the AFR response was correct, but for the other half the response was incorrect. Their findings replicated Fysh and Bindemann's (2018) finding that humans were influenced by the fictitious AFR responses. One of the criticisms that has been made of this research is that the fictitious labels that were provided were arbitrary and not based on real decisions by AFR algorithms; however, there is some research that has addressed this issue (Carragher & Hancock, 2022).

Carragher and Hancock (2022) conducted a series of experiments with human participants and simulated responses from an ARF algorithm that were based on real performance from a DCNN. In all the experiments face matching tasks were employed and participants had to decide if pairs of faces were the same person or two different people. Previous research had been used to construct the face pairs so that some were known to be difficult and others easy to match (Phillips et al., 2011). In all

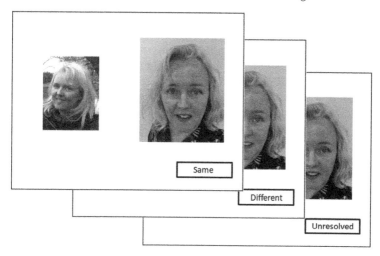

Figure 7.3 Example of AFR task with response.

the experiments, the face matching task was initially conducted by participants without any additional information to create a baseline, and then for the other half of the study they were presented with the face pairs and also the simulated response from the AFR system, to see if this influenced their decisions. In experiments where the AFR had a high accuracy rate (97.6%) this was found to increase the accuracy of participants' decisions, as compared to the control condition with no AFR information. In experiments where the AFR had lower accuracy (54.8%) this was found to not influence matching performance. The same results were found if participants knew in advance how accurately the AFR performed, so it appeared that knowing the accuracy of the AFR didn't influence responses. Interestingly when the responses were compared to a the real DCNNs responses, it was found that when face pairs were the same person (match) the DCNN and humans made similar responses; however, when the faces were different identities (mismatch) responses for some face pairs were different for the DCNN as compared to humans, which suggests that humans and DCNN are making decisions about the faces in slightly different ways when they are two different identities. Overall, using the algorithm improved the human participants' matching accuracy; however, there were times when the algorithm had the correct responses and the human participants overruled that response and in doing so made an error, and there were other times where the humans failed to correct an error made by the AFR algorithm.

Psychological research has also investigated whether AFR systems are more accurate than humans performing the same task, by comparing how well humans and AFR algorithms perform on face recognition and matching tasks. One study by Phillips et al. (2018) compared state-of the-art DCNNs' face matching accuracy with groups of humans who had varying degrees of experience and predetermined ability to do the task. The human participants were made up of different groups, including forensic facial examiners and reviewers, who have been trained to compare facial images, super recognisers who are untrained, but have superior face recognition ability (this will be discussed in more detail in Chapter 10), and students and fingerprint examiners. They found DCNNs outperformed most human participants, apart from some of the top performing facial examiners.

Another study comparing humans and machines' face recognition was conducted by Hancock, Somai and Mileva (2020) who tested six commercial AFR systems using a series of one-to-one face matching tasks against human participants. For some of the matching tasks one of the face pairs had been transformed using specialist software, so that the face was a different sex or race from the other face. For example, the original female face had been transformed to a male face, and the original white face had been transformed to a Black face. When it came to matching faces that had not been transformed in any way, the AFR algorithms outperformed the human participants (average around 70%), with some of the AFR algorithms performing at very high levels, over 99% accuracy. However, when it came to the transformed faces the pattern was quite different, especially when it came to the faces that were transformed by sex. Many of the AFR algorithms were not able to perceive a difference and often declared the two faces to be the same identity despite them being different sexes. When it came to judging face pairs that had been transformed by race, in general, the AFR algorithms were slightly more accurate as compared to sex, but in many cases they still suggested the two different faces were the same identity irrespective of the race transform. Hancock et al. (2020) suggested that the AFR systems found same identity face pairs more difficult to match than those that were different identities. When AFR algorithms suggest two different people are the same person this has some real-world implications, especially when it comes to law enforcement and the misidentification of innocent suspects.

Face recognition technology use in law enforcement

In the US, face recognition technology is now widely used to try and identify criminal suspects, with at least 786 local police departments in 40 states using face recognition technology. The New York Police Department conducted over 7,000 searches for suspects using face recognition technology in 2018, while the FBI conducted 152,500 searches from 2017 to 2019. (Benedict, 2022). Despite its wide use, face recognition technology used by the police has not always been accurate and there have been a number of cases where innocent people have been wrongly arrested as a result of misidentification. There are two main reasons for misidentification from AFR and these result from the quality of images being used as a reference point, and also the biases in algorithm due to the images in the database, which will be discussed in more detail later in this chapter.

When using images (e.g. stills from CCTV) to identify suspects from the police database or to match to driving licences, or existing mugshots, the AFR algorithms work best when high-quality images are used and faces are facing forwards rather than in profile or three-quarters view. However, high-quality images are often unavailable, and the police may have to rely on whatever images are available, for example grainy and taken from different angles and/or under poor lighting, which increases the risk of misidentification (Benedict, 2022). It has been suggested the failure of the AFR system used during the Boston Marathon bombing was due to the poor-quality images that were gained by CCTV at the event, combined with the suspects Tamerian and Dzhokhar Tsarnaev both wearing hats that day, and one was also wearing sunglasses. As a result of the poor images and the faces being concealed (this will be discussed in more detail in Chapter 8) the

AFR system did not identify the attackers prior to the incident (Klontz & Jain, 2013).

The image quality that is captured not only for a police database but that is being used to drive the identification is important to ensure accurate identification; however, even when high-quality images are used there can still be misidentifications through AFR technology. There have been several examples where members of the public have been misidentified and wrongfully arrested because of AFR technology. Some of the examples of misidentification through AFR are described in the text box.

Real-world examples of misidentifications by law enforcement

In January 2020 Robert Williams was at work when he received a call claiming to be from the Detroit Police Department telling him to go to the police station to be arrested. He thought it was a prank call. When he arrived home from work the police arrested him and took him to the police station. It wasn't until he was interviewed that he was told he was being accused of shoplifting watches worth several thousand dollars. The police's face recognition software falsely identified Robert Williams as being the thief from the shop's CCTV footage from his driving licence photograph, although when comparing the image of the real culprit they were clearly two different people. Furthermore, if the police had checked, Williams had an alibi and therefore could not have been in the shop on the day of the incident. Two weeks later the prosecutors dropped the case saying that they had insufficient evidence; however, Williams and his family had already faced unnecessary stress and humiliation due to the whole incident (Hill, 2020).

There have been other misidentifications made by the Detroit police's face recognition software. Michael Oliver was another innocent person who was wrongly identified from the algorithm as grabbing a mobile from someone in a car, throwing it and damaging it. When the two images of both men were compared, it was very clear that Oliver was not the culprit as he had tattoos all over his arms, while the culprit did not, and the case was finally dismissed (Anderson, 2020).

In February 2019, Nijeer Parks was arrested for aggravated assault, unlawful possession of weapons, using a fake ID, shoplifting and resisting arrest, as well as nearly hitting a police officer with a car. What led to his arrest was that the face recognition technology used by the New Jersey police matched the fake ID left at the scene of the crime, to a photo in the database of Parks. It was clear looking at the images of both men that the suspect and Parks were two different people, as the suspect had his ears pierced, while Parks did not. Likewise, if the police had checked, Parks had an alibi as he was over 30 miles away from the scene of the crime. After Parks spent ten days in jail and paid $5,000 to defend himself, the case was dismissed for lack of evidence (General & Sarlin, 2021).

Police in the UK have also used face recognition technology. The Metropolitan (Met) Police force have used live face recognition (LFR) technology since August 2016 to monitor crowds at the Notting Hill Carnival (Manthorpe & Martin, 2019). In LFR technology, a camera is set up taking live footage of members of the public and the algorithm tries to match the faces to any faces that exist in the database. If the algorithm finds a possible match, it can inform the human operator who can then decide if they think the match is a credible identification (Fussey, Davies & Innes, 2021). The Met's LFR system has also come under criticism, as research by Professor Fussey and colleagues from Essex University found that the LFR technology was only successful at making correct identifications 19% of the time and not 70%, of the time as the Met had previously claimed (Rosseau, 2020).

Police in South Wales have also used AFR technology for live scanning of the general public to try and locate individuals they may have already in their database, and also to try and identify individuals who have been caught on CCTV. Davies, Innes and Dawson (2018), researchers from the University of Cardiff, evaluated the deployment or the face recognition technology and found that image quality significantly influenced the accuracy of the system. They found initially there were high rates of false positives (72%), where the algorithm suggested matches that, once examined by the human operator, were found to be two different people. The ARF also produced a low rate of true positives (3%), where the AFR suggested the identities were the same and the human operator agreed the identities were the same. Over time the algorithm did appear to increase its true positive rate (from 3% to 46%); however, it still resulted in very few arrests.

Biased AFR algorithms

Many of real-life examples of misidentifications due to AFR technology have a common theme and that is the persons misidentified were of Black ethnic origin, which suggests the algorithms used by the police were racially biased and less accurate with faces that have darker skin. In all cases in the US described above, if the police had checked whether those who had been misidentified had alibis, or even closely looked at the images of the real culprits compared to the images flagged by the algorithm, they would have seen that they were in fact two different people, and this would have saved lots of unnecessary stress, police time and court costs.

AFR algorithms are only as good as the set of faces they learnt from. For example, when creating a new algorithm to recognise faces, if all that algorithm has learnt to recognise are white male faces, then it can become fairly accurate at recognising faces from that group; however, when it comes to recognising faces from other groups, it will be much more error prone. In a way it is like the contact hypothesis and expertise explanations for the own-race bias in humans that you read about in Chapter 4. These explanations for the own-race bias in humans suggest that the more contact one has with different groups, the better one should be at recognising the faces of people from those groups, while not being as accurate at recognising the faces of people where there is very little contact. In the same vein, if algorithms learn to recognise faces from a diverse database with a variety of racial groups, different ages and genders, then the recognition technology should be more accurate; however, this does not seem to be happening in practice (Vaughan, 2021).

It's not just AFR employed by the police that have been found to be biased towards certain groups. In the UK there have been problems with the procedures of obtaining a passport through the online system. An investigation by the BBC found that problems with the Home Office's face recognition technology associated with passports can begin even before the person has obtained a passport, as there are problems with the automatic online checkers that ensure an image that is submitted to be used in a passport is suitable. The BBC research found that dark-skinned women (22%) were much more likely to have their photos rejected as compared to light-skinned women (14%) and men with light (9%) or dark skin (15%). Photos of dark-skinned women were also four times more likely than photos of light-skinned women to be categorised as poor quality. It seems that, like humans, the software appears to have a racial and also gender bias (Maryam, 2020).

Research conducted by Buolamwini and Timnit (2018) in their Gender Shades project (see http://gendershades.org) investigated the influence of gender and skin colour when using AFR systems. They tested three different commercially available AFR systems; IBM, Microsoft and Face ++. The first two are based in the US and the third from China. The findings revealed that all systems were more accurate with male faces as compared to female faces, and more accurate with lighter-skinned faces as compared to darker skinned faces. The findings demonstrated that the commercially available AFR algorithms were biased for race and gender and were much more likely to misidentify or misclassify darker-skinned females. This included not detecting a darker-skinned female face in an image of a scene and also misclassifying a darker-skinned female face as being male. Findings from the Gender Shades project concluded that biased algorithms have created a real threat for gender equality and civil rights.

There have been several systematic evaluations of AFR used around the world, that have found AFR can demonstrate bias. The National Institute of Standards and Technology (NIST) tested 106 different face recognition algorithms from 24 countries from different global regions; such as Europe, the US, China, Russia, Singapore, India and Israel, to name a few (Grother et al., 2019). The findings from their research revealed many of the algorithms produced high false positive rates, suggesting faces were the same identity when they were in fact two different people, when the faces belonged to people from African and East Asian ethnic groups. There were some exceptions; for example, algorithms that had been developed in China were more accurate with East Asian faces, while US algorithms produced high rates of false positives with Native American, African American and Asian ethnic groups compared to faces from a white ethnic background. These are interesting findings as they lend further evidence that there is a racial bias in the algorithms, most probably because of the set of faces that have been used to train the systems to identify faces. For example, algorithms developed in China, that were most likely trained with Chinese faces, did not give high rates of false positives to East Asian faces, but those developed in other countries, e.g. the US, where presumably most of the training faces were white, had high levels of false positives for East Asian faces, as well as Black faces. There was also an influence of gender and age with higher false positive rates for women as compared to men and for elderly and children's faces (Grother et al., 2019). The same study also found that many of the systems failed to associate two images as being the same person, and thus created false negatives. For the US systems, there were higher false negatives for Native Americans, and Asians as compared to white and African American faces. However, when the image quality was reduced there were more false negatives for faces from African ethnic backgrounds.

The ethical issues of using face recognition technology

There are several ethical issues about using live AFR systems with members of the public and they relate to the purpose the technology is being used for, for example for safety of the public, the protection of property, or for maintaining order and ensuring laws are being adhered to in public spaces. There is also the issue of how face databases that are crucial for accurate AFR algorithms are created, whether the individuals whose faces are on the systems have consented to having their data stored and how long the information might be stored for.

For face recognition algorithms to work they need to have a large database or gallery of images of all the different identities they want to recognise, that is a database to compare a current image of the person they want to identify. There are some ethical issues when it comes to creating these databases and that is whether people whose images are within a database have consented to having their biometric data stored. In some cases, for example, police forces might have existing images of suspects that have been taken in custody suite images, or mugshots; other databases may have images from driving licenses. In creating the FBI's Next Generation Identification (NGI) system many of the civilians in the database are unaware that their images have been provided by the government and could potentially be implicated in criminal investigations. Some researchers have suggested that the FBI's database could be used for conducting unlawful searches for the identification and it violates the Fourth Amendment, which prohibits unreasonable searches and seizures (Snyder, 2018).

There are companies that support the use of AFR systems and organisations who market AFR systems claim they have the potential to be used to protect the public, for example to try and prevent terrorist attacks by identifying threat in public spaces. AFR technology is also being used more widely in the retail sector to identify shoplifters, whose images are already stored in databases of known offenders. The use of AFR in supermarkets has caused some controversy in the UK, where a number of Southern Co-op stores in England employed AFR to identify and ban individuals from their stores. A privacy group called Big Brother complained to the Information Commissioner's Office, stating this was unlawful as the system stores images and information about individuals who have been identified as being offenders (Grierson, 2022).

Another ethical issue about the use of AFR in public spaces is related to the purpose of its use and when it is used to enforce certain laws. In some Islamic countries, such as Iran, it is mandatory for women to wear a hijab (head covering or headscarf) while out in public. In 2022, the Iranian government suggested using face recognition in public spaces to police hijab law and identify any individuals and make arrests of those who were not adhering to this law. This is especially worrying as in 2022 a Kurdish woman, Jina Mahsa Amini, was arrested by the morality police for not wearing a hijab and died in police custody. Her death provoked the biggest wave of protests seen in Iran for decades, and this resulted in an estimated 19,000 arrests and 500 deaths. Many of the arrests did not occur during the protests but took place a few days later, suggesting that face recognition was being employed at the scene to identify individuals at a later date (Johnson, 2023).

As mentioned earlier, in the UK, South Wales Police have been using AFR at public events and in shopping malls recording images of people without their consent. In a landmark case, Edward Bridges, from civil rights group Liberty, took South Wales Police to court over the use of his images that had been recorded without his consent on two different occasions and argued this contravened his human rights and also the data protection act. The Court of Appeal found that under these particular circumstances the AFR was deployed in an unlawful way (Gordon, 2021). However, this has not prevented South Wales Police continuing to use live face recognition in public and a trial deployment was undertaken in Cardiff in March 2022 (Jones, 2022).

Conclusion

Automatic face recognition systems are becoming more prevalent in everyday life, with individuals using them for unlocking phones, laptops and banking apps. In public spaces we are now all more likely to be inadvertently watched by AFR systems implemented by law enforcement and retail outlets, and to use ePassport gates at border control. However, AFR systems are not always accurate, and they can make mistakes, especially when they have learnt to only recognise particular groups of people, which has meant some people, particularly women and those with darker skin, are more likely to be misidentified. There have been several cases where innocent people have been wrongly identified as a result of racially biased AFR. Therefore automatic face recognition is more likely to 'go wrong' and misidentify or misclassify Black women.

Psychological research has shown that in many circumstances AFR algorithms can be more accurate than humans at determining whether two different images are the same identity (Hancock et al., 2020), especially when humans have not been trained adequately to do a face comparison task (Phillips et al., 2018), or have a poor face recognition ability. However, many decisions made by AFR must be verified by a human, which can also reduce accuracy for identification, especially if the human is swayed by inaccurate information provided by the AFR (Fysh & Bindemann, 2018; Howard et al., 2020).

There are ethical issues of using AFR in public spaces as individuals may have not consented to their images being filmed and stored on databases. There is also the double-edged sword of using the AFR technology, as it has the potential to make the public safer by identifying terrorists prior to any attacks, but can be used to curtail women's rights, or single out people from particular ethnic groups in certain nations. Ritchie et al. (2021) suggest that organisations who use AFR need to do more to explain why it is being used, understand how accurate their systems are and adhere to data protection policies. Similarly, Gordon (2021) suggests that ARF's systems should ensure accuracy and fairness, and be compliant with the law. As AFR use is increasing globally we need to continue the conversation of when and why the systems are being used, and not assume they are always accurate.

References

Alturki, R., Alharbi, M., AlAnzi, F., & Albahli, S. (2022). Deep learning techniques for detecting and recognizing face masks: A survey. *Frontiers in Public Health*, 10(March). https://doi.org/10.3389/fpubh.2022.955332.

Anderson, E. (2020). Detroit facial recognition technology has misidentified suspects. https://eu.freep.com/story/news/local/michigan/detroit/2020/07/10/facial-recognition-detroit-michael-oliver-robert-williams/5392166002/.

Benedict, T. J. (2022). The computer got it wrong: Facial recognition technology and establishing probable cause to arrest. *Washington and Lee Law Review*, 79(2).

Buolamwini, J., & Timnit, G. (2018). Gender shades: Intersectional accuracy disparities in commercial gender classification. *Proceedings of Machine Learning Research*, 81, 1–15.

Buolamwini, J., Ordóñez, V., Morgenstern, J., & Learned-Miller, E. (2020). Facial recognition technologies: A primer. www.ajl.org/federal-office-call

Carragher, D. J., & Hancock, P. J. B. (2022). Simulated automated facial recognition systems as decision-aids in forensic face matching tasks. *Journal of Experimental Psychology: General*, 1–57.

Davies, B., Innes, M., & Dawson, A. (2018). An evaluation of South West Police automated facial recognition. https://static1.squarespace.com/static/51b06364e4b02de2f57fd72e/t/5bfd4fbc21c67c2cdd692fa8/1543327693640/AFR+Report+%5BDigital%5D.pdf.

Fussey, P., Davies, B., & Innes, M. (2021). 'Assisted' facial recognition and the reinvention of suspicion and discretion in digital policing. *British Journal of Criminology*, 61(2), 325–344. https://doi.org/10.1093/bjc/azaa068.

Fysh, M. C., & Bindemann, M. (2018). Human–computer interaction in face matching. *Cognitive Science*, 42(5), 1714–1732. https://doi.org/10.1111/cogs.12633.

General, J., & Sarlin, J. (2021). Nijeer Parks was arrested due to a false facial recognition match. https://edition.cnn.com/2021/04/29/tech/nijeer-parks-facial-recognition-police-arrest/index.html.

Gordon, B. J. (2021). Automated facial recognition in law enforcement: *The Queen (on application of Edward Bridges) v the Chief Constable of South Wales Police*. *Electronic Law Journal*, 24(24). https://doi.org/10.17159/1727-3781/2021/V24I0A8923.

Grierson, J. (2022). Facial recognition cameras in UK retail chain challenged by privacy group. *The Guardian*, 26 July. www.theguardian.com/world/2022/jul/26/facial-recognition-cameras-in-uk-retail-chain-challenged-by-privacy-group.

Grother, P., Ngan, M., & Hanaoka, K. (2019). Face Recognition Vendor Test (FRVT) Part 3: Demographic Effects. *Nistir*, 8280 (December), https://doi.org/10.6028/NIST.IR.8280.

Hancock, P. J. B., Somai, R. S., & Mileva, V. R. (2020). Convolutional neural net face recognition works in non-human-like ways. *Royal Society Open Science*, 7(10), 1–7. https://doi.org/10.1098/rsos.200595.

Hill, K. (2020). Wrongfully accused by an algorithm. *The New York Times*, 24 June. www.nytimes.com/2020/06/24/technology/facial-recognition-arrest.html.

Howard, J. J., Rabbitt, L. R., & Sirotin, Y. B. (2020). Human-algorithm teaming in face recognition: How algorithm outcomes cognitively bias human decision-making. *PLoS ONE*, 15(8 August), 1–18. https://doi.org/10.1371/journal.pone.0237855.

Johnson, K. (2023). Iran says face recognition will ID women breaking hijab laws. *Wired*, 10 January. www.wired.com/story/iran-says-face-recognition-will-id-women-breaking-hijab-laws/.

Jones, E. R. (2022). South Wales Police deploy controversial facial recognition cameras in Cardiff. *The Cardiffian*, 22 March. https://cardiffjournalism.co.uk/thecardiffian/2022/03/22/south-wales-police-deploy-controversial-facial-recognition-cameras-in-cardiff/.

Klontz, J. C., & Jain, A. K. (2013). A case study of automated face recognition: The Boston marathon bombings suspects. *Computer*, 46 (11), 91–94. https://doi.org/10.1109/MC.2013.377.

Manthorpe, R., & Martin, A. J. (2019). 81% of 'suspects' flagged by Met's police facial recognition technology innocent, independent report says. https://news.sky.com/story/met-polices-facial-recognition-tech-ha s-81-error-rate-independent-report-says-11755941.

Maryam, A. (2020). UK passport photo checker shows bias against dark-skinned women. www.bbc.co.uk/news/technology-54349538.

Noyes, E., & Hill, M. Q. (2021). Automatic recognition systems and human computer interaction in face matching. In M. Bindemann (ed.), *Forensic face matching: Research and practice* (pp. 193–215). Oxford University Press. https://doi.org/10.1093/oso/9780198837749.003.0009.

Payal, P., & Goyani, M. M. (2020). A comprehensive study on face recognition: methods and challenges. *Imaging Science Journal*, 68(2), 114–127. https://doi.org/10.1080/13682199.2020.1738741.

Phillips, P. J., Beveridge, J. R., Draper, B. A., Givens, G., O'Toole, A. J., Bolme, D. S., Dunlop, J., Lui, Y. M., Sahibzada, H., & Weimer, S. (2011). An introduction to the good, the bad, & the ugly face recognition challenge problem. In *2011 IEEE International Conference on Automatic Face and Gesture Recognition and Workshops, FG 2011*, 346–353. https://doi.org/10.1109/FG.2011.5771424.

Phillips, P. J., Yates, A. N., Hu, Y., Hahn, C. A., Noyes, E., Jackson, K., Cavazos, J. G., Jeckeln, G., Ranjan, R., Sankaranarayanan, S., Chen, J. C., Castillo, C. D., Chellappa, R., White, D., & O'Toole, A. J. (2018). Face recognition accuracy of forensic examiners, superrecognizers, and face recognition algorithms. *Proceedings of the National Academy of Sciences of the United States of America*, 115(24), 6171–6176. https://doi.org/10.1073/pnas.1721355115.

Ritchie, K. L., Cartledge, C. I., Growns, B., Yan, A., Wang, Y., Guo, K., Kramer, R. S. S., Edmond, G., Martire, K. A., San Roque, M., & White, D. (2021). Public attitudes towards the use of automatic facial recognition technology in criminal justice systems around the world. *PLoS ONE*, 16(10), e0258241. https://doi.org/10.1371/journal.pone.0258241.

Rosseau, S. (2020). Met police to begin using live facial recognition cameras in London. *The Guardian*, 24 January. www.theguardian. com/technology/2020/jan/24/met-police-begin-using-live-facial-recog nition-cameras.

Shaieles, S. (2021). Facebook will drop its facial recognition system – but here's why we should be sceptical. https://theconversation.com/fa cebook-will-drop-its-facial-recognition-system-but-heres-why-we-should -be-sceptical-171186.

Snyder, E. (2018). Faceprints and the Fourth Amendment: How the FBI uses facial recognition technology to conduct unlawful searches. *Syracuse Law Review*, 68(1), 68. www.fbi.gov/services/cjis/.

Vaughan, A. (2021). UK still using racially biased passport tool despite available update | New Scientist. https://institutions-newscientist-com. libezproxy.open.ac.uk/article/2271078-uk-still-using-racially-biased-passport-tool-despite-available-update/.

White, D., Dunn, J. D., Schmid, A. C., & Kemp, R. I. (2015). Error rates in users of automatic face recognition software. *PLoS ONE*, 10(10), 1–14. https://doi.org/10.1371/journal.pone.0139827.

8 Disguises, face masks and appearance change

Introduction

As you have read earlier in this book, face recognition by humans and machines is not always 100% accurate, and there are a number of different factors that can influence whether a face is recognised or not. This chapter is going to focus on the research that has investigated whether humans and machines are still able to identify persons when they have disguised their face or their appearance has been changed in some way.

From my own personal experience, I find when I am out walking my dog in the cold winter weather, it sometimes takes me longer to recognise people I know because they have hats and scarves on. You might have also noticed that when you watch a film you might not always recognise a well-known actor right away if they have changed their appearance from how you are used to seeing them. Some actors have gained or lost significant amounts of weight and used prosthetics and/or make-up to change the way their faces look for a specific character. These are examples of when people who are familiar have changed their appearance, but there are times when people who are unfamiliar have changed their appearance and/or tried to deliberately disguise their face.

Criminals have used disguises for many years to try and evade being identified by the police; one famous bank robber in the US was William Sutton Jr, who was nicknamed 'The Actor' due to his use of disguises. In 1950 Sutton was added to the FBI's 'Ten most wanted' list; he was arrested several times and escaped prison six

DOI: 10.4324/9781003177128-8

times, before finally serving his last sentence in 1952. Seventeen years later he was released and he became an actor and book author (FBI, n.d.).

Criminals are still using disguises to try and prevent being recognised while committing robberies. One example is Martin Reilly, who used various disguises including wigs, hats, false beards and moustaches; he also dressed up as Elvis Presley while he committed armed robberies of banks and betting shops (Press Association, 2012). However not all criminals have employed disguises successfully. Matthew Davies failed to cut eye holes in the pillowcase he was wearing over his head to disguise his appearance while robbing a bank in Scotland (BBC News, 2020). This resulted in him having to remove the head covering so that he could see what he was doing, and as a result it was not a very effective disguise and he was later identified!

Criminals also change their appearance if they are trying to look like another person, for example to use a fraudulent passport or other form of identification. As passports become more difficult to forge and creating believable fake passports is costly, this has led to an increase in criminals using stolen passports that are used by lookalike imposters. In the UK, there has been a rise of imposters using stolen passports from 24% in 2005 to over 50%, and almost 400,000 passports are reported lost or stolen each year. In the US, it has been estimated that 80–85% of all fraudulent documents that were intercepted at border control involved stolen passports (Stevens, 2021). Interpol's STLD database of stolen travel and identity documents has over 40 million entries; the UK searched the database more than 140 million times and the US 238 million times in 2013 (Interpol, 2014). These figures demonstrate the challenge that border control staff face when trying to determine whether someone is the same identity as the passport they are carrying.

For individuals to get away with using a stolen passport they must have some resemblance to the photograph on the passport, such as being the same sex, ethnicity and approximate age, and sharing a general appearance. However, as you read in Chapter 1, when Kemp et al. (1997) conducted their study where cashiers were tasked to match shoppers to a photograph on their credit card, they found that fraudulent cards were accepted 50% of the time, especially when the person looked similar to the photograph on the card (Kemp et al., 1997). In research with real passport officers it was also found that they can make errors when trying to match a person to their photographic ID and length of service as a passport officer did not appear to make performance any more accurate (White et al., 2014).

Disguises are not just employed by criminals trying to hide their identity; they have also been employed by individuals working for organisations like the CIA, to try and blend their agents into different situations across the globe. In these cases, disguises must be convincing and not look like disguises, unlike those employed by a bank robber who uses a disguise to cover their face to stop them from being identified. Disguises employed by CIA operatives can have life or death consequences if they are not convincing and as a result the CIA created a Department of Disguise and sought advice from magicians and actors to help create realistic disguises. Jonna Mendez was the former CIA chief of disguise and an expert in surveillance photography until she retired in 1993. Her role involved creating disguises for agents and other individuals who were working for the CIA, and trying to recognise people who were disguised (e.g. terrorists) and trying to hide their identity (Atwell, 2022). Mendez's top tips for effective disguises are listed in the box.

Figure 8.1 Example of a face wearing a disguise.

Jonna Mendez's Top 10 CIA Disguise Tips

1   Blend in if you don't want to be noticed. If you have time, buy local clothing.
2   Change your hair. If you can't colour it or wear a wig, a change of style may help change your appearance.
3   Avoid fake moustaches. If you are going to be uncomfortable or at risk of perspiring, avoid extra facial hair.
4   Glasses. Horn-rimmed glasses can change a face.
5   Makeup. Makeup can be a game-changer for men or women who want to smooth out a rough complexion.
6   Accessorize. A person carrying a leather portfolio and a cigar will likely be remembered for their leather portfolio and cigar.
7   Footwear. You can often tell where someone is from based on their shoes.
8   Less can be more. You don't need a full, *Mission Impossible*-style face mask. Your disguise should allow you to smoke, talk, eat, drink, and use your phone.
9   Think of disguise as an onion. Whether you're building it or peeling it off, you're dealing with layers. When you have the right amount, you disappear, and another person is in the room.
10 Own it. Just as important as your disguise is your demeanour. Stride in like you own the room and the character.

Source: Spyscape (2022)

Looking at Jonna Mendez's top tips for disguises, you can see that only numbers 2–5 are directly related to face recognition, whereas many of the other tips are related to other aspects of a person's appearance that can be altered to blend into different situations. As the focus of this book is face recognition going wrong, the next section will look at some of the psychological research that has investigated whether using facial disguises can influence face recognition.

Disguises and face recognition

One of the first studies to investigate the effect of disguises on face recognition presented faces that were either the identical image seen during study, or disguised in appearance via a changed hair style, or the addition or removal of beard and/or moustache. Unsurprisingly, when faces were disguised, participants were less accurate than when they saw the exact same image that they had seen during the study phase (Patterson & Baddeley, 1977). One of the criticisms of this study is that it used the identical image from study to test in the control (undisguised) condition and therefore the argument is that it was testing image recognition, rather than face recognition (Bruce, 1982). Another more recent study by Righi et al. (2012) investigated which type of disguise (wigs, glasses or both) might have a greater influence over face recognition. They found that changing hair via a wig was more likely to reduce recognition than wearing glasses, and that wearing both reduced recognition accuracy even further. Interestingly, if faces were seen at study with glasses, the removal of glasses at test was a greater detriment to recognition than when faces were seen without glasses at study and then added during a test phase. They suggested that when faces are initially seen with disguises (e.g. glasses or wigs), the disguise becomes encoded as a part of the face, and this is why, when the face is seen without the disguise, it is more detrimental than a face that was learnt without a disguise which is then seen with a disguise. They suggest that people should be trained to try and ignore hairstyles and glasses and focus on other areas of the face accurate recognition.

A more recent study investigating the influence of disguises by Noyes and Jenkins (2019) made the distinction between two different ways people might disguise themselves. Faces can be disguised so that a person changes their usual appearance so they don't look the same as they would usually: they called this evasion, and this is what a thief might do so they aren't identified. The other way a disguise might be used is when a person tries to look like another person, i.e. impersonation, and this is what individuals do when they use a stolen passport. To investigate the influence of these different types of disguises, Noyes and Jenkins (2019) created a dataset of faces where the models were asked to deliberately disguise themselves in one of two ways; either to hide their identity (evasive condition), or to look like another person (impersonation condition). Participants were presented with a face matching task with the disguised and undisguised faces and had to decide whether the face pairs were the same person or two different people. When faces were unfamiliar, participants were less accurate at matching disguised faces as compared to undisguised faces. Furthermore, participants were less able to detect that two faces were the same person if one of those faces had been disguised in the evasive condition. When the faces were personally familiar to the participants then they were able to correctly decide whether a face pair were the same identity, regardless of whether the faces were disguised, although there was still a small influence on the evasive condition. Noyes and Jenkins' (2019) research demonstrates how familiarity with a person can reduce the effectiveness of a disguise; however, in many real-life scenarios, such as eyewitness identification, a disguised person may not be familiar to a witness.

Disguises and eyewitness memory

As mentioned earlier, criminals sometimes wear disguises when committing crime in public spaces, such as robbing a bank, to prevent them from being later identified either through CCTV or by eyewitnesses who may be asked to try and make an identification from a police lineup. There have been a number of studies that have investigated the influence of disguises on subsequent eyewitness identification. Often participants view a mock crime of a perpetrator wearing some type of disguise and then after a delay are presented with a lineup to see if they can identify the person that they previously saw. Mansour et al. (2020) investigated the influence of different disguises on eyewitness identification and found that when a perpetrator wore a disguise that this not only made recognition less accurate for seen perpetrator, but participants were more likely to make a false identification if that perpetrator was absent from a subsequent lineup. Over two different eyewitness experiments they found that when it came to correctly recognising a previously seen culprit from a target present lineup, wearing a hat and/or sunglasses, or a stocking that covered the face, reduced subsequent identification from a lineup as compared to no disguise. Wearing sunglasses was more detrimental than a hat and wearing both a hat and sunglasses reduced correct identification more than either alone. Wearing sunglasses also increased false identifications from target absent lineups that did not contain the previously seen culprit, while wearing a hat appeared to make little difference. For targets that wore the stocking disguise, this was found to increase false identifications from target absent lineups if the stocking covered two-thirds or the whole face, but not when it only covered the top half of the face. They concluded that the more areas of a face that are covered by a disguise not only means a witness is less likely to subsequently recognise the face again, but they are also more at risk of making a false identification of an innocent person.

Manley et al. (2022) also investigated the influence of wearing a disguise upon the accuracy of eyewitness identification. Employing an eyewitness study, participants saw a masked perpetrator in a mock crime video and then saw either a lineup where all the individuals were masked, or they were unmasked. They found that participants were more likely to correctly identify a perpetrator from a masked lineup than an unmasked lineup; however, when shown a target absent lineup there was little difference between performance for the masked and unmasked lineups. Manley et al. (2022) suggest that their study has real-world applications to make eyewitness identification more accurate, without increasing false identification if innocent persons are wrongfully arrested. This is only one study, however, and until it is replicated by further research we should be cautious about the findings.

Although not looking specifically at disguises, Zarkadi et al. (2009) looked at the influence of suspects with distinctive features, such as tattoos, scars and piercings, upon subsequent identification from a lineup. They found identification was more accurate when the distinctive features of a previously seen culprit were replicated onto all lineup members through image manipulation software, rather than removed. The findings of Zarkadi et al. (2009) coupled with those of Manley et al. (2022) imply that identification accuracy should be improved if the viewing conditions during the police lineup match with those during the crime. Researchers Or et al. (2023) suggest that if a witness sees a culprit with a mask then the faces in the lineup should all be masked, or if the suspect has a facial scar then all lineup members should have that same scar. The idea that viewing conditions of the lineup should match the viewing conditions of the witnessed crime is supported by the encoding specificity principle, which suggests that contextual information is encoded during memory creation and that retrieval will be more accurate if that contextual information is present (Tulving & Thomson, 1973). Carlson et al. (2021) found support for encoding specificity principle with their study where identification was more accurate when viewing conditions were matched from an initial viewing to identification. However, Carlson et al. (2021) only compared faces that had the external features masked to viewing the whole faces and therefore could not conclude whether this would generalise to other more complex disguises.

Which type of disguise is the most effective?

There are several ways faces can be disguised or masked, such as using wigs, hats, sunglasses and face masks and some researchers have investigated which disguises have the greatest impact on reducing face recognition accuracy. A face matching study by Kramer and Ritchie (2016) found that even when only one face in a face pair wore a pair of glasses this could reduce matching accuracy, and participants were less likely to make a correct decision when both sets of faces were wearing glasses. Graham and Ritchie (2019) extended research looking at the effect of eyewear and found that sunglasses reduced matching decisions as compared to no glasses. Also, if one face wore glasses or sunglasses, face matching was more error prone than if both faces wore glasses or no glasses. Bennetts et al. (2022) extended the research even further by conducting a face matching task where faces had sunglasses, face masks or both, or were unedited. They found that the addition of sunglasses or a face mask reduced face matching, and there was no difference between these two types of disguise. When faces wore both sunglasses and a face mask, matching performance was even less accurate. Studies using face recognition paradigms have also investigated how disguises influence face recognition and whether certain types of disguises are more detrimental for later recognition compared to others. Nguyen and Pezdek (2017) found that sunglasses were more likely to reduce face recognition than a bandana. Noyes et al. (2021) conducted a face matching task comparing decisions for face pairs where one face either wore sunglasses or a surgical mask, or was not concealed in anyway. They found that any face covering reduced matching decisions, but masks appeared to be the most detrimental for decisions.

Much of the research that has looked at the influence of disguise on face recognition has found that the more of a face that is covered the less likely it will be recognised later. One way to completely cover a face, while also not drawing attention to oneself, is to wear a hyper-realistic prosthetic mask. These masks, as their name suggests, are realistic and allow the wearer to look exactly like another individual, including changing their ethnicity and even gender. Once part of the storyline in films like *Mission Impossible*, now hyper-realistic silicone masks can be bought from a variety of places including the internet so that anyone can make themselves look like, say, Donald Trump or Kim Jong Un, if they so desire. There have been several incidents where criminals have worn hyper-realistic masks to impersonate people and then commit identity fraud, such as using stolen travel documents or stealing money (Robertson et al., 2020). Sanders and Jenkins (2021) found that cases where silicone masks were reportedly used in crimes have increased on a yearly basis from 2009 to 2019, suggesting that they are either being more frequently used or more frequently reported. The box has some real-life examples of when masks were used by criminals.

Figure 8.2 Example of a hyper-realistic mask.

Real-life examples of hyper-realistic masks

A case of impersonation

One of the most famous cases of the use of a realistic silicone mask involved several people impersonating Jean-Yves Le Drian, a French politician, who has served as the Minister of Europe and Foreign Affairs (2017–2022) and the Minister of Defence (2012–2017). There were several incidents where persons impersonating Jean-Yves Le Drian contacted individuals such as CEOs and government officials, often via Skype from a makeshift office, to ask for financial help, and they were able to scam €80 million before finally being arrested (Schofield & Hugh, 2019).

Changing appearance to evade being recognised

One prolific bank robber nicknamed the 'Geezer Bandit' wore the silicone mask of an elderly man, although as he ran speedily away from the crime scenes this alluded to him being a young person, rather than an elderly man. He robbed 16 banks in the US from 2009 to 2011 and is still wanted by the FBI who are offering a $20,000 reward for information (Weisman, 2022). Another example was John Colletti, who was able to steal over $100,000 from casino patrons, by wearing a silicone mask of an elderly man and using counterfeit driving licenses to withdraw funds from their bank accounts (Setty, 2020). Conrad Zdzierak, a white Polish man, was able to not only change his general appearance but also his appeared ethnicity as he disguised himself as an African-American using a silicone mask, and carried out a string of robberies. This lead to an innocent Black individual being wrongly arrested by the police as the suspect and misidentified from a lineup (Dwyer, 2010).

The real-life examples demonstrate people can change the outward appearance of their age, ethnicity and impersonate another person, but can those around them tell if someone is wearing a silicone mask? Several researchers have investigated whether individuals are able to tell if someone is wearing a hyper-realistic mask and have found people often fail to notice that the individuals were wearing silicone masks. Research by Sanders et al. (2017, Experiment 1) found that when shown a series of face images, 30% of participants failed to notice that one of the faces was a mask and not a real face. In the same study, Sanders et al. (2017, Experiment 3) found that even in a live setting participants failed to notice when a confederate was wearing a mask if they were 20 metres away and very few (6%) noticed the confederate was wearing a mask when they were 5 metres away. In another study by Robertson et al. (2020) a mock passport checking scenario was created and participants were asked to try and decide if a confederate matched the image on their passport. The confederate wore a silicone mask and either carried a passport with a photo of the masked face, or a photograph of another identity. They found only 13% of participants spontaneously reported the confederate was wearing a mask, and a further 11% when prompted with a question about whether the confederate was wearing a mask. Even when participants were explicitly told the confederate might be wearing a mask, 10% of the participants still did not think he was wearing a mask. Robertson et al.'s (2020) study demonstrates that even when a person is seen relatively close up (2 metres away) many people were still unable to detect that they were wearing a silicone mask. This has serious implications for identity theft.

Face masks

Up until the COVID-19 pandemic the wearing of face masks in public was a rare phenomenon in the majority of countries, although in some countries like China and Japan the wearing of face masks was more common in public spaces. However, during the pandemic many countries made it compulsory to wear face masks in public spaces, in an attempt to slow down the spread of the virus. As the face masks (if worn correctly) cover the nose, mouth and chin, several researchers set out to investigate how wearing face masks would influence face recognition and face matching, in both humans and for automatic face recognition (AFR) technology.

In relation to face recognition studies, many have found that when unfamiliar faces are seen with face masks people are less likely to recognise them, especially when faces have masks both in the study and test phase (Garcia-Marques et al., 2022). Also, if the mask is worn correctly, covering the nose and mouth, then face recognition is less accurate than if the face mask is worn incorrectly and only covers the mouth (Chen et al., 2023). Face recognition studies have also found that when familiar faces are seen wearing face masks this can also reduce recognition accuracy (Kollenda & de Haas, 2022).

Estudillo and Wong (2022) investigated how accurate humans were at deciding whether pairs of faces were the same identity when one or both faces are wearing face masks. They used an adapted version of the Glasgow Face Matching Task (Burton et al., 2010), where participants saw either both faces unmasked, both faces masked or where one face was masked and the other unmasked. They found that when it came to faces that were the same identity (match), unsurprisingly participants were more accurate when the faces were unmasked; however, when one face wore a mask and the other was unmasked this was more detrimental than when both the faces were wearing masks. When the faces were different identities (mismatch), decisions were more accurate when both faces were unmasked, but there was no difference in accuracy when both faces were masked, compared to when one face was masked and the other was unmasked. This study demonstrates that there is a different process between telling faces apart (mismatch) where there are two different identities and telling faces together (match) that are the same identity (Andrews et al., 2015), and Estudillo and Wong (2022) suggest their findings demonstrate how important it is that there is congruency between face stimuli when faces are the same identity.

As you will have read in previous chapters, there are individual differences in face recognition and some people are more accurate at face recognition as compared to others. Estudillo et al. (2021) investigated whether people who were more accurate at matching faces without masks might also be more accurate at matching faces wearing masks. Like other research that has investigated the effect of face masks they found that participants were less accurate when one or both faces were masked as compared to being unmasked. They also found that performance on the unmasked faces predicted performance on the masked face conditions, such that many of those who were very accurate at matching unmasked faces were also very accurate at matching masked faces.

Many of the initial studies investigating the effect of wearing face masks during the pandemic on face processing were conducted at the beginning of the pandemic, when wearing face masks was still relatively novel. Freud et al. (2022) conducted a longitudinal study to see if people became more accurate at face recognition as wearing face masks in public became a more common everyday occurrence over the pandemic. They were interested in whether people were able to adapt to seeing individuals wearing face masks, so that this no longer reduced face recognition. They adapted the Cambridge Face Memory Test, by having some conditions where the faces were edited to have a face mask and conducted the experiments at six different time points over a 20-month period from 2020 to 2022. They found that there was no improvement in face recognition of masked faces over time and that masked faces were still more difficult to recognise as compared to unmasked faces. They suggest the reason that people did not improve their recognition of masked face is that face processing is more malleable in childhood and by adulthood face recognition ability is unlikely to be influenced by experience.

Automatic face recognition and disguises

As you read in Chapter 7, AFR technology is now being used more frequently and research has also been conducted to investigate how accurate algorithms are for identifying faces that are disguised. Research by the National Institute of Standards and Technology (NIST) Information Technology Laboratory tested a series of available AFR algorithms to see how effective they were at verifying faces that were wearing surgical masks (Ngan et al., 2020). They found when faces were masked, the algorithms were more likely to make a false non-match, i.e. stating two different images of the same person are two different people, as compared to unmasked faces. Furthermore, the larger the area of the face that was occluded by the mask, the higher the chance of a false non-match. Interestingly, their data suggested the wearing of masks appeared not to increase the false match rate, i.e. saying that two different people are the same person. The researchers suggest there were a few limitations of their research, one being the masks were all superimposed via photo manipulation software, and not real face masks, so they may not be realistic images. Also, in their one-to-one verification task only one image of each face was seen was seen wearing a mask and therefore they cannot make any inferences about when both images of faces are wearing masks. Also only the wearing of surgical masks was examined and therefore they do not know how the AFR algorithms would be influenced by the wearing of glasses, sunglasses or other disguises such as wigs, etc.

Noyes et al. (2021) investigated how accurate a deep convolutional neural network (DCNN) that had been trained for face recognition would be able to verify faces that were disguised. Using the same set of faces they had used in their study with human participants (Noyes & Jenkins, 2019), faces were disguised in one of two ways either to evade identification (not look like oneself), or to impersonate another person. They found that when faces were not disguised the DCNN performed at a high level of accuracy; however, when the faces were disguised in the evade condition, the DCNN had a much lower accuracy level. Interestingly, the pattern of results they found was similar to that found by humans trying to verify disguised faces.

A number of studies have compared whether humans or automatic face recognition systems are more accurate at identifying faces that are disguised. Carragher and Hancock (2020) investigated how accurately humans and a deep neural network (DNN) could match face pairs that were wearing surgical face masks. They employed the Glasgow Face Matching Task (Burton et al., 2010) mentioned above. Participants also completed the Stirling Famous Face Matching Task, which is also a one-to-one matching task; however, some of the faces are famous celebrities (familiar faces) while others are non-famous models (unfamiliar faces). All image pairs were also edited to include face masks. When it came to the human participants, face masks significantly reduced face matching accuracy for both familiar and unfamiliar faces and this was the case if even only one of the faces wore a mask as well as when both faces wore a mask. They found when humans saw faces with masks they were more likely to make false positives (incorrectly saying two faces are the same person) for familiar faces, while for unfamiliar faces they were more likely to make false rejections (incorrectly saying two faces are two difference people). When it came to the DNN's performance on the face matching tasks when the faces were masked this did reduce the DNN's accuracy. Interestingly, however, when one of the faces wore a mask and the other did not the DNN seems to be less accurate, especially when both faces were the same identity, compared to when both faces wore a mask. Carragher and Hancock (2020) suggest that if both faces are wearing masks the DNN can compare both masks and the top half of the face which is uncovered to make a similarity judgment; however, when only one face wears a mask, it may occlude some of the facial landmarks (e.g. nose, mouth, chin) of one face that the DNN compared across the two faces, and can thereby reduce the similarity rating for faces that are the same identity.

In a further study investigating the influence of surgical masks on identification from AFR systems Damer et al. (2022) tested 14 AFR algorithms and concluded that wearing face masks had a negative influence on verification. However, unlike Carragher and Hancock (2020), they found that having both faces masked did not increase accuracy as compared to when only one face was masked. They did use a simulated face mask in one of their conditions in addition to the surgical face mask. A number of researchers have suggested that AFR algorithms should be trained to recognise masked faces to increase verification accuracy (Damer et al., 2022; Ngan et al., 2020); however, there is a growing movement of individuals who want to deliberately disguise themselves to prevent being identified by AFR algorithms.

There are various methods that can be used to try and disguise a person to fool AFR systems into not identifying the face, or not detecting a face is present. One method involves disguising a live person's face from which an image is captured, so that the face is not recognisable. Apart from the use of paraphernalia such as glasses, hats, etc. described earlier there is also anti-surveillance makeup, which often includes geometric shapes painted onto the face to fool the AFR algorithm; however, this is not a good method for anyone trying to be inconspicuous as the face will stand out from other faces (Shein, 2022). Another method is to wear clothing that fools AFR systems into not detecting a human face; this involves wearing bright colours in specific patterns that fool the algorithm (Thys et al., 2019). There are some clothing companies who have designed whole clothing ranges they claim will fool AFR systems into thinking that the wearer is not even human, but some other animal such as a giraffe (Flower, 2023). However there has been little research that has investigated how effective this clothing is in reality and this is certainly an area that warrants further inquiry. As disguises become more elaborate to try and deceive AFR systems, in response researchers try to develop algorithms that can still recognise faces under disguised conditions (Dhamecha et al., 2014).

Conclusion

Perhaps unsurprisingly, research that has investigated the influence of disguises and changes of appearance has found that, when faces are disguised, face recognition is more likely to 'go wrong' as faces are more difficult to recognise and also correctly match. This is the case for unfamiliar faces and familiar faces. What is surprising is that disguises do not have to be elaborate for 'face recognition to go wrong'; even the addition of glasses has been found to reduce subsequent face recognition (Graham & Ritchie, 2019; Kramer & Ritchie, 2016) and the more of the face that is covered the less likely the face will be recognised (Mansour et al., 2020).

The wearing of disguises by criminals has some real-world issues in relation to police investigations as eyewitness research has found that when a perpetrator is seen wearing a disguise they are less likely to be correctly recognised if they are placed in a police lineup. Furthermore, if an innocent person is placed in a lineup they are more likely to be falsely identified if the culprit wore a disguise while committing a crime. Much of the research cited in this chapter demonstrates the importance between what a face looks like when it is being encoded and what it then looks like when it is being recognised, upon retrieval. One of the problems with recognising faces that are disguised is that when they are encoded, parts of the face may be occluded or look quite different to when the face is presented for identification. For example, if a witness to a bank robbery sees a thief wearing a hat or a hoodie, then seeing their full face in a police lineup might not make that witness as likely to identify them as if they see the thief wearing a hat or hoodie mask in a lineup, and they might be more accurate if all the lineup members are wearing the same disguise (Carlson et al., 2021; Manley et al., 2019). Therefore according to the encoding specificity principle, when a suspect is placed in a lineup they should appear along with the other lineup members in the same way they were seen to commit the crime (e. g. wearing a mask or hat), or face recognition is more likely to go wrong.

Automatic face recognition algorithms, although they can be more accurate than humans at recognizing unfamiliar faces, are also less accurate at identifying faces that are disguised. However, the majority of the research investigating AFR systems have disguised faces with surgical masks rather than other deliberate disguises and therefore this is an area that warrants further research. Another area that needs further exploration is the effectiveness of specialist clothing that has been designed to fool AFR in preventing identification.

References

Andrews, S., Jenkins, R., Cursiter, H., & Burton, A. M. (2015). Telling faces together: Learning new faces through exposure to multiple instances. *Quarterly Journal of Experimental Psychology*, 68(10), 2041–2050. https://doi.org/10.1080/17470218.2014.1003949.

Atwell, H. (2022). The art of disguise. https://spyscape.com/podcast/the-art-of-disguise.

BBC News. (2020). Bank robber pillow case disguise had no eye holes. www.bbc.co.uk/news/uk-scotland-edinburgh-east-fife-51154331.

Bennetts, R. J., Johnson Humphrey, P., Zielinska, P., & Bate, S. (2022). Face masks versus sunglasses: limited effects of time and individual differences in the ability to judge facial identity and social traits. *Cognitive Research: Principles and Implications*, 7(1). https://doi.org/10.1186/s41235-022-00371-z.

Bruce, V. (1982). Changing faces: Visual and non-visual coding processes in face recognition. *The British Journal of Psychology*, 73(1), 105–116.

Burton, A. M., White, D., & McNeill, A. (2010). The Glasgow face matching test. *Behavior Research Methods*, 42(1), 286–291. https://doi.org/10.3758/BRM.42.1.286.

Carlson, C. A., Hemby, J. A., Wooten, A. R., Jones, A. R., Lockamyeir, R. F., Carlson, M. A., Dias, J. L., & Whittington, J. E. (2021). Testing encoding specificity and the diagnostic feature-detection theory of eyewitness identification, with implications for showups, lineups, and partially disguised perpetrators. *Cognitive Research: Principles and Implications*, 6(1). https://doi.org/10.1186/s41235-021-00276-3.

Carragher, D. J., & Hancock, P. J. B. (2020). Surgical face masks impair human face matching performance for familiar and unfamiliar faces. *Cognitive Research: Principles and Implications*, 5(1). https://doi.org/10.1186/s41235-020-00258-x.

Chen, Y., Wu, C., Li, S., & Yu, T. (2023). Effect of mask coverage on face identification in Taiwanese men and women. *Frontiers in Psychology*, 14(January). https://doi.org/10.3389/fpsyg.2023.1082376.

Damer, N., Boutros, F., Süßmilch, M., Fang, M., Kirchbuchner, F., & Kuijper, A. (2022). Masked face recognition: Human versus machine. *IET Biometrics*, 11(5), 512–528. https://doi.org/10.1049/bme2.12077.

Dhamecha, T. I., Singh, R., Vatsa, M., & Kumar, A. (2014). Recognizing disguised faces: Human and machine evaluation. *PLoS ONE*, 9(7). https://doi.org/10.1371/journal.pone.0099212.

Dwyer, D. (2010). White man used lifelike Black mask to evade arrest in robberies. *ABC News*, 1 December. https://abcnews.go.com/US/white-man-lifelike-black-mask-evade-arrest-robberies/story?id=12288529.

Estudillo, A. J., Hills, P., & Wong, H. K. (2021). The effect of face masks on forensic face matching: An individual differences study. *Journal of Applied Research in Memory and Cognition*, 10(4), 554–563. https://doi.org/10.1016/j.jarmac.2021.07.002.

Estudillo, A. J., & Wong, H. K. (2022). Two face masks are better than one: congruency effects in face matching. *Cognitive Research: Principles and Implications*, 7(1). https://doi.org/10.1186/s41235-022-00402-9.

FBI. (n.d.). Criminal history of bank robber William Sutton. www.fbi.gov/history/artifacts/criminal-history-of-bank-robber-william-sutton.

Flower, L. (2023). Clothes that fool surveillance technology. www.bbc.co.uk/sounds/play/p0dyv93p.

Freud, E., Di Giammarino, D., Stajduhar, A., Rosenbaum, R. S., Avidan, G., & Ganel, T. (2022). Recognition of masked faces in the era of the pandemic:

No improvement despite extensive natural exposure. *Psychological Science*, 33(10), 1635–1650. https://doi.org/10.1177/09567976221105459.

Garcia-Marques, T., Oliveira, M., & Nunes, L. (2022). That person is now with or without a mask: how encoding context modulates identity recognition. *Cognitive Research: Principles and Implications*, 7(1). https://doi.org/10.1186/s41235-022-00379-5.

Graham, D. L., & Ritchie, K. L. (2019). Making a spectacle of yourself: The effect of glasses and sunglasses on face perception. *Perception*, 48(6), 461–470. https://doi.org/10.1177/0301006619844680.

Interpol. (2014). INTERPOL confirms at least two stolen passports used by passengers on missing Malaysian Airlines flight 370 were registered in its databases. www.interpol.int/en/News-and-Events/News/2014/INTERPOL-confirms-at-least-two-stolen-passports-used-by-passengers-on-missing-Malaysian-Airlines-flight-370-were-registered-in-its-databases.

Kemp, R., Towell, N., & Pike, G. (1997). When seeing should not be believing: Photographs, credit cards and fraud. *Applied Cognitive Psychology*, 11(3), 211–222. https://doi.org/10.1002/(sici)1099-0720(199706)11:3<211:aid-acp430>3.3.co;2-f

Kollenda, D., & de Haas, B. (2022). The influence of familiarity on memory for faces and mask wearing. *Cognitive Research: Principles and Implications*, 7(1). https://doi.org/10.1186/s41235-022-00396-4.

Kramer, R. S. S., & Ritchie, K. L. (2016). Disguising Superman: How glasses affect unfamiliar face matching. *Applied Cognitive Psychology*, 30(6), 841–845. https://doi.org/10.1002/acp.3261.

Manley, K. D., Chan, J. C. K., & Wells, G. L. (2019). Do masked-face lineups facilitate eyewitness identification of a masked individual? *Journal of Experimental Psychology: Applied*, 25(3), 396–409. https://doi.org/10.1037/xap0000195.

Manley, K. D., Chan, J. C. K., & Wells, G. L. (2022). Improving face identification of mask-wearing individuals. *Cognitive Research: Principles and Implications*, 7(1). https://doi.org/10.1186/s41235-022-00369-7.

Mansour, J. K., Beaudry, J. L., Bertrand, M. I., Kalmet, N., Melsom, E. I., & Lindsay, R. C. L. (2020). Impact of disguise on identification decisions and confidence with simultaneous and sequential lineups. *Law and Human Behavior*, 44(6), 502–515. https://doi.org/10.1037/lhb0000427.

Ngan, M., Grother, P., & Hanaoka, K. (2020). Ongoing face recognition vendor test (FRVT) part 6B: Face recognition accuracy with face masks using post-COVID-19 algorithms. https://nvlpubs.nist.gov/nistpubs/ir/2020/NIST.IR.8311.pdf.

Nguyen, T. B., & Pezdek, K. (2017). Memory for disguised same- and cross-race faces: The eyes have it. *Visual Cognition*, 25(7–8). https://doi.org/10.1080/13506285.2017.1329762.

Noyes, E., Davis, J. P., Petrov, N., Gray, K. L. H., & Ritchie, K. L. (2021). The effect of face masks and sunglasses on identity and expression recognition with super-recognizers and typical observers. *Royal Society Open Science*, 8(3). https://doi.org/10.1098/rsos.201169.

Noyes, E., & Jenkins, R. (2019). Deliberate disguise in face identification. *Journal of Experimental Psychology: Applied*, 25(2), 280–290. https://doi.org/10.1037/xap0000213.

Noyes, E., Parde, C. J., Colón, Y. I., Hill, M. Q., Castillo, C. D., Jenkins, R., & O'Toole, A. J. (2021). Seeing through disguise: Getting to know you with a deep convolutional neural network. *Cognition*, 211(May). https://doi.org/10.1016/j.cognition.2021.104611.

Or, C. C. F., Lim, D. Y., Chen, S., & Lee, A. L. F. (2023). Face recognition under adverse viewing conditions: Implications for eyewitness testimony. *Policy Insights from the Behavioral and Brain Sciences*, 10(2), 264–271. https://doi.org/10.1177/23727322231194458.

Patterson, K. E., & Baddeley, A. D. (1977). When face recognition fails. *Journal of Experimental Psychology: Human Learning and Memory*, 3 (4), 406–417. https://doi.org/10.1037/0278-7393.3.4.406.

Press Association. (2012). 'Elvis' gets life for armed robbery spree. *The Guardian*, 2 April. www.theguardian.com/uk/2012/apr/02/elvis-gets-life-for-armed-robbery.

Righi, G., Peissig, J. J., & Tarr, M. J. (2012). Recognizing disguised faces. *Visual Cognition*, 20(2), 143–169. https://doi.org/10.1080/13506285.2012.654624.

Robertson, David J., Sanders, J. G., Towler, A., Kramer, R. S. S., Spowage, J., Byrne, A., Burton, A. M., & Jenkins, R. (2020). Hyper-realistic face masks in a live passport-checking task. *Perception*, 49(3), 298–309. https://doi.org/10.1177/0301006620904614.

Robertson, David James, Towler, A., Sanders, J., & Kramer, R. (2020). Hyper-realistic masks are extremely hard to spot – as our new research shows. *The Conversation*, 4 February. https://theconversation.com/hyper-realistic-masks-are-extremely-hard-to-spot-as-our-new-research-shows-131166.

Sanders, J. G., & Jenkins, R. (2021). Realistic masks in the real world. In *Forensic face matching: Research and practice* (pp. 193–215). Oxford University Press. https://doi.org/10.1093/OSO/9780198837749.003.0010.

Sanders, J. G., Ueda, Y., Minemoto, K., Noyes, E., Yoshikawa, S., & Jenkins, R. (2017). Hyper-realistic face masks: a new challenge in person identification. *Cognitive Research: Principles and Implications*, 2(1). https://doi.org/10.1186/s41235-017-0079-y.

Schofield, & Hugh. (2019). The fake French minister in a silicone mask who stole millions. *BBC News*, 20 June. www.bbc.co.uk/news/world-europe-48510027.

Setty, G. (2020). A man using a prosthetic mask stole more than $100,000 at casinos, prosecutors say. *CNN*, 25 July. https://cbs58.com/news/a-man-using-a-prosthetic-mask-stole-more-than-100-000-at-casinos-prosecutors-say.

Shein, E. (2022). Using makeup to block surveillance. *Communications of the ACM*, 65(7), 21–23. https://doi.org/10.1145/3535192.

Spyscape. (2022). Jonna Mendez: Ex-CIA disguise chief's top 10 spy tips for undercover ops. https://spyscape.com/article/master-of-disguise-how-the-cias-ex-chief-of-disguise-stared-down-a-terrorist.

Stevens, C. (2021). Person identification at airports during passport control. In M. Bindemann (ed.), *Forensic face matching: Research and practice* (pp. 1–14). Oxford University Press. https://doi.org/10.1093/OSO/9780198837749.003.0001.

Thys, S., Ranst, W. Van, & Goedeme, T. (2019). Fooling automated surveillance cameras: Adversarial patches to attack person detection. In *IEEE Computer Society Conference on Computer Vision and Pattern Recognition Workshops, 2019-June*, 49–55. https://doi.org/10.1109/CVPRW.2019.00012.

Tulving, E., & Thomson, D. M. (1973). Encoding specificity and retrieval processes in episodic memory. *Psychological Review*, 80(5), 352–373. https://doi.org/10.1037/H0020071.

Weisman, D. (2022). Move over D.B. Cooper for Geezer Bandit. *The Escondido Grapevine*, 17 December. www.escondidograpevine.com/2022/12/17/move-over-d-b-cooper-for-geezer-bandit/.

White, D., Kemp, R. I., Jenkins, R., Matheson, M., & Burton, A. M. (2014). Passport officers' errors in face matching. *PLoS ONE*, 9(8). https://doi.org/10.1371/journal.pone.0103510.

Zarkadi, T., Wade, K. A., & Stewart, N. (2009). Creating fair lineups for suspects with distinctive features. *Psychological Science*, 20(12), 1448–1453. https://doi.org/10.1111/J.1467-9280.2009.02463.X.

9 Prosopagnosia
Face blindness

Introduction

Prosopagnosia, also called face blindness, is an impairment in recognising familiar faces and learning new faces. As prosopagnosia is such an unusual condition where face recognition 'goes wrong', it deserves a whole chapter of its own in this book. The term prosopagnosia comes from the Greek words '*prosopon*' meaning 'face' and '*agnosia*' meaning 'not knowing' or 'lack of knowledge'. It can affect people differently, with some people not being able to tell the difference between unfamiliar faces, while others cannot recognise familiar faces, such as family and friends, or even their own face in a mirror or photographs. Although some people with prosopagnosia may have problems in distinguishing between certain objects (e.g. different types of cars), recognising emotions on people's faces, or determining their gender, and age, what makes prosopagnosia so unique is the problem in processing and recognising faces, making it a face-specific disorder (Busigny et al., 2010).

Why faces? Faces are a special class of visual stimulus; that is, faces are generally very similar in overall appearance as they usually contain the same set of features, e.g. two eyes, one nose and one mouth, and they are all in the same general layout. Despite their overall similarity, the majority of humans have become particularly good at noticing subtle differences in faces. This includes observing small variations in the features of faces that are encountered and the spatial relationships between the features, which can help learn new faces and recognise familiar individuals. So much so that we have become expert at identifying people we know and can recognise

DOI: 10.4324/9781003177128-9

familiar faces even from poor-quality images (Burton et al., 1999). This so-called 'expertise' means we can recognise familiar faces, such as friends and family, and also distinguish between faces that might be the same person or two different people, such as verifying a person's identity at border control using a photograph in their passport. It has been argued that humans have developed this expertise in face perception through exposure to faces, although there is still a debate about whether humans can also gain expertise in identifying other classes of visual stimuli (Tanaka & Philibert, 2022).

Although most people can recognise the faces of people they know, not everyone is able to recognise faces that are familiar and one of the most researched face recognition deficits is prosopagnosia. There are two types of prosopagnosia: apperceptive prosopagnosia and associative prosopagnosia. People who have apperceptive prosopagnosia often cannot make sense of faces at the perceptual level and can have difficulties in deciding if two faces are the same person or two different people. Individuals who are able to process faces, but who cannot recognise them or extract any memory associated with the face, have associative prosopagnosia. You may remember in Chapter 1 we looked at the Bruce and Young model of face recognition (Bruce & Young, 1986) and in the first stage of the model the structural encoding occurs and people who have problems perceiving and cognitively processing faces at this stage have apperceptive prosopagnosia, and this affects all the other stages of face recognition. According to the Bruce and Young model, those who have associative prosopagnosia cannot access

Figure 9.1 A graphic portrayal of prosopagnosia.

the face recognition units (FRUs) and/or personal identity nodes (PINs) and therefore cannot identify who the face belongs to (De Renzi et al., 1991). This chapter will focus more on associative prosopagnosia, research that has been conducted to investigate it and the types of issues that people who have it face every day.

The majority of people do not have any problems in recognising faces and they take this ability for granted, until they have some type of error where they fail to recognise someone they know. This can often be a bit embarrassing, but for most people it's a rare occurrence. For individuals who have prosopagnosia, failing to recognise people they know is an everyday reality, and in the text box there are some personal anecdotes from people who

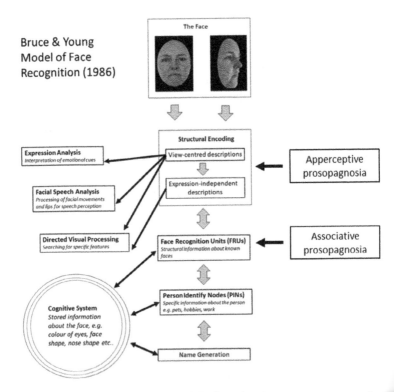

Figure 9.2 Bruce and Young's model adapted to demonstrate apperceptive prosopagnosia and associative prosopagnosia.

have prosopagnosia illustrating the types of issues they face every day when they fail to recognise the faces of people they know.

Personal anecdotes from prosopagnosics

My brother and I are both face blind, but his is much more severe. Growing up, we tended to rely on context clues and specific hats to identify each other. So if he encountered someone in the hallway in the middle of the night, it was pretty safe to assume it was me. But one night I snuck out for some teenage escapades, returning well after curfew. There was no reason for someone to be entering the house at this time, so my brother thought someone was breaking in! He met me at the top of the stairs with a katana, and said only one word: 'intruder'. Of course he recognised my (panicked) voice as soon as I explained the situation, and we both had a good laugh about it. We didn't tell our parents for years!

* * *

My wife and I are both radiographers. For a few years, we worked in the same department. One day, a woman walked into reception, bringing her son with her. This woman didn't speak to me, but gave me a huge smile as she walked in and spoke with the clerical staff. She turned and gave me another big smile as she went off to the waiting room. I was pretty unnerved by this, it was weird as far as I was concerned. I went to find my wife, asked her to go and find out who that creepy smiley woman in the waiting room was. She did so; my wife came back to me and explained who this woman was who'd been smiling at me. 'It's your sister', she said.

* * *

I once went to someone's house to collect something I'd bought on marketplace and another lady was there doing the same. She smiled really warmly at me and said 'fancy meeting you here!'. I had no idea who she was and was forced to say 'sorry, how do you know me?' She couldn't believe it because we had sat next to each other at a dinner party the night before and talked for about 4 hours!

* * *

I got out of the car at my son's soccer game and saw my 'brother'. My brother had recently lost a lot of weight and I saw a man with the same body shape. OK, I was not expecting him to be at his nephew's game, but there he was, and it wasn't out of the realm of possibility. And he had obviously run into a friend because they were deep in conversation. So, I followed them and waited for a break in their conversation. My long-suffering husband ran me down. 'You think that's your brother, don't you? It's not. You're stalking a stranger.'

* * *

I was waiting for my sister in front of a restaurant. I hadn't been diagnosed yet. I was getting annoyed because it was cold, she was late, and this girl was blocking the door so I couldn't get in. Apparently, I was awkwardly pacing and looking increasingly frustrated, so the girl tapped me. It was my sister; she'd gotten a haircut. She couldn't figure out what I was doing.

* * *

I got in my husband's car who was picking me up after a workout in the gym, and unleashed a tirade of 'Where have you been! I've been waiting 15 mins, you're always late', etc. Unusually for him, my husband did not argue back, and in fact as my annoyance died down I noticed a look of fear on his face. I also wondered why he hadn't started the car engine to take me home. It occurred to me that this might be another one of those 'I got it wrong again' situations. 'You're not my husband, are you?' I said. He shook his head with a look of pure horror as I slunk out muttering 'I think I got in the wrong car' in apology. His partner was just coming up to his car as I rushed out of it. I think he had some explaining ahead of him.

Some of the personal accounts from people who have prosopagnosia are funny anecdotes; however, as these types of issues can crop up every day it can be embarrassing for prosopagnosics when they do not recognise people they should know. If someone has had trouble recognising people all of their life they may not realise until adulthood that their poor face recognition ability can be labelled, and they may think that they are just a bit bad with faces and names, and therefore it can often be a relief to finally get a diagnosis to explain why they struggle to recognise people's faces (Gilbert, 2020).

Prosopagnosia not only has two different types which distinguish whether people can perceive or recognise faces, but prosopagnosia has also been subdivided in relation to how the person came to have the condition. One of the subtypes is called acquired prosopagnosia, where the individual didn't always have problems recognising faces, but after some specific event now has acquired a face recognition impairment. The other subtype is developmental or congenital prosopagnosia, where a person has always had difficulty recognising faces since childhood. Although both can have similar symptoms, they have different origins, and this will be explored in the next sections of the chapter.

Acquired prosopagnosia

Acquired prosopagnosia is caused by damage to specific brain regions, and individuals who have this condition were usually able to recognise faces until the brain damage occurred and then only experience problems after the damage. The first case of acquired prosopagnosia was recorded 150 years ago; however, the condition was not studied until Bodmer's report in 1947, which described an injured soldier's impaired face recognition ability (cited in Corrow et al., 2016). The damage can be caused by a stroke, a traumatic brain injury or by certain neurodegenerative diseases all of which damage certain areas of the brain. There are some specific areas of the brain responsible for recognising faces, such as the fusiform face area (FFA), which is in the right hemisphere of the brain; this area is known to be involved in face processing (Kanwisher et al., 1997) and damage to this area can lead to problems in face perception (Barton et al.,

2002). Although the FFA plays a vital role in face processing, there are other areas of the brain that have also been found to be involved in face processing, such as the occipital face area, anterior face selective region and damage to these areas can result in prosopagnosia. More recent research suggests that the different brain areas work together like a network and that it is damage to the what is called the occipitotemporal face-processing network that results in acquired prosopagnosia (Cohen et al., 2019). Many people who have acquired prosopagnosia also have other associated problems, such as problems with navigation, like getting lost (Corrow et al., 2016), problems with object recognition (Barton et al., 2019) and also sometimes colour perception (Bouvier & Engel, 2006). These associated issues could be due to the location of brain regions that have been damaged, as often brain damage can be to several areas of the brain and as many of the regions associated with these tasks are near to those associated with face processing and there can be overlaps in lesion sites in the ventral occipital cortex (Bouvier & Engel, 2006). Although most cases of acquired prosopagnosia are usually the result of brain damage due to trauma, tumour, a stroke or some other degenerative condition, there has been an unusual case that appears to be the result of COVID-19 (Kieseler & Duchaine, 2023)

Case study of prosopagnosia following COVID-19

Annie is 28 years old and is a customer service representative and part-time portrait artist. She had COVID-19 in March 2020 and felt unwell, with many of the typical symptoms: coughing fits, shortness of breath, loss of smell and taste. Then after 3 weeks she felt well enough to return to work. However, 4 weeks later her symptoms returned, and she felt something wasn't quite right when she looked at faces. She was referred for a CT scan, but she did not have any active bleeds in her brain. Later that year she went to stay with her family and realised that she did not recognise her father's face, and that she could not distinguish between her father and her uncle. She found that she was now relying on hearing a person's voice to identify them rather than their face. She also now found it much more difficult to draw faces, relying much more on looking at a photograph than she had previously. Another issue was she also found it more difficult to navigate her environment, and had difficulties finding her way around the grocery store. She would have difficulties finding where she had parked her car, and giving and following directions (Kieseler & Duchaine, 2023).

In their study Kieseler and Duchaine (2023) gave Annie four face recognition tests and she performed significantly lower than an age-matched control sample. However when it came to face detection and perception Annie's scores where similar to those of control participants, suggesting that her problems with faces related to memory, and therefore she had associative and not apperceptive prosopagnosia.

Annie's experience demonstrates that there was a specific event in her life that led to her having prosopagnosia, although in this case there was no obvious sign of brain damage. However, Annie's health insurance would not cover an MRI scan, therefore it cannot be ruled out that she might have suffered a stroke and had some damage to her brain that may be an alternative cause for the prosopagnosia she experiences. Not all cases of prosopagnosia can be linked to specific events in a person's life, and for some they have experienced difficulties in recognising faces their whole life. That is the topic of the next section.

Developmental prosopagnosia

Individuals who have acquired prosopagnosia are aware that at one time they were able to recognise faces, but now after a specific incident where they received brain damage, they have problems with face recognition. However, not all people who have prosopagnosia have it because of brain damage. Some individuals with prosopagnosia have no history of brain damage. This is referred to as developmental, hereditary or congenital prosopagnosia, and I shall refer to it as developmental prosopagnosia for the rest of this chapter. Individuals who have developmental prosopagnosia often have normal vision and memory, and do not have any obvious signs of brain damage, but still have problems recognising faces. This less understood condition has begun to receive a significant amount of research over the last twenty years, some of which will be explored in this section.

When someone has developmental prosopagnosia they have usually experienced a lifelong difficulty in recognising faces from childhood. Some researchers suggest that there is a pathological aspect to developmental prosopagnosia which might result from genetic mutations. Evidence to support the idea that developmental prosopagnosia might have a genetic component comes from research that has found that prosopagnosia can run in families with a number of family members all having difficulties in recognising faces (Duchaine et al., 2007; Grueter et al., 2007; Lee et al., 2010; Schmalzl et al., 2008). Duchaine et al. (2007) investigated the face recognition abilities of a group of family members who all had impaired face recognition abilities to some degree. They found seven siblings, their parents and a maternal uncle all with face recognition deficiencies compared to control participants; they all performed less accurately on a number of tests of face recognition (e.g. CFMT). In a further study, Schmalzl et al. (2008) also found a family where prosopagnosia appeared to run through four generations, adding more evidence to the genetic basis for this condition. Lee et al. (2010) also tested a father and his two daughters, who all presented impaired face recognition skills. Taken together the findings from these studies appear to demonstrate that there can be a genetic component responsible for developmental prosopagnosia.

Some researchers have been interested in examining whether there are differences between people who have acquired prosopagnosia and those with developmental prosopagnosia in the way they process faces, and whether this is linked to object processing. Some research revealed that people elicit different eye movements when viewing faces, and the individuals with acquired prosopagnosia were less accurate at recognising facial expressions and matching pairs of faces as compared to those with developmental prosopagnosia (Behrmann et al., 2011). There can be other differences between individuals with acquired prosopagnosia and developmental prosopagnosia, and this might be due to the brain lesions experienced by those with acquired prosopagnosia as this could affect other perceptual systems such as object recognition in addition to face processing (Geskin & Behrmann, 2018).

Geskin and Behrmann (2018) reviewed 716 cases of developmental prosopagnosia from 1976 to 2016 to see if there was a relationship between deficits in face recognition and deficits in object recognition. Of the cases of developmental prosopagnosia they examined, 62% also had impaired object recognition and 38% did not. They also examined the relationship between scores on face recognition tests to see if they correlated with scores on object recognition tests and found that the majority of individuals showed an association between the two types of tasks, i.e. those who had low scores on face recognition tests also had low scores on object recognition tests. However, there was a minority of individuals where there was no association between the scores and there was a dissociation between the performance on face recognition and object recognition tests. One of the criticisms in comparing performance on face recognition and object recognition tasks is that prior experience is usually greater for faces than it is for certain classes of stimulus that might be used in object recognition tasks (e.g. flowers, cars, shoes, etc.), meaning that object recognition might be at a disadvantage.

Looking at the prevalence of this condition, developmental prosopagnosia is thought to affect 2–2.5% of the population, although this can vary according to what diagnosis criteria and cut-offs are used (DeGutis et al., 2023). According to Barton and Corrow (2016) face recognition is an ability that varies among the population and is normally distributed so that some people, such as super recognisers (see Chapter 11), are at the high-performing end of the curve. Then it also makes sense that there are some people who are poor at recognising faces and at the other end of the curve. The issue is when does just being generally poor at recognising faces become prosopagnosia? Regardless of whether a person is formally diagnosed with prosopagnosia or just at the lower end of the population when it comes to recognising faces, they may face everyday difficulties in recognising those around them, and this can affect people's careers and the social interactions they have (Adams et al., 2020). There is a growing body of research that has looked at methods to treat people who have prosopagnosia and offer coping strategies.

Getting a diagnosis for prosopagnosia

There are several different ways to confirm that someone has prosopagnosia, in addition to their own anecdotes of difficulties recognising faces. Although there is no universal agreement on the best method to diagnose prosopagnosia (Burns et al., 2022), there are a number of objective tests that have been developed to investigate face recognition ability, such as the Benton Facial Recognition Test (Murray et al., 2022), the Warrington Recognition Memory Test (cited in Duchaine & Weidenfeld, 2003) and (currently the most commonly used) the Cambridge Face Memory Test (Duchaine & Nakayama, 2006). All these tests involve showing faces to participants and then seeing if they can identify them, and then performance is compared to normative data, to determine if their performance fits in with the normal range. If it is below (usually two standard deviations below the mean of control group performance) then they may be diagnosed as having prosopagnosia. Another face recognition test is the Famous Faces Memory Test (FFMT), where participants are presented with famous celebrities faces and they have to name them, in order to demonstrate that they recognise the faces. One of the issues with using famous faces is that they may only be familiar to certain people of a certain age, education, cultural background and with specific interests, and so they may not be reliable indicators of face recognition deficits (Albonico & Barton, 2019).

In addition to face recognition tests that measure a person's ability to recognise faces, there is a self-report questionnaire that individuals can complete, the 20-Item Prosopagnosia Index (PI20), which has 20 different statements and participants respond on a 1–5-point scale, with 1 being strongly disagree to 5 being strongly agree (Shah et al., 2015). Here's a sample of some of the statements used in the task:

- My face recognition ability is worse than most people.
- I often mistake people I have met before for strangers.
- Without hearing people's voices, I struggle to recognise them.
- I sometimes find movies hard to follow because of difficulties recognising characters.

- It is hard to recognise familiar people when I meet them out of context (e.g. meeting a work colleague unexpectedly while shopping).

As you can see many of the statements are similar to the anecdotes of real accounts from people with prosopagnosia, and that is because they were generated after reviewing research and surveying those with prosopagnosia. When the questionnaire was evaluated, scores from the PI20 were found to correlate with objective measures from face recognition tests such as the CFMT, demonstrating its usefulness in assisting to diagnose those with prosopagnosia (Shah et al., 2015).

When it comes to which measure might be the most effective to diagnose someone with prosopagnosia, some researchers have suggested employing objective measures such as the CFMT and FFMT often uses cut-offs that are too conservative, and that there could be those who have prosopagnosia, but still perform within the accepted range and therefore might not be diagnosed (DeGutis et al., 2023). Murray and Bate (2020) suggest that using objective tests such as the CFMT may not be effective for diagnosing prosopagnosia as individuals' scores can vary with repeated testing and testing location (e.g. online or in person) could also influence performance, making diagnosis for borderline cases inconsistent. Furthermore, it could also be argued that the faces in the CFMT are not naturalistic images of faces that one would see every day, as the faces have been cropped to remove the hair and even the face shape, which can be extremely useful when trying to recognise unfamiliar faces (Young et al., 1985). Findings such as these have recommended that self-report measures such as the PI20 index should be employed as an initial screening measure before employing any other objective measures of face recognition (Burns et al., 2022). Once an individual has a diagnosis of prosopagnosia it can be a relief to explain why they may have been experiencing difficulties with faces; however, it does not necessary help the issue at hand. Psychological research has suggested a few different methods to try and help individuals with prosopagnosia, which will be outlined in the next section.

Treatments and coping strategies

Having prosopagnosia can have an enormous impact on every-day life for individuals who have this condition, many of whom avoid social interactions and interpersonal relations, and who report that their condition has damaged their career, and even caused depression and social anxiety. Children with proso-pagnosia also can struggle with social interactions and in school as teachers often do not fully understand what prosopagnosia is and can attribute children's behaviour to other conditions such as autism (Adams et al., 2020). There is a developing body of work that aims to investigate methods to help those with prosopagno-sia, and this can be separated into two different approaches. First, there is research that examines rehabilitation techniques, which involve some form of training and are employed to try and improve face recognition deficits by changing the way people look at and try to remember faces. Then there are coping and/or compensation strategies, which can be used by prosopagnosics in their daily lives, as they try to navigate social and workplace interactions. Davies-Thompson et al. (2017) made a further dis-tinction between mnemonic treatments and perceptual training. Mnemonic training involves associating faces with specific semantic information, such as names and/or semantic data. While perceptual approaches involve training individuals to look at faces in a specific manner and attending to facial features and the spatial relationships between them to improve the dis-crimination among different faces. They suggest for training to be ecologically valid, that is relevant in the real world and beneficial to individuals with prosopagnosia, training should not only improve recognition of faces learnt during the training period, but the skills should be transferable and improve face recognition in everyday life.

DeGutis et al. (2014) found that using strategies that involve verbalising distinctive features was found to be the most useful strategy for those with acquired prosopagnosia. For those with developmental prosopagnosia, training that involved looking at the holistic properties of faces, including feature configuration and the administration of oxytocin, could improve face proces-sing ability. However, unfortunately they were unable to conduct a follow-up study to see if the benefits from training presented in the long term, or generalised to face recognition in everyday life. In another study, Bate et al. (2022) developed a training tool using an adapted version of the game 'Guess Who' and found that this appeared to help adults and some children with prosopagnosia; however, it was not known if the benefits were maintained in the long term, or were effective outside of the laboratory.

Gobbo et al. (2022) conducted a systematic review of the literature examining rehabilitation treatments and found that many published studies had limited generalisability as they were based on small sample sizes and were often case studies with one or two individuals, and although improvements did transfer to new faces in the lab it was not clear if this also benefitted everyday interactions. Gobbo et al. (2022) did suggest that there could be different treatments that might be beneficial depending on the type of prosopagnosia condition. For example, perceptual training that involved analysing facial features, face matching and face discrimination could be more useful for apperceptive prosopagnosia, while associative prosopagnosia might benefit more from mnemonic training, where semantic information is learnt alongside faces that can be used as memory aid upon recognition.

One of the criticisms of much of the research that has used training or rehabilitation techniques is that they often use artificially created faces that have been manipulated so that they only vary by small degrees and are not necessarily representative of faces that are seen in everyday life. Face recognition is also often measured before and after training, sometimes using the same tests, and often using faces with little natural variation between images, or with the external features removed, such as in the CFMT (Duchaine & Nakayama, 2006). Therefore, although some techniques do appear to be beneficial and improve face recognition within the study parameters (Bate et al., 2022), so far there has not been one particular method that has been found to be beneficial for long-term improvements in face recognition in everyday life for prosopagnosics.

Other researchers have investigated the use of coping strategies that can be employed in everyday life to help those with prosopagnosia recognise those around them. Adams et al. (2020)

conducted interviews with adults with prosopagnosia and also parents of children with prosopagnosia, and discovered some of the issues they faced and strategies they had put in place to try and reduce recognition failures. When it came to adults with prosopagnosia, some found it beneficial to disclose their condition in the workplace and socially, as it not only raised awareness, but could explain why they appear to be rude when they fail to recognise friends and colleagues they should know. The parents of children with developmental prosopagnosia sometimes told the child's school of their condition, which then allowed the school to apply additional aids, such as wearing of name tags. However, there were some parents and also adults with the condition who did not want to disclose any information as they felt they would be judged or be put in a vulnerable position if people knew they had prosopagnosia. Adams et al. (2020) also found several recognition strategies that those with prosopagnosia used, although they also came with associated risks. Table 9.1 presents some of these strategies.

Looking at the table of recognition strategies and their associated risks it appears that using these strategies requires significant cognitive resources and can be mentally exhausting (Adams et al., 2020). Furthermore, employing these strategies still doesn't guarantee that someone's identity will be figured out and there could be embarrassing consequences if there are misidentifications. You can see why those with prosopagnosia might want to raise awareness of their condition so that they can feel comfortable disclosing this in the workplace and in social situations.

Prosopagnosia is a condition recognised by the NHS and you can be referred by your GP for assessment (NHS, 2023). The NHS states that there is no treatment for prosopagnosia, but there is a list of suggestions for things to try when you have this condition, such as telling people you have the condition before you meet them, and using people's voices and body language as cues. Face Blind UK is a community interest company that was created by those whose lives are affected by prosopagnosia to raise awareness and understanding of face blindness and to provide services to people who have this condition, including support, networking and information. If you know anyone affected by prosopagnosia, their website has lots of useful information (see www.faceblind.org.uk).

Table 9.1 Summary of recommended recognition strategies and their associated risks.

Strategy	Potential risks
Ask significant others for identity prompts	Need to be discreet, requires to be present
Using other cues – e.g. voice, gait, hairstyle, mannerisms, clothing and body shape	Can be unreliable when appearance has changed, or person met out of context; multiple strategies might need or be combined
Visual association – creating links between the persons appearance and the location they might found, objects, etc.	Requires regular contact with the person and some familiarity, also requires imagery, that isn't always available
Use distinguishing facial cues – memorise distinguishing facial cues, e.g. distinctive features	Requires regular contact to maintain associations and also studying a person's face in detail which might be socially inappropriate
Identifying others through conversation – use small talk to cue identity, introduce oneself and hope they do the same, use voice as an identity cue	Might not be appropriate in some contexts, can appear to be odd, especially if introducing oneself to a familiar person
Recognition aids – memorise detailed notes on the person's appearance, study photographs, write down name during meetings etc.	Might not be reliable in some contexts, person can change their appearance, notes can be difficult to read
Avoidance – avoid uncomfortable situations, be the first person to arrive at the location, use humour to hide difficulties	Might not be appropriate in some contexts, sometimes can appear to be rude, or absent-minded

Source: adapted from Adams et al. (2020)

Conclusion

Prosopagnosia is a condition where people have problems recognising faces of people they know, and in some cases it also affects recognising facial emotions, gender and age. There are two main types of prosopagnosia: apperceptive prosopagnosia, which affects how faces are perceived and processed, and associative prosopagnosia, which affects how faces are remembered and later recognised. There is a further distinction with the categories of prosopagnosia, and this comes from how the condition was obtained, with acquired prosopagnosia resulting from some type of brain injury while developmental prosopagnosia is present without injury and can run in families. There are various methods to diagnose prosopagnosia, including objective face recognition tests and self-report questionnaires. It has been suggested that diagnostic cut-offs for face recognition tests have been too conservative and that diagnosis should rely on more than one method (e.g. objective measures and also self-report questionnaire) to ensure a valid diagnosis.

There have been several types of experimental treatments and rehabilitation techniques that have been designed to try and help those with prosopagnosia process faces more accurately and aid recognition. However, although many of these techniques have allowed participants to learn new faces in the lab, many of the benefits have not transferred to everyday life. It could be that employing coping strategies might be the best way forward to prevent face recognition from 'going wrong'. Raising awareness in society for this condition so that prosopagnosics do not feel they need to avoid social situations would also be helpful.

References

Adams, A., Hills, P. J., Bennetts, R. J., & Bate, S. (2020). Coping strategies for developmental prosopagnosia. *Neuropsychological Rehabilitation*, 30(10), 1996–2015. https://doi.org/10.1080/09602011.2019.1623824.

Albonico, A., & Barton, J. (2019). Progress in perceptual research: The case of prosopagnosia [version 1; peer review: 2 approved]. *F1000Research*, 8, 1–9. https://doi.org/10.12688/f1000research.18492.1.

Barton, J. J. S., Albonico, A., Susilo, T., Duchaine, B., & Corrow, S. L. (2019). Object recognition in acquired and developmental prosopagnosia. *Cognitive Neuropsychology*, 36(1–2), 54–84. https://doi.org/10.1080/02643294.2019.1593821.

Barton, J. J. S., & Corrow, S. L. (2016). The problem of being bad at faces. *Neuropsychologia*, 89, 119–124. https://doi.org/10.1016/j.neuropsychologia.2016.06.008.

Barton, J. J. S., Press, D. Z., Keenan, J. P., & O'Connor, M. (2002). Lesions of the fusiform face area impair perception of facial configuration in prosopagnosia. *Neurology*, 58(1), 71–78. https://doi.org/10.1212/WNL.58.1.71.

Bate, S., Dalrymple, K., & Bennetts, R. J. (2022). Face recognition improvements in adults and children with face recognition difficulties. *Brain Communications*, 4(2), 1–12. https://doi.org/10.1093/braincomms/fcac068.

Behrmann, M., Avidan, G., Thomas, C., & Nishimura, M. (2011). Impairments in face perception. In A. J. Calder *et al.* (eds), *Oxford handbook of face perception*. Oxford University Press. https://doi.org/10.1093/OXFORDHB/9780199559053.013.0041.

Bouvier, S. E., & Engel, S. A. (2006). Behavioral deficits and cortical damage loci in cerebral achromatopsia. *Cerebral Cortex*, 16(2), 183–191. https://doi.org/10.1093/cercor/bhi096.

Bruce, V., & Young, A. (1986). Understanding face recognition. *British Journal of Psychology*, 77(3), 305–327. https://doi.org/10.1111/j.2044-8295.1986.tb02199.x.

Burns, E. J., Gaunt, E., Kidane, B., Hunter, L., & Pulford, J. (2022). A new approach to diagnosing and researching developmental prosopagnosia: Excluded cases are impaired too. *Behavior Research Methods*, 55, 4291–4314. https://doi.org/10.3758/s13428-022-02017-w.

Burton, A. M., Wilson, S., Cowan, M., & Bruce, V. (1999). Face recognition in poor-quality video: Evidence from security surveillance. *Psychological Science*, 10(3), 243–248. https://doi.org/10.1111/1467-9280.00144.

Busigny, T., Graf, M., Mayer, E., & Rossion, B. (2010). Acquired prosopagnosia as a face-specific disorder: Ruling out the general visual similarity account. *Neuropsychologia*, 48(7), 2051–2067. https://doi.org/10.1016/j.neuropsychologia.2010.03.026.

Cohen, A. L., Soussand, L., Corrow, S. L., Martinaud, O., Barton, J. J. S., & Fox, M. D. (2019). Looking beyond the face area: Lesion network mapping of prosopagnosia. *Brain*, 142(12), 3975–3990. https://doi.org/10.1093/brain/awz332.

Corrow, J. C., Corrow, S. L., Lee, E., Pancaroglu, R., Burles, F., Duchaine, B., Iaria, G., & Barton, J. J. S. (2016). Getting lost: Topographic skills in acquired and developmental prosopagnosia. *Cortex*, 76, 89–103. https://doi.org/10.1016/j.cortex.2016.01.003.

Corrow, S. L., Dalrymple, K. A., & Barton, J. J. S. (2016). Prosopagnosia: Current perspectives. *Eye and Brain*, 8(2016), 165–175. https://doi.org/10.2147/EB.S92838.

Davies-Thompson, J., Fletcher, K., Hills, C., Pancaroglu, R., Corrow, S. L., & Barton, J. J. S. (2017). Perceptual learning of faces: A rehabilitative study of acquired prosopagnosia. *Journal of Cognitive Neuroscience*, 29(3), 573–591. https://doi.org/10.1162/jocn.

De Renzi, E., Faglioni, P., Grossi, D., & Nichelli, P. (1991). Apperceptive and associative forms of prosopagnosia. *Cortex*, 27(2), 213–221. https://doi.org/10.1016/S0010-9452(13)80125-80126.

DeGutis, J., Bahierathan, K., Barahona, K., Lee, E., Evans, T. C., Shin, H. M., Mishra, M., Likitlersuang, J., & Wilmer, J. B. (2023). What is the prevalence of developmental prosopagnosia? An empirical assessment of different diagnostic cutoffs. *Cortex*, 161, 51–64. https://doi.org/10.1016/j.cortex.2022.12.014.

DeGutis, J. M., Chiu, C., Grosso, M. E., & Cohan, S. (2014). Face processing improvements in prosopagnosia: Successes and failures over the last 50 years. *Frontiers in Human Neuroscience*, 8(August), 1–14. https://doi.org/10.3389/fnhum.2014.00561.

Duchaine, B. C., & Weidenfeld, A. (2003). An evaluation of two commonly used tests of unfamiliar face recognition. *Neuropsychologia*, 41(6), 713–720. https://doi.org/10.1016/S0028-3932(02)00222-00221.

Duchaine, B., & Nakayama, K. (2006). The Cambridge Face Memory Test: Results for neurologically intact individuals and an investigation of its validity using inverted face stimuli and prosopagnosic participants. *Neuropsychologia*, 44(4), 576–585. https://doi.org/10.1016/j.neuropsychologia.2005.07.001.

Duchaine, B., Germine, L., & Nakayama, K. (2007). Family resemblance: Ten family members with prosopagnosia and within-class object agnosia. *Cognitive Neuropsychology*, 24(4), 419–430. https://doi.org/10.1080/02643290701380491.

Geskin, J., & Behrmann, M. (2018). Congenital prosopagnosia without object agnosia? A literature review. *Cognitive Neuropsychology*, 35(1–2),4–54. https://doi.org/10.1080/02643294.2017.1392295.

Gilbert, J. (2020). *The Picasso mirror*. Rogue House Publishing.

Gobbo, S., Calati, R., Silveri, M. C., Pini, E., & Daini, R. (2022). The rehabilitation of object agnosia and prosopagnosia: A systematic review. *Restorative Neurology and Neuroscience*, 1–24. https://doi.org/10.3233/rnn-211234.

Grueter, M., Grueter, T., Bell, V., Horst, J., Laskowski, W., Sperling, K. Halligan, P. W., Ellis, H. D., & Kennerknecht, I. (2007). Hereditary prosopagnosia: The first case series. *Cortex*, 43(6), 734–749. https://doi.org/10.1016/S0010-9452(08)70502-70501.

Kanwisher, N., McDermott, J., & Chun, M. (1997). The fusiform face area: A module in human extrastriate cortex specialized for face perception. *The Journal of Neuroscience*, 17(11), 4302–4311.

Kieseler, M.-L., & Duchaine, B. (2023). Persistent prosopagnosia following COVID-19. *Cortex*, 162, 56–64. https://doi.org/10.1016/j.cortex.2023.01.012.

Lee, Y., Duchaine, B., Wilson, H. R., & Nakayama, K. (2010). Three cases of developmental prosopagnosia from one family: Detailed neuropsychological and psychophysical investigation of face processing. *Cortex*, 46(8), 949–964. https://doi.org/10.1016/j.cortex.2009.07.012.

Murray, E., & Bate, S. (2020). Diagnosing developmental prosopagnosia: Repeat assessment using the Cambridge Face Memory Test. *Royal Society Open Science*. 7(9). https://doi.org/10.1098/rsos.200884.

Murray, E., Bennetts, R., Tree, J., & Bate, S. (2022). An update of the Benton Facial Recognition Test. *Behavior Research Methods*, 54(5), 2318–2333. https://doi.org/10.3758/s13428-021-01727-x.

NHS. (2023). Prosopagnosia (face blindness). www.nhs.uk/conditions/face-blindness.

Schmalzl, L., Palermo, R., & Coltheart, M. (2008). Cognitive heterogeneity in genetically based prosopagnosia: A family study. *Journal of Neuropsychology*, 2(1), 99–117. https://doi.org/10.1348/174866407X256554.

Shah, P., Gaule, A., Sowden, S., Bird, G., & Cook, R. (2015). The 20-item prosopagnosia index (PI20): A self-report instrument for identifying developmental prosopagnosia. *Royal Society Open Science*, 2(6), 1–11. https://doi.org/10.1098/rsos.140343.

Tanaka, J. W., & Philibert, V. (2022). *The expertise of perception: How experience changes the way we see the world*. Cambridge University Press. https://doi.org/10.1017/9781108919616.

Young, A. W., Hay, D. C., McWeeny, K. H., Flude, B. M., & Ellis, A. W. (1985). Matching familiar and unfamiliar faces on internal and external features. *Perception*, 14(6), 737–746. https://doi.org/10.1068/p140737.

10 Delusions of misidentification

Introduction

This chapter looks at several delusions of misidentification clas-
sed as mistaken identity or face recognition disorders that are
quite different from prosopagnosia or face blindness. Individuals
with delusions of misidentification (DMI) often have normal face
recognition ability; however, they believe that certain individuals
are not who they appear to be and are in fact other people. In this
chapter we are going to explore several delusional misidentification disorders where face recognition 'goes wrong'; not necessarily for every face that is encountered, but sometimes when it
comes to identifying loved ones, friends and colleagues.

Delusions of misidentification are sometimes also called delusional misidentification syndromes (DMS). They are rare disorders
whereby an individual falsely believes that a person, part of the
body, object or place are not what they appear to be, but have been
replaced. People who have DMI are able to recognise the person,
object or place, looking as they should; however, they fail to correctly identify or recognise what they are seeing, and create a false
belief or delusion. For this chapter, we will only explore conditions
that influence the misidentification of humans' faces, although there
are DMI that have been found to involve objects, places and parts
of the body. Many of the DMI are thought to result from either brain
abnormalities, such as lesions, or psychological problems (mental
health issues), or they could be a combination of both. However,
there have been cases where they have been thought to be purely
psychological (Volkan, 2020).

DOI: 10.4324/9781003177128-10

There are a variety of DMI that were first recorded in the 1900s and current estimates suggest they occur in 1–4% of psychiatric patients, most commonly with those who have schizophrenia, and also those with dementia (Garrett & Leighton, 2022). Different types of DMI are associated with different symptoms, but the common theme is the person with the disorder can no longer correctly identify a particular person and thinks they are now someone else. DMI can often influence an individual's behaviour and can pose difficulties for those around them, and also for health professionals. This chapter will look at the four DMI that involve face recognition problems, beginning with Capgras syndrome, which has received the most research.

Capgras syndrome

Although DMI are rare by their nature, the most common one is Capgras syndrome, and this is the belief that some individuals, often a family member or close friend, are not who they say they are and instead they have been replaced by an identical imposter. In some cases, the individual with Capgras syndrome believes the imposter is an alien or robot. It has been suggested that Capgras syndrome was the inspiration for the science fiction film *Invasion of the Body Snatchers*, where people have been replaced by aliens for nefarious purposes, and numerous other body swap science fiction and horror movies. Capgras syndrome is often accompanied with a

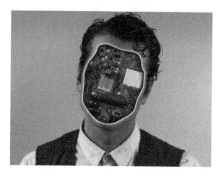

Figure 10.1 In Capras syndrome loved ones are often thought to be an imposter or robot in disguise.

diagnosis of schizophrenia, but can also occur due to brain damage or neurological issues. A person with Capgras recognises the face of a particular person that they know ('that person looks like my mother, brother, husband etc.') but then they deny that it is that person. The example in the box illustrates an example of an individual who developed Capgras syndrome.

The case of the imposter wife

In 1995 Mr and Mrs Davies were involved in a car accident, and both were taken to hospital for their injuries. Mr Davies became convinced that his wife of 31 years, Christine, had died in the accident and even when she returned home he would not accept that she was his wife. He did not feel any affection for his wife and referred to her as 'Christine two', treating her like a stranger. Mr Davies was diagnosed by a psychiatrist as having Capgras syndrome and awarded damages as a result of the disorder he developed after the crash (Gentleman, 1999).

Capgras syndrome gets its name from the psychiatrist Joseph Capgras, who co-authored a paper in 1923 with Jean Reboul-Lachaux, recording the first case of Madame M (Freeman, 2019). Madame M was in her fifties, and had a bout of anxiety after the death of her two daughters and twin boys, which was thought to have brought on the disorder. She became convinced her remaining daughter had been replaced many times by doubles over a period of 4 years (1914–1918), claiming she had encountered 2,000 doubles of her daughter. She also believed that her husband had been murdered and replaced by a double, and as a result asked for a divorce from her husband's replacement.

Historically, Capgras syndrome was classified as a psychiatric disorder, often using psychodynamic explanations whereby a person has negative feelings and emotions towards a significant other (Garrett & Leighton, 2022). The negative emotions, often unconscious, could induce feelings of guilt, thereby creating the delusion that the loved one has been replaced, to reduce the feelings of guilt. For example: 'I loathe this person, but they are my husband, therefore he cannot be my real husband, he must be a double.' It was not until the 1980s that Caprgras syndrome was first associated with brain lesions and dementia, suggesting that it could be a combination of a neurological and psychiatric disorder (Coltheart & Davies, 2021). Other research has revealed that Capgras syndrome can manifest as a symptom of Parkinson's disease and could be related to a dopamine deficiency. Approximately 15.8% of patients with Alzheimer's disease have Capgras syndrome. It has been estimated that approximately 16.6% to 27.8% of patients with dementia with Lewy bodies, where clumps of protein form inside brain cells, also have Capgras syndrome. Capgras syndrome can also develop from brain injuries, specifically to the right hemisphere and temporal lobes, which can result from strokes or brain tumours (Perkins, 2021). Other research has estimated that 80% of Capgras syndrome cases are people who have schizophrenia or dementia (Davis, 2023), pointing to neurological and psychiatric causes.

The main theoretical explanation for Capgras syndrome is that it results from a disconnection between the brain areas associated with face recognition and the emotional component associated with familiarity (Ellis & Lewis, 2001). There is evidence to support these suggestions as many individuals with Capgras syndrome have been found to have brain abnormalities, often in the right hemisphere (Bell et al., 2017), which is known to be involved in face recognition. Studies that have measured autonomic responses to face recognition have demonstrated that some familiar faces do not produce the same reactions in people with Capgras syndrome (Lewis et al., 2001).

Researchers Coltheart and Davies (2022) also suggest that a key finding to understanding Capgras syndrome is that personally familiar faces normally activate the sympathetic nervous system much more strongly than unfamiliar faces; however, in Capgras syndrome this familiarity is absent, prompting the person with the delusion to feel that a familiar person such as a loved one is in fact a stranger even though they recognise the person's face. There have been several studies that have tested skin conductance response (SCR), a measure of the electrical conductivity of the skin, which is linked to the sympathetic nervous system and associated with emotion. These studies have found that when individuals were shown photographs of faces of familiar people, healthy controls show larger SCR as compared to unfamiliar faces. However, individuals with Capgras syndrome did not show any differences when viewing unfamiliar versus familiar faces, demonstrating that there was a disconnection between their emotional responses and seeing a familiar face, which then led them to create a false belief that the familiar individuals had been replaced by strangers (Ellis et al., 1997; Lewis et al., 2001).

Coltheart and Davies (2021) claim that although Capgras syndrome results from a failure of emotional response to familiar faces, this is not enough to explain why some individuals have Capgras syndrome and create a delusion that those individuals are imposters. They have suggested a two-factor theory to explain why a person develops Capgras syndrome. Initially the individual develops a disconnect between the face recognition system and the emotional response linked to familiarity, which creates the delusion that the familiar person is a stranger. However, an important second factor is that the individual cannot dismiss or reject this delusion, as a healthy individual might when faced with this situation (Coltheart & Davies, 2022). Therefore, Capgras syndrome is about impaired reasoning and decision making in addition to being a face recognition disorder. In the box is an example of a case study of someone with Capgras syndrome.

Case study of Capgras syndrome

Nuara et al. (2020) reported the case of IF, an 87-year-old man who developed the delusion that his son had been substituted by an imposter. However, he did not believe his daughter or any other relatives were imposters. IF had been diagnosed as having a cyst on his right hemisphere; however, he had no other neurological symptoms or psychiatric issues. IF believed his son was an imposter when he saw his son, but not when listening to his son's voice if he was on the phone or wasn't able to see him in another room. IF took part in a series of cognitive tests including face recognition tests, and performed within the normal parameters. When autonomic measures were obtained, they found increased activity when he was shown the face of his daughter, demonstrating familiarity as compared to an unfamiliar face and the face of his son. However, when it came to hearing voices of his son and daughter, both elicited higher activity as compared to the voice of an unfamiliar person. Nuara and colleagues suggested there was an impairment in communication between the limbic system that is involved in emotions and the face recognition system, so that when IF looked at his son, he did not feel the emotions he should feel and then this lack of input created the belief that the son was an imposter.

Nuara et al. (2020) proposed that the reason the delusion was only associated with the son and not the daughter, is the face identity units for his two children could be located in different brain neurons. There is some support for this idea, as a study by Quiroga et al. (2005) found that a single neuron in the right hemisphere could be activated by seeing a photograph of the face of the actress Jennifer Aniston, suggesting that identity can be stored in a single neuron. If the pathway between the neuron that held the identity of IF's son and the emotional centre were disconnected, this may have been the precursor for his delusion that his son was an imposter and created the delusion.

The findings from Nuara et al. (2020) suggest that Capgras syndrome is related specifically to faces and not to other means of identification, such as voice recognition, as often someone with Capgras only feels that their loved one has been replaced by an imposter when they see them and not when they hear their voice without seeing their face (e.g. on the telephone). This was a finding from the case of DS, who believed, after a brain injury, that his parents were imposters when he looked at them, but not when he talked to them on the phone (Hirstein & Ramachandran, 1997). However there has been one case, that of HL, who had voice-specific Capgras syndrome and did not recognise the voice of her son, although she did recognise his face (Lewis et al., 2001). Voice-specific Capgras syndrome appears to be extremely rare, and this is the only reported case of a sighted individual that has been published at this time of writing, all the other published cases have been related to face recognition.

Much of the research that has been published on Capgras syndrome has focused on case studies of individuals who have this DMI; however, more recently Pandis, Agrawal and Poole

(2019) conducted a large systematic review of research articles that had reported cases of Capgras syndrome. They examined 175 papers from 1963 to 2016 detailing 258 cases of Capgras syndrome, and categorised Capgras syndrome as having two different aetiologies, or causes. Just over half (56%) of cases coincided with a mental health issue (functional causes), with the most common being schizophrenia, while just under half (43%) also had some type of neurological disorder (organic causes), such as organic delusional disorder and dementia, which were the most commonly occurring conditions. Interestingly, those in the functional group were on average younger and more likely to believe the imposter was a parent, and were likely to have auditory hallucinations, aggression and other misidentification syndromes. Those in the organic causes group were more likely to be older, believe that their spouse was the imposter, and have visual hallucinations and thought disorders. One of the commonalities between all the cases was that 80% of those who had undergone neuroimaging (e.g. CT or MRI scans) had abnormalities involving the right hemisphere. When it came to treatment, the most frequently offered were antipsychotic drugs, antidepressants and antidementia medication; however, there were other rarely used treatments such as electroconvulsive therapy (ECT). Of all cases, 65% responded well to treatment; although many still believed in the delusion, they were able to not let it affect their behaviour.

Another method to investigate the prevalence and symptoms of rare conditions such as Capgras syndrome is by looking at medical records of the general public. Bell et al. (2017) conducted a large-scale search of a medical records database in south London, and found that out of 250,000 cases only 84 had the diagnosis of Capgras syndrome. Of those cases, 69 had also had a diagnosis of a mental health condition, with 23 being diagnosed with schizophrenia. They found that out of the 84 cases, 71 believed that close family members were imposters. Only 40 of the cases (less than half) also had neuroimaging data such as CT and MRI scans. Only 14 of the cases had abnormal neuroimaging assessments, and of those there was little evidence of dominance in right hemisphere abnormalities. Bell et al. (2017) made the conclusion there was no evidence for right hemisphere damage in Capgras syndrome. However, since its publication other researchers have suggested it could be because the sample were more likely to have functional (psychiatric/mental health) causes for Capgras as opposed to organic (neurological/brain abnormality) causes (Coltheart & Davies, 2022). Furthermore, many of the cases had not received any neuroimaging investigations so it could be that there were some individuals who had undiagnosed neurological issues.

Many people who have Capgras syndrome believe that not only have their loved ones been replaced by imposters, but these imposters have malicious intentions. As a result of feelings of persecution, some individuals with Capgras syndrome can become aggressive towards the person they believe is an imposter, putting the so called 'imposter' at risk. One study that examined 110 cases of Capgras syndrome found that just over 60% of individuals had acted violently towards family members and caregivers, with more acts of violence from males. Some of these acts of violence had deadly consequences, resulting in murder or attempted murder (Karakasi et al., 2019). Many people with Capgras syndrome also have additional mental health issues (e.g. schizophrenia), with symptoms such as hallucinations, and they can also have other DMI (Pandis et al., 2019). In the rest of this chapter some other DMI will be described, beginning with Fregoli syndrome.

Fregoli syndrome

Fregoli syndrome is another form of DMI, where individuals believe those around them, who look outwardly like different people, are not who they appear to be, but are the same person in disguise. The name originates from the Italian twentieth-century actor Leopoldo Fregoli, who was famous for being able to quickly change characters and costumes during his performances, to the extent that some believed he was not just one man but that there were several 'Fregolis' (Greener, 2017).

Fregoli syndrome was first described by Courbon and Fail in 1927, who described a young woman who believed that she was being constantly followed by two actresses (cited in Langdon et al., 2014). She believed that the actresses were unrecognisable as they were disguising themselves as other people, including her friends, doctor, previous employer and strangers. For example, when the young woman saw the actress Sarah Bernhardt in a play, she then believed that she saw her again the next day disguised in the street as another person. In the text box is a more recent case study of an individual with Fregoli syndrome.

Case study of Fregoli syndrome

In their paper, Hentati et al. (2022) report the case of Ms F, who was a 50-year-old widow living with her mother and her 18-year-old daughter. The onset of her disorder could be traced back several years. When she was 34 years old she developed the belief that one of her colleagues, Mr S, had developed feelings for her, and she became convinced that he wanted to have a sexual relationship without her consent and to force her to change from being a Muslim to become a Jew. She was also convinced that all her work colleagues were gossiping about this and eventually she quit her job. However, even though she had left her job, she began to believe that Mr S was disguising himself as other individuals to look for her. More recently one of those people Mr S was thought to be disguising himself as was her daughter's fiancé. As you can imagine this created a lot of family conflicts as Ms F was convinced that her daughter's fiancé wanted to have sex with her and force her to change her religion. To try and avoid Mr S finding her she would often disguise herself and hide her face with a scarf so that he would not recognise her.

Ms F was diagnosed with schizophrenia, as she also experienced auditory and visual hallucinations, and was treated with antipsychosis medication. After two years, the hallucinations had stopped. Although she still had the misidentification delusion, it no longer affected her behaviour, and she was able to cope with her false beliefs.

As the case of Fregoli syndrome described in the box demonstrates, for many individuals it can have huge implications on the social and work life of those who suffer from this condition, and also creates some difficult relationships with family and friends. If the individual with Fregoli syndrome believes people around them are disguised and persecuting them, then it can put those around them at risk of harm. There have been incidents in hospital settings whereby patients with Fregoli syndrome have misidentified members of the health team (e.g. doctors and nurses) and believed they were other people with evil intent, and then have behaved aggressively towards those staff (Ashraf et al., 2011).

There have been several explanations for the underlying mechanism for Fregoli syndrome; like Capgras syndrome, it has been suggested that it is related to the pathways between face recognition areas of the brain and also emotional areas of the brain. However, while in Capgras syndrome there is a disconnection between face recognition for certain familiar faces and the corresponding emotion, in Fregoli it has been suggested that there is a superfluous connection between unfamiliar faces and emotion. Therefore when seeing some unfamiliar person it is associated with a feeling or sense of emotional arousal/familiarity, and the individual with Fregoli creates the delusion that this must be a known person in disguise (Langdon et al., 2014). However, like Capgras syndrome, the process to create and perpetuate the delusion involves impaired decision-making, so individuals with Fregoli syndrome continue to believe that the people around them are others in disguise.

There are suggestions that certain medications to treat Parkinson's disease appear to be linked to Fregoli syndrome (Sunitha et al., 2018). Fregoli has also been found after brain trauma, especially the temporal and parietal areas (Feinberg et al., 1999). One unusual case found a woman, who had no previous history of mental health issues, or brain trauma, developed Fregoli as a result of acute pneumonia and an infection (Salviati et al., 2014). Another rare case also found a young woman who developed Fregoli as a result of typhoid fever (Stanley & Andrew, 2002); however, these cases are very rare indeed. Most cases of Fregoli syndrome, like Capgras syndrome, have involved some underlying mental health or neurological condition.

Teixeira-Dias et al. (2023) conducted an individual patient meta-analysis of 83 studies of Fregoli syndrome and found that over half also had additional psychiatric diagnoses, including a diagnosis of schizophrenia. Many also had some type of neuro-logical problems, such as stroke, traumatic brain injury, epilepsy, substance issues or a neurodegenerative disease. Many shared neuroimaging abnormalities, with the majority having lesions in the right hemisphere and the right frontal lobe. Those with schizo-phrenia were more likely to have bilateral lesions. Dysfunction in the right hemisphere and frontal lobes is thought to be associated with misplaced feelings of familiarity, as well as problems with rea-lity monitoring and memory integration. Those who had feelings of being persecuted were more likely to have a primary diagnosis of a psychiatric disorder (e.g. schizophrenia). These findings replicate those of Pandis et al. (2019), who also found those who had feelings of persecution associated with Capgras syndrome symptoms were more likely to have a diagnosis of schizophrenia.

Although Fregoli and Capgras syndromes usually occur sepa-rately in individuals, there has been a case of an individual who had both Fregoli and Capgras syndromes. Flores-Medina et al. (2021) reported on the case of Miss G, who had a history of mental health issues. She began to believe that her children had been kidnapped, and those that lived with her were in fact dou-bles. She also believed that the imposters had implanted her with a chip to alter her perception of reality so that her real children would appear as strangers. She began to believe that several of the customers who frequented the shop where she worked were her real children (in disguise), who would only reveal themselves if she answered a set of questions correctly. She was never able to answer the questions correctly and as a result would spend a couple of hours most days walking around her neighbourhood trying to find her real children. Fortunately, Miss G was still able to work and maintain relationships with her co-workers and boss, but she had limited interpersonal relationships. Fregoli syndrome has also been found to co-exist with another rare DMI, namely inter-metamorphosis syndrome, which is described in the next section.

Intermetamorphosis syndrome

Intermetamorphosis syndrome could be described as a combination of Capgras and Fregoli syndromes, and it is the rarest among the delusions of misidentification (Kandeğer et al., 2017). As a result there is less published research into this extraordinary condition. Individuals who have this delusion believe that familiar people around them have exchanged identities in both physical appearance and personality. It was first described in 1932 by Courbon and Tusques (cited in Leis et al., 2019), who described a patient who claimed that people around her, including her family, had changed themselves physically and mentally.

There have been more recent cases of those with intermetamorphosis syndrome where an individual believed that her daughter was her mother, while another individual believed that his wife was his sister. Hermanowicz (2018) examined two case studies of intermetamorphosis syndrome, where both individuals also had Parkinson's disease. One of the individuals kept mistaking her husband for her deceased mother, and the other individual believed his husband was a friend and co-worker from many years previous. Individuals who have intermetamorphosis syndrome often also have other symptoms, such as visual hallucinations. Another case study was reported by Narayanaswamy et al. (2012), about a 40-year-old woman, Ms A, who was diagnosed with schizophrenia and both intermetamorphosis and Fregoli syndromes. Ms A. claimed that her husband would transform in front of her into a demon, and although he would look the same in appearance he would become darker and had a strange facial expression, and act as if he was going to harm her. She also believed that strangers around her were the same person in disguise who were planning to harm her family.

Similar to other cases of DMI, intermetamorphosis syndrome also appears to coincide with other mental health problems such as schizophrenia, bipolar, substance misuse and often in conjunction with hallucinations (Leis et al., 2019). This seems to suggest that of the few cases of intermetamorphosis syndrome reported in the literature, that this delusion appears to be more closely linked to mental health conditions, rather than through neurological abnormalities. However, it could be that there has simply been less research investigating this syndrome and therefore any neurological causations have yet to be thoroughly researched and reported. Treatment for intermetamorphosis syndrome usually involves antipsychotic medication, and although this does not always completely remove all the symptoms, often it can reduce their frequency, or helps in their management.

There is also a subtype of this DMI called reverse inter-metamorphosis syndrome, whereby the individual believes that they have been exchanged with another person. In one case study reported by Breen et al. (2000b), RZ, a 40-year-old woman who had been diagnosed with schizophrenia in her twenties, had the delusional belief that she was a man. The majority of the time RZ claimed she was her father and occasionally that she was her grandfather. RZ would only answer to her father's name and would sign his name on forms, and if asked any biographical information would give that of her father rather than her own. Reverse intermetamorphosis is interesting as it is about self-identity and not being able to recognise oneself as being the correct identity, which is similar to the delusion in the next section.

Mirrored self-misidentification syndrome

Mirrored self-misidentification syndrome (MSMS), as the name suggests, is linked to the self and self-recognition of one's face. People who have this condition often have normal face recognition ability and are able to recognise other individuals, but when it comes to looking at their own face in the mirror they do not recognise themselves and think that the person looking at them is a stranger. In many cases individuals with mirrored self-misidentification typically see the person in the mirror as being a younger or older version of themselves, a relative, or a complete stranger.

Figure 10.2 Individuals with mirrored self-misidentification syndrome often do not recognise themselves in the mirror.

Mirrored self-misidentification syndrome case study

One example of someone with mirrored self-misidentification syndrome is that of a 77-year-old retired primary school teacher, who had a probable Alzheimer's disease diagnosis as he had experienced progressive short term memory loss (Fernandes et al., 2021). He also was found to have atrophy in the hippocampus, an area of the brain known to be involved in memory. His wife took him to the clinic as he had started to complain about seeing a strange man in their house whenever he saw his own face in the mirror. His symptoms grew worse over the COVID-19 pandemic and imposed lockdown. More often he became anxious and irritable when seeing his own face in the mirror, questioning who the man was and what he was doing in their house. It was suggested that the isolation and reduced social contact during lockdown may have been a trigger for his DMI. In the clinic he was shown his own face in a mirror and stated that it was the face of a stranger. However, he was able to recognise other people such as his wife when he saw her reflection in the mirror. He was prescribed antipsychotic medication, and the mirrors in his house were removed or covered up, and this seemed to relieve his symptoms and reduce his anxiety.

Studies that have examined individuals with MSMS often report a dysfunction of the right hemisphere, and early signs of dementia (Roane et al., 2019). MSMS, similar to Capgras and Fregoli syndromes, not only involves issues with face recognition, but also problems with reasoning (Breen et al., 2000a, 2000b). In their paper Roane et al. (2019) examined 24 cases of MSMS and found 22 had cognitive deficits, such as memory impairments and visual spatial issues. Neuroimaging also showed neurological abnormalities, especially in the right hemisphere; however, Roane et al. (2019) point out that brain abnormalities are often found in patients with dementia or other neuropsychological conditions who do not develop MSMS. They suggest that, unlike Capgras syndrome, MSMS is nearly always associated with neurological illnesses or neurodegenerative conditions.

In contrast to the conclusion drawn by Roane et al. (2019) that MSMS is always associated with neurological illnesses and brain abnormalities, Rong et al. (2020) reported the first case of MSMS in a patient with schizophrenia and no other brain abnormalities. Rong et al. (2020) published a paper about a 52-year-old woman who claimed that the person in the mirror was not her, but she was able to recognise other people and objects she saw in the mirror. CT and MRI scans showed no brain abnormalities, and she performed as normal on tests for dementia, which suggested that the MSMS was a result of schizophrenia rather than any neurological issue. This isn't the first time it's been reported that individuals with schizophrenia can have had strange reactions to seeing their own face in the mirror. Bortolon et al. (2017) found that when they asked a group of individuals with schizophrenia to look at themselves in a mirror for 2 minutes, many said they had feelings of strangeness as compared to healthy controls. Perhaps feelings of strangeness towards one's own face are a precursor to MSMS, when it results from psychological causes. Furthermore, as many of the other DMI are associated with psychological issues as well as neurological ones, it could be that there is just less prevalence of psychological causes for MSMS.

Conclusion

Delusions of misidentification are quite different from other face recognition deficits such as prosopagnosia, as often people who have them can have normal face recognition abilities and they only have issues with specific faces. DMI are rare conditions; the most commonly experienced one is Capgras syndrome, whereby people believe that those closest to them have been replaced by doubles, or robots. Less common is Fregoli syndrome, which is the delusional belief that people, often family friends or strangers, are other individuals in disguise. The rarest of the DMI is intermetamorphosis syndrome, which is the false belief that familiar people change into someone or something else, both in external appearance and internal personality. Mirrored self-misidentification syndrome relates to self-recognition and is when the person fails to recognise themself in a mirror.

Some researchers have suggested that DMI are not separate disorders, and as such should not be treated as separate neuropsychological conditions. For example, it has been suggested that Capgras and Fregoli are located along the same continuum of an underlying psychosis (Sinkman, 2008, cited in Leighton et al., 2022). There is some evidence to support the idea that DMI are not separate conditions as there have been some reported cases where the same individuals have had several DMI, such as Fregoli and Capgras syndromes (Flores-Medina et al., 2021), or intermetamorphosis and Fregoli syndromes (Narayanaswamy et al., 2012).

When looking at the causes of DMI, the majority of studies have found they coincide with mental health issues, most commonly schizophrenia (especially paranoid schizophrenia). Among the symptoms there are often hallucinations and paranoid thoughts of persecution. Many DMI involve brain abnormalities, especially in relation to the right hemisphere, which is known to be involved in face recognition and sometimes neurodegenerative conditions such as dementia, Alzheimer's disease and Parkinson's disease. However, there have been some rare cases where DMI have been reported in individuals with no known brain injuries or neurological deficits, and with no history of mental health issues (Leighton et al., 2022).

Theoretical explanations suggest that DMI can result when there are communication problems between areas of the brain involved in face recognition and areas of the brain involved in emotions (Ellis et al., 2000; Ellis & Lewis, 2001). There is some neuroimaging evidence to support this theory (Roane et al., 2019). Some researchers have suggested a two-factor theory for DMI. The first factor is a neuropsychological impairment that initially creates the belief, usually involving face recognition and emotion pathways. The second factor is a neuropsychological impairment that influences reasoning and decision making that does not reject the delusion or false belief (Coltheart, 2010; Coltheart & Davies, 2021).

When it comes to treatment for people with DMI, some antipsychotic drugs appear to help relieve symptoms, and in some rare cases ECT has been employed when medication has not been beneficial (Pandis et al., 2019). Often individuals with DMI can feel persecuted by those around them, and they can feel anxious, which can not only make the person with the DMI unhappy, but can be very difficult for the loved ones who have to deal with their behaviour. Talking therapies can be beneficial for those suffering from DMI and their loved ones to help to understand and cope with their behaviour.

One of the problems with mental health and neurological conditions like DMI is that, unlike other physical health conditions (e. g. diabetes), there is often not an objective medical test, such as a blood test, that can demonstrably diagnose that a person has a specific mental health condition. As result of this lack of objective measures some researchers have been critical of psychiatric diagnosis (Szasz, 1974). Research investigating DMI can cross the boundaries between neurology, neuroscience, psychology and psychiatry. The findings from researching DMI illustrate that we still have more to learn about these conditions. Researchers from psychology, psychiatry and neuroscience need to continue to work together to try and understand why face recognition 'goes wrong' for those who have delusions of misidentification, and how to effectively treat and support them and their loved ones.

References

Ashraf, N., Antonius, D., Sinkman, A., Kleinhaus, K., & Malaspina, D. (2011). Fregoli syndrome: An underrecognized risk factor for aggression in treatment settings. *Case Reports in Psychiatry*, 2011, 1–3. https://doi.org/10.1155/2011/351824.

Bell, V., Marshall, C., Kanji, Z., Wilkinson, S., Halligan, P., & Deeley, Q. (2017). Uncovering Capgras delusion using a large-scale medical records database. *BJPsych Open*, 3(4), 179–185. https://doi.org/10.1192/bjpo.bp.117.005041.

Bortolon, C., Capdevielle, D., Altman, R., Macgregor, A., & Raffard, S. (2017). Mirror self-face perception in individuals with schizophrenia: Feelings of strangeness associated with one's own image. *Psychiatry Research*, 253, 205–210. https://doi.org/10.1016/j.psychres.2017.03.055.

Breen, N., Caine, D., & Coltheart, M. (2000a). Models of face recognition and delusional misidentification: A critical review. *Cognitive Neuropsychology*, 17(1–3),55–71. https://doi.org/10.1080/026432900380481.

Breen, N., Caine, D., Coltheart, M., Hendy, J., & Roberts, C. (2000b). Towards an understanding of delusions of misidentification: Four case studies. *Mind and Language*, 15(1), 74–110. https://doi.org/10.1111/1468-0017.00124.

Coltheart, M. (2010). The neuropsychology of delusions. *Annals of the New York Academy of Sciences, 1191*, 16–26. https://doi.org/10.1111/j.1749-6632.2010.05496.x.

Coltheart, M., & Davies, M. (2021). Failure of hypothesis evaluation as a factor in delusional belief. *Cognitive Neuropsychiatry, 26*(4), 213–230. https://doi.org/10.1080/13546805.2021.1914016.

Coltheart, M., & Davies, M. (2022). What is Capgras delusion? *Cognitive Neuropsychiatry, 27*(1), 69–82. https://doi.org/10.1080/13546805.2021.2011185.

Davis, J. (2023). What is Caprgras syndrome?www.webmd.com/mental-health/impostor-syndrome-capgras.

Ellis, H. D., Lewis, M. B., Moselhy, H. F., & Young, A. W. (2000). Automatic without autonomic responses to familiar faces: Differential components of covert face recognition in a case of Capgras delusion. *Cognitive Neuropsychiatry, 5*(4), 255–269. https://doi.org/10.1080/13546800050199711.

Ellis, H. D., Young, A. W., Quayle, A. H., & De Pauw, K. W. (1997). Reduced autonomic responses to faces in Capgras delusion. *Proceedings of the Royal Society B: Biological Sciences, 264*(1384), 1085–1092. https://doi.org/10.1098/rspb.1997.0150.

Ellis, Hadyn D., & Lewis, M. B. (2001). Capgras delusion: A window on face recognition. *Trends in Cognitive Sciences, 5*(4), 149–156. https://doi.org/10.1016/S1364-6613(00)01620-X

Feinberg, T. E., Eaton, L. A., Roane, D. M., & Giacino, J. T. (1999). Multiple Fregoli delusions after traumatic brain injury. *Cortex, 35*(3), 373–387. https://doi.org/10.1016/S0010-9452(08)70806-70802.

Fernandes, C., Taveira, I., & Nzwalo, H. (2021). Mirrored-self misidentification in a patient with probable Alzheimer dementia. *JAMA Neurology, 78*(9), 1150. https://doi.org/10.1001/jamaneurol.2021.2142.

Flores-Medina, Y., Rosel-Vales, M., Adame, G. A., & Ramírez-Bermúdez, J. (2021). The loss of familiarity: A case study of the comorbidities of Capgras and Fregoli. *Neurocase, 27*(5), 385–390. https://doi.org/10.1080/13554794.2021.1970188.

Freeman, D. (2019). Capgras: The 'illusion of doubles'. www.bbc.co.uk/sounds/play/m0007rvd.

Garrett, M., & Leighton, E. (2022). Capgras syndrome and other delusions of misidentification: Integrating neuropsychological models of delusion formation with psychoanalytic object-relations theory. *Current Behavioral Neuroscience Reports, 9*(3), 84–92. https://doi.org/10.1007/s40473-022-00249-w.

Gentleman, A. (1999). Car crash victim wins £130,000 for 'impostor' wife. *The Guardian*, 5 March. www.theguardian.com/uk/1999/mar/05/amelia gentleman.

Greener, M. (2017). New insights into delusional misidentification syndromes. *Progress in Neurology and Psychiatry*, 21(2), 33–35. https://doi.org/10.1002/pnp.469.

Hentati, S., Masmoudi, R., Guermazi, F., Cherif, F., Feki, I., Baati, I., Sallemi, R., & Masmoudi, J. (2022). Fregoli syndrome in schizophrenia: About a case report. *Archives of Psychiatry and Mental Health*, 2022, 6. https://doi.org/10.29328/journal.apmh.1001038.

Hermanowicz, N. (2018). Delusional misidentification in Parkinson's disease: report of two cases and a review. *Postgraduate Medicine*, 130 (2), 280–283. https://doi.org/10.1080/00325481.2018.1411161.

Hirstein, W., & Ramachandran, V. S. (1997). Capgras syndrome: A novel probe for understanding the neural representation of the identity and familiarity of persons. *Proceedings of the Royal Society B: Biological Sciences*, 264(1380), 437–444. https://doi.org/10.1098/rspb.1997.0062.

Kandeğer, A., Tekdemir, R., & Selvi, Y. (2017). Delusional misidentification syndromes: A case of intermetamorphosis. *Klinik Psikiyatri Dergisi*, 20(2), 150–154. https://doi.org/10.5505/kpd.2017.22931.

Karakasi, M. V., Markopoulou, M., Alexandri, M., Douzenis, A., & Pavlidis, P. (2019). In fear of the most loved ones: A comprehensive review on Capgras misidentification phenomenon and case report involving attempted murder under Capgras syndrome in a relapse of a schizophrenia spectrum disorder. *Journal of Forensic and Legal Medicine*, 66 (October 2018), 8–24. https://doi.org/10.1016/j.jflm.2019.05.019.

Langdon, R., Connaughton, E., & Coltheart, M. (2014). The Fregoli delusion: A disorder of person identification and tracking. *Topics in Cognitive Science*, 6(4), 615–631. https://doi.org/10.1111/tops.12108.

Leighton, E., Garrett, M., Beltrani, A., Min, J. Y., & Schilder, V. (2022). Capgras syndrome and other delusions of misidentification: A summary of the psychological, psychiatric, and neurophysiological literature on DMI. *Current Behavioral Neuroscience Reports*, 9(3), 93–99. https://doi.org/10.1007/s40473-022-00248-x.

Leis, K., Mazur, E., Racinowski, M., Jamrożek, T., Gołębiewski, J., Gałązka, P., & Pąchalska, M. (2019). Delusional misidentification syndrome: Dissociation between recognition and identification processes. *Acta Neuropsychologica*, 17(4), 455–467. https://doi.org/10.5604/01.3001.0013.6551.

Lewis, M. B., Sherwood, S., Moselhy, H., & Ellis, H. D. (2001). Autonomic responses to familiar faces without autonomic responses to familiar voices: Evidence for voice-specific Capgras delusion

Cognitive Neuropsychiatry, 6(3), 217–228. https://doi.org/10.1080/13546800143000041.

Narayanaswamy, J. C., Gopinath, S., Rajkumar, R. P., Bhargava Raman, R. P., & Math, S. B. (2012). Co-occurrence of intermetamorphosis and Frégoli syndrome in schizophrenia: A case report. *The Primary Care Companion to CNS Disorders*, 14(2). https://doi.org/10.4088/PCC.11L01279.

Nuara, A., Nicolini, Y., D'Orio, P., Cardinale, F., Rizzolatti, G., Avanzini, P., Fabbri-Destro, M., & De Marco, D. (2020). Catching the imposter in the brain: The case of Capgras delusion. *Cortex*, 131, 295–304. https://doi.org/10.1016/j.cortex.2020.04.025.

Pandis, C., Agrawal, N., & Poole, N. (2019). Capgras' delusion: A systematic review of 255 published cases. *Psychopathology*, 52(3), 161–173. https://doi.org/10.1159/000500474.

Perkins, A. (2021). Capgras' syndrome: Familiar unfamiliar faces. *Nursing Made Incredibly Easy*, 19(6), 38–45. https://doi.org/10.5958/2454-2660.2021.00028.4.

Quiroga, R. Q., Reddy, L., Kreiman, G., Koch, C., & Fried, I. (2005). Invariant visual representation by single neurons in the human brain. *Nature*, 435(7045), 1102–1107. https://doi.org/10.1038/nature03687.

Roane, D. M., Feinberg, T. E., & Liberta, T. A. (2019). Delusional misidentification of the mirror image. *Current Neurology and Neuroscience Reports*, 19(8). https://doi.org/10.1007/s11910-019-0972-5.

Rong, C., Issac, A. G., Alkan, E. S., Fashina, O., Ding, K., & Selek, S. (2020). A case of mirror image agnosia and mirrored self-misidentification syndrome in schizophrenia without dementia or structural abnormalities. *Neurocase*, 26(5), 317–319. https://doi.org/10.1080/13554794.2020.1799019.

Salviati, M., Carlone, C., Provenzano, A., Valeriani, G., Melcore, C., Macrì, F., Terlizzi, S., & Biondi, M. (2014). Fregoli syndrome in course of infection-related delirium: A case report. *Journal of Psychopathology*, 20(2), 180–185.

Stanley, P. C., & Andrew, A. E. (2002). Fregoli syndrome: a rare persecutory delusion in a 17 year old sufferer of psychosis associated with typhoid fever at Jos University Teaching Hospital, Jos, Nigeria. *Nigerian Medical Journal*, 11(1), 33–34.

Sunitha, P. S., Rashmi, P., Vidya, & Saraswati, P. (2018). Fregoli Syndrome – A Review Article. *International Journal of Advances in Nursing Management*, 6(3), 269. https://doi.org/10.5958/2454-2652.2018.00060.4.

Szasz, T. S. (1974). *The myth of mental illness: Foundations of a theory of personal conduct*. HarperCollins.

Teixeira-Dias, M., Dadwal, A. K., Bell, V., & Blackman, G. (2023). Neuropsychiatric features of Fregoli syndrome: An individual patient meta-analysis. *The Journal of Neuropsychiatry and Clinical Neurosciences*, 35, 171–177. https://doi.org/10.1176/appi.neuropsych.22010011.

Volkan, K. (2020). Delusional misidentification syndromes: Psychopathology and culture. *Journal of Health and Medical Sciences*, 3(3), 288–301. https://doi.org/10.31014/aior.1994.03.03.124.

11 Super recognisers

Introduction

This book has focused on when face recognition 'goes wrong', looking at the errors humans and machines can make when trying to recognise individuals, and the different factors that can influence whether a face is identified or not. It therefore felt necessary to also look at the reverse situation and see when faces are correctly recognised, even under conditions that are not optimal. Most people are relatively good at recognising the faces of people they know, either personally or through the media (e.g. celebrities), but can be quite error prone when it comes to recognising the faces of unfamiliar people they have seen, e.g. eyewitness identification. However, there are a minority of individuals who possess extraordinary abilities for recognising and remembering faces and they have been called super recognisers. Super recognisers (SRs) can often remember unfamiliar faces even from a fleeting glance, or under poor conditions and over long periods of time.

The first published study to use the term 'super recogniser' was by Russell et al. (2009). In their lab they usually studied individuals with prosopagnosia or face blindness (see Chapter 9). They stated that due to media coverage of their research on prosopagnosia, they were contacted by several individuals who claimed to have the opposite condition and have superior face recognition abilities. They invited these individuals to come to their lab and administered several face identification tests. The tests revealed that all the individuals who claimed to have

DOI: 10.4324/9781003177128-11

superior face recognition abilities performed more accurately, as compared to the control participants. Russell and colleagues concluded that there are a subset of people in the population who are exceptionally good at face recognition and perception.

Although the first study investigating SRs' abilities was published by Russell and colleagues in 2009; by 2017 there was still only a handful of studies that had been published in this area (Noyes et al., 2017) and very few studies compared to the large number of papers on face recognition in general (Ramon, 2021). Over the last few years research investigating SRs' abilities has begun to increase and their talents have also received media attention with news articles (Mitchell, 2023; Potts, 2015), radio programmes (Hammond, 2010), television programmes (Jones, 2015) and even a short science fiction film (Sheridan, 2017). This chapter is going to explore some of the research that has investigated SR's abilities and how their skills might be utilised in the workforce to benefit society.

What is a super recogniser?

Despite the increasing number of studies over the last few years that have investigated SRs' abilities, there still appears to be no unified definition of what an SR is. Research has found that SRs generally outperform healthy control participants on most face recognition and face matching tasks (Bobak et al., 2016d). Also, SRs usually have superior face recognition skills for both familiar (Robertson et al., 2016) and unfamiliar faces (Bobak et al., 2016c; Davis et al., 2016). However, although SRs are usually more accurate for different face processing tasks (e.g. matching and recognition), they do not always excel at both tasks, e.g. they may well excel at matching but not recognition and vice versa (Bobak, et al., 2016a). It appears that SRs are not a homogeneous group, and levels of ability can vary among a group of SRs as well as their performance varying across different face processing tasks (Moreton et al., 2019).

In her search to find a definition of an SR, Ramon (2021) surveyed a small number of police officers and civilians and asked them 'what is a super recogniser?'. Although there was more agreement in the police officers group as compared to the civilians, only 64% claimed that SRs are 'people who excel at recognising others using various cues, such as face, posture and gait', 27% agreed with the statement that SRs are '1–2% of the population who can remember 80% of faces they have seen' and 9% said 'people who are above average at face matching'. There was even less agreement among civilians as to what defined an SR, although 41% said SRs are '1–2% of the population who can remember 80% of faces they have seen'. Ramon (2021) concluded there is no formal definition of what constitutes an SR and therefore the term means different things to different people.

Other researchers, while trying to define what a super recogniser is, have compared the concept to deficits in face processing ability, namely prosopagnosia. Bate et al. (2021) suggested that as prosopagnosia has two different subtypes resulting from two different face processing deficits, e.g. apperceptive prosopagnosia, which relates to a perceptual face processing deficit, and also Associative prosopagnosia, which is a face memory deficit, it could be that super recognisers may also have different subtypes. This might help to explain why SRs are not a homogeneous group and perform differently on various tests of face processing.

There is some evidence to support a range of 'super recognition' skills in both perception and memory. Studies have found that not only can SRs have superior memory for previously seen faces (Bate et al., 2018), but they can also be super matchers, and excel not only at matching simultaneously presented faces, but other visual stimuli such as fingerprints (Growns et al., 2022). Those who are super matchers may have extraordinary visual perception abilities, rather than face recognition abilities per se, as the task does not rely on memory for faces. In their study Growns and colleagues only investigated matching tasks, so it is not clear if those who were super matchers were also super recognisers.

Although there has been research that has investigated SR abilities, what hasn't received any research at the time of writing this chapter is any investigation of the lived experienced of what it is like to be an SR. In the text box are two examples of some of the real-life experiences of SRs and how their abilities have influenced their lives.

Personal experiences of super recognisers

There is still relatively little research that has looked at the personal experiences of people who possess SR abilities. Yenny Seo is one individual who through online testing was classified as an SR. She claims she has had super ior face recognition skills since childhood, when she would recognise strangers she had seen briefly in the street weeks later in a grocery store. She would also recognise extras from movies who often only appeared fleetingly in other films. Her mother thought she was just very observant, and it wasn't until she was older that she began to realise that not everyone else shared her special ability (Adcock, 2022).

Seo said that she has always enjoyed looking at different faces, and it wasn't until she was older and started using social media that she became self-conscious of her unique talent. She said:

> I would start a new class in uni or I would meet people through social gatherings and I would remember visually what kind of photos I'd seen them in. I'd already be so familiar with them and I'd know in my head: 'Oh, you are that person's sibling', or 'You used to date so-and-so', but I also knew it'd be really creepy if I said that out loud, so I'd keep it on the down low and just say: 'Oh, nice to meet you.'
>
> (Adcock, 2022)

Her special ability did come in handy when she worked in a clothes shop and was shown a grainy photo of a shoplifter and then next time the person entered the shop Seo recognised them and alerted the security guard (Adcock, 2022).

Another SR known only as CS also felt she had to hide her extraordinary abilities as it could make people feel uncomfortable. She said, 'I often pretend not to recognize someone because it scares them if I say, "Oh, I remember you, you were behind me in line at a supermarket in 1996 wearing a yellow soccer jersey!".' Furthermore, she claims 'It doesn't matter how many years pass; if I've seen your face before I will be able to recall it' (Hawthorn, 2023).

Looking at the two SR experiences, both felt they needed to hide their abilities to prevent making other people uncomfortable as it might seem 'creepy' if they knew information about a person who they had only met briefly or seen online. There are, however, ways in which their abilities could be used as a benefit to society, for example in security or border control settings where being able to identify faces is part of the job, which is discussed later in this chapter. Firstly, however, before employing SRs in the field they need to be correctly identified through some type of objective testing process.

Classifying super recognisers

To classify an individual as being a super recogniser, most studies have usually administered one or more face recognition tests and then compared performance from those who claim to have extraordinary face recognition ability to data from a control group of participants. In their initial study Russell, Duchaine and Nakayama (2009) tested potential super recognisers on three different recognition tasks. The Before They Were Famous (BTWF) Test where participants are presented with images of people, often as children and before they were famous and try to name them, or give some type of identifying information, e.g. she is an actress who was in a film called *The Hunger Games* (Jennifer Lawrence). The Cambridge Face Memory Test–Long Form (CFMT +) was adapted from the original CFMT (Duchaine & Nakayama, 2006) to include additional trials that were more difficult to try and distinguish between those who could perform at a higher ability from those in the normal population. Also, the Cambridge Face Perception Test (CFPT; Duchaine et al., 2007) is a face perception test whereby participants are presented with a target face in a three quarters view and also six other faces in a front view and they need to sort them into order according to which looks more like the target face. In their study, Russell et al. (2009) found that SRs outperformed the control participants by a large margin, with some scoring 2 standard deviations (SD) above participants in the control group. They suggested scores should be above 2 SD above mean control data for an individual to be classified as a super recogniser. Conversely, to diagnose for prosopagnosia, individuals need to perform 2 SD below the control mean score.

Researchers have suggested that for someone to be classified as an SR they should score a minimum of 95/102 on the CFMT+ (Bobak, et al., 2016c) and that this ability should be present in about 2% of the population (Robertson et al., 2020). Others have suggested that for someone to be classified or diagnosed as an SR they should be administered with a minimum of two different face recognition tests, and should perform significantly more accurately than average control data on the different tests (Bate et al., 2018; Mayer & Ramon, 2023).

Adding to the discussion of what tests are appropriate to identify SR, Ramon (2021) suggests that some tests that have been previously used to identify SRs are not appropriate, for example the GFMT (Burton et al., 2010) as it suffers from ceiling effects and the CFMT short version (Duchaine & Nakayama, 2006) as it was designed to diagnose face recognition impairments. Ramon proposes a diagnostic framework for classifying SRs including face recognition and perception components that are sensitive enough to ensure that SRs can be distinguished from other high performing individuals. This would involve administering a battery of tests to assess the different processes of face processing including the CFMT+, Yearbook Test–Long (YBT-long), and Facial Identity Card Sorting Test (FICST) and that SRs should score highly on two out of the three tests. Furthermore, as the different tests involves different skills then SRs can be categorised according to the results from the test (de Haas, 2022).

One of the criticisms of studies that have used face recognition tests to try and classify SRs is that most tests have been designed primarily to diagnose individuals with prosopagnosia, or to try and investigate individual differences in the general population, rather than to classify individuals with superior face recognition abilities. A further criticism of face recognition tests is that often the images used are filmed under optimum conditions and have been manipulated, such as removing hair and face shape and do not vary as much as naturally occurring images in the real world (Ramon et al., 2019). The most commonly used test to identify SRs is the CFMT+, and although this test has been validated by a large number of studies (Ramon et al., 2019), it has also received some criticism in the way it was constructed. The CFMT+ images were all collected on the same day and under tightly controlled conditions, and although there are some variations in viewpoint, lighting and expression, it does not illustrate the natural variation and variability that exists when seeing faces in different real-world settings. Furthermore, the CFMT+ only presents target present trials and therefore does not test the applied scenario of when a target is absent (Bate et al., 2018).

Researchers Dunn et al. (2020) created an online tool specifically designed to classify super recognisers using naturally occurring images of faces at different ages, from different angles and wearing different accessories. The University of New South Wales (UNSW) Face Test combines both face recognition memory and face perceptual tasks. They have the data from over 20,000 participants who took part in the online tests and from those scores produced normative data whereby they were able to set thresholds to identify SRs. They recommend to be classified as a super recogniser individuals should also complete the GFMT (Burton et al., 2010), the GFMT2-H (White et al., 2022), which is a more difficult version of the GFMT, and the CFMT (Duchaine & Nakayama, 2006) in addition to the UNSW Face Test (Dunn et al., 2020).

Theoretical explanation for super recognisers

Although objective tests such as the CFMT+ and the UNSW can help researchers to identify SR, what they cannot do is explain why a person is an SR and the mechanisms that underly this extraordinary ability. There has been very little academic discussion about theoretical explanations for SR abilities and why these individuals are better at recognising faces as compared to the majority of the population. In 2017, Noyes, Phillips and O'Toole reviewed the small body of literature that had accumulated to investigate SR abilities and as a result proposed two different theoretical explanations for SR abilities (Noyes et al., 2017). The first explanation is that face recognition is an ability that is normally distributed in the general population and that SRs are simply in the top tail of the distribution (see Figure 11.1). In contrast the second suggestion is that SRs have skills which are qualitatively and quantitively different as compared to most people.

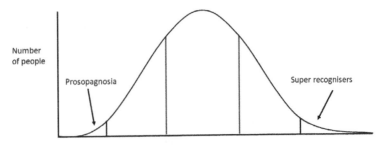

Figure 11.1 A normal distribution curve. Super recognisers and those with prosopagnosia are at the extremes of the distribution.

Noyes et al. (2017) suggest that the first explanation is more likely and that super recognisers are simply in the top section of the population when it comes to face recognition. There is some evidence to support the theory that natural ability in face recognition may have a genetic component, for example where cases of developmental or congenital prosopagnosia have been all found in the same family (Duchaine et al., 2007; Lee et al., 2010). As prosopagnosia appears to have a hereditary component it could be those with extraordinary face recognition skills may have inherited their abilities; however, there is currently no research evidence for this.

To investigate the mechanisms behind SRs' abilities and whether they are limited to faces, or if they had superior recognition of other visual objects, Bobak et al. (2016a) presented a group of SRs and control participants with images of hands, houses and cars. Their results revealed that SRs were no better than control participants at recognising or matching objects, apart from one SR who performed at almost perfect accuracy on the cars task. For the majority of SRs, their skills did not extend from faces to other objects. They also administered matching tasks and found that some SR, but not all, had superior perceptual skills as compared to the controls. They suggest that their findings support the theory that face recognition ability is normally distributed in the population, and at one end of the spectrum there are prosopagnosics who struggle to recognise faces and the other end are super recognisers with enhanced ability to recognise faces.

Although there seems to be little evidence that SRs might be exceptional at recognition of matching other visual objects (Bobak et al., 2016a), there is some evidence that their skills do extend beyond faces. Jenkins et al. (2021) investigated whether people who were exceptional at recognising faces would also demonstrate superior voice recognition abilities. They administered a series of face recognition and voice recognition tasks and found that those who performed at the top end on face recognition tasks as compared to controls, also were more accurate on voice recognition tasks. They suggest that there are some individuals that are not only super recognisers when it comes to face recognition, but they are also super voice recognisers.

In a further study to explore whether SRs process faces differently compared to other people, Bobak et al. (2017) used eye tracking methods to investigate whether SRs looked at faces differently from other people (controls) and also those diagnosed with prosopagnosia. They found SRs were quicker to look at a face in a scene as compared to the other groups and SRs spent more time looking at the nose of faces as compared to controls. Although there were individual differences in viewing strategies for SRs and controls, there were no overall consistent strategies that distinguished the SRs from the control participants. The findings suggest that SRs do not necessarily use qualitatively different processing strategies compared to most people; they are just more effective at face recognition.

Another study to employ eye tracking methods to explore an SR's abilities was a case study of an adolescent who was found to have extraordinary face recognition skills (Bennetts et al., 2017). The adolescent, known only as O.B., was 14 years of age and reported herself to the psychology lab as she believed she had exceptional face recognition skills. No other family members reported to have superior face recognition skills. O.B. completed a series of face recognition tests and was found to be not only more accurate than other children her age, but also more accurate than adults, and her performance was comparable to adult SR scores. When eye tracking methods were used to investigate how she looked at faces, she was found to spend more time looking at the nose region of faces as compared to the control participants, replicating the pattern found by Bobak et al. (2017)

with adult SRs. O.B.'s recognition skills did not extend to object recognition, where she performed within the normal range; her extraordinary ability was exclusively for faces. This is the only study at the time of writing this chapter where an adolescent SR has been reported in the literature and so any conclusions need to be tentative; however, it does appear to show that SR abilities can manifest relatively early in life and before adulthood. This coincides with adult SRs' reports of their childhood, where they have said their abilities were present earlier in their lives (Bobak et al., 2016a; Russell et al., 2009).

Super recognisers may look at faces in a slightly different way to other people, as they appear to look at the nose area of the face more than other people. However there does not appear to be any evidence that SRs process faces in a qualitatively different way to other people; they are just better at processing and remembering faces they have seen. Often SRs have received no formal training and therefore they may have a natural ability, rather than being trained to be accurate at recognising faces. There are some jobs where people have been specifically trained to compare images of faces for forensic or security purposes, and having above average face recognition abilities would be advantageous.

Super recognisers versus face recognition experts

One way to investigate SRs' abilities is to not only compare their performance to other control participants from the general population, but to compare their performance to individuals who have been trained to be experts in face processing. Facial examiners are (FEs) often employed by the police or forensic services and have undergone a considerable amount of training to identify faces at a high level of accuracy. FEs are employed to conduct image comparisons, such as matching people caught on CCTV to images taken in custody when a person is arrested, or to try and determine whether someone caught on CCTV footage at several different crime scenes is the same individual. Phillips et al. (2018) compared SRs' with FEs' performance on a simultaneous face matching task, where they had to decide if a pair of faces was the same person. They found that SRs and FEs performed equally well, and both groups were more accurate than students and fingerprint examiners. This study led other researchers to question whether FEs were a subset of SRs, with the added benefit of training and credentials (Hahn et al., 2022). What is not known is whether those who become FEs already have superior face recognition skills before their training; one would assume that they will have an interest in looking at faces in general and so it could be that they have above average abilities in face recognition prior to beginning their employment.

Hahn et al. (2022) set out to investigate whether FEs were a subset of SRs by comparing SRs, FEs and control participants and asked them to judge whether a face pair was the same person on a 7-point scale and to rate how difficult they found each decision on a 5-point scale. They found that FEs used the full scale, while SRs tended to select the extreme ends of the scale and avoid the midpoints. SRs were also much more confident when pairs of faces were the same identity, while FEs did not show any confidence bias. FEs' decisions were more consistent and agreed with one another across the face pairs; in contrast SRs did not show consistent agreement. Hahn et al. (2022) suggest that FEs and SRs demonstrate distinct behaviours; however, they still could not determine whether FEs had pre-existing SR skills prior to their training and whether training alters behaviour. To investigate whether SRs are a subset of FEs, longitudinal research should be conducted testing forensic examiners prior to their training, to establish if they already possess SR abilities. It would then be interesting to test the FEs during their training and finally once it is completed and see if their behaviour has changed.

Another study comparing FE and SR behaviour by Towler et al. (2023) administered a number of different face identification tasks and compared the accuracy of SRs, FEs and control participants. They found that SRs outperformed control participants across all unfamiliar face identification tasks and were also more accurate than FEs when faces were seen for a short amount of time, such as 2 seconds, while FEs were only more accurate than control participants when faces were seen for longer, e.g. 30 seconds. They concluded the SRs can achieve a high level of accuracy after viewing faces for a short amount of time, while FE require more time to make accurate decisions. Furthermore, FEs appear to use a feature-by-feature approach when trying to determine whether two images depict the same person. Another difference was that SRs were more likely to incorrectly say that two faces were the same person, which has serious ramifications in relation to wrongful convictions due to misidentification. In contrast FEs did not show a bias (neutral bias) and were just as likely to say the face images were the same or two different people, and were also more likely to say they were unsure as compared to the SRs.

Other-group recognition

As you read earlier in this book, people often demonstrate cognitive biases when looking at faces and can demonstrate an own-race bias where they are more accurate at recognising faces that are the same race as they are (see Chapter 4). People can also be more accurate at recognising faces from the same age group that they belong to, which is an own-age bias (see Chapter 6). More recently, researchers have been interested in whether SRs, with their enhanced skills in face recognition, also demonstrate an own-group bias when it comes to recognising faces that are perceived as coming from a different group to the one they belong to.

Bate et al. (2019a) investigated whether SRs elicited an own-race bias (ORB) by comparing their performance using the CFMT+ (Duchaine & Nakayama, 2006), which has Caucasian faces, and the CFMT-Chinese, which as the name suggests consists of Chinese faces (McKone et al., 2012). They found that the SRs (who were all Caucasian) performed more accurately than the Caucasian control participants on both tests and were very accurate when identifying faces that were the same race as them from the CMFT+. However, SRs were less accurate on the Chinese version of the CFMT and did not outperform the Asian control participants on this task. In a second experiment, face matching tasks were employed, one with Caucasian faces and the other with Asian faces. Replicating the results from the first experiment, SRs (who were all Caucasian) were more accurate than Caucasian control participants, and again were more accurate with own-race faces as compared to faces of a different race. However, when matching Asian faces, SRs were not more accurate than Asian control participants. Bate et al. (2019a) suggesting that SRs are subject to the same biases as othe people in the population and rather than processing faces in a qualitatively different way, SRs are simply at the top percentile of the population.

Some researchers have criticised the Bate et al. (2019a) study, as they only used a small number of SRs, eight in total (Robertson et al., 2020). Following on from that area of research, Robertson et al. (2020) tested a large number of participants on a battery of face memory and face matching tasks, where participants had to identify own-race (Caucasian) and other-race (Egyptian and Chinese) faces. Out of over 700 participants they identified 35 individuals who met the criteria to be classified as SRs, as they performed above the control participants on the majority of tasks. SRs also outperformed control participants not only on tasks that involved own-race faces, but also on tasks that contained other-race faces; however, SRs were still less accurate with other-race faces compared to own-race faces. Robertson et al. (2020) suggest that when recruiting SRs for their ability in certain roles, e.g. police and passport control, that not only should face tests include same race-faces, but they should also include other-race faces too, to ensure that SRs can also be highly accurate at recognising people outside of their ethnic group. I would further suggest that when recruiting SRs to do jobs that involve identifying people from different ethnic backgrounds that recruiters try and ensure they have ethnic diversity within their workforce, to reduce any own-race bias.

Another bias that has been found in the face recognition literature is the own-age bias, where people are better at recognising faces of individuals who belong to their own age group. Belanova et al. (2018) investigated the own-age bias by presenting a large group of SRs and control participants with face recognition tests employing adult faces and also infant faces (aged 4 and 6 months). Their findings revealed that SRs were more accurate at recognising both the adult and infant faces compared to control participants; however, SRs were more accurate when it came to making decisions for the adult faces as compared to the infant faces, and therefore demonstrated an own-age bias.

Bate et al. (2020) also investigated the own-age bias, but using a slightly different face processing task. They presented SRs and control participants with a simultaneous face matching task where participants have to decide if two faces were the same person or two different people. Half of the face pairs were adults and the other half were children (aged between 1–5 years of age). They found that the SRs were very accurate on the task, often more so than the control participants; however, they were more accurate at matching adult faces as compared to child faces, and therefore they demonstrated an own-age bias.

The studies described in the section replicate the general findings that SRs are more accurate than many people at recognising and matching faces. However, what the studies also reveal is that SRs are not immune to own-group biases, and they are less accurate with faces that they perceive as being outside of their group, such as those from a different race, or a different age group. This research shows SRs are not always 100% accurate, and do not necessarily process faces in a qualitatively different way to other individuals and they can be vulnerable to making mistakes. With that in mind, as SRs do demonstrate more accurate face processing skills than the general population, they have been recruited to take on roles that will benefit from their enhanced abilities.

Employing super recognition skills in the field

Super recognisers' skills have the potential to be employed in a number of different fields, to make society a fairer and safer place by preventing wrongful convictions, identity fraud and terrorist events (Ramon et al., 2019). Super recognisers' abilities have mainly been utilised in security checking and law enforcement. Several police forces in the UK now employ super recognisers for a variety tasks, such as the Metropolitan (Met), City of London, Jersey and West Midlands Thames Valley Police force. For example, Thames Valley have employed super recognisers to identify known sex offenders in public spaces, by emailing photographs to super recognisers to see if they can identify the sex offenders outside of nightclubs (Mitchell, 2023). The Met have also employed super recognisers to identify people from CCTV who have committed various crimes caught on video footage (Potts, 2015), including creating a specialist team of super recognisers to identify suspects caught on CCTV during the 2011 London riots (Murugesu, 2020). Psychological researchers have also investigated the accuracy of SRs who have been employed by police forces. Before exploring this research there are two examples of SRs who have been employed for their extraordinary abilities (see box).

Real-life super recognisers

Andy Pope (nicknamed the 'memory cop') is a super recogniser who has been employed at West Midlands Police as a Police Community Support Officer (PCSO). In 2018 Pope received the Chief Constable's Award for having identified 1,000 criminal suspects between 2012 and 2017. Some of the suspects were identified through watching CCTV footage and connecting it to mugshots, and at other times he identified people while travelling on public transport in Birmingham (Moshakis, 2018). By 2020 Andy had identified more than 2,000 suspects and every time he begins his shift he looks through images of people that the police are looking for; his record is 17 identifications in one day (BBC News, 2020). Although many of the identifications have led to arrests, convictions and prison sentences, it would be interesting to know how many false positives Andy Pope made, that is how many people he identified who were later found to be innocent and not the person he claimed they were.

Another SR who was employed for her special abilities was Louise Bruder, who discovered she was an SR after completing an online test one evening. After completing several more tests to confirm her SR status she was offered a new career at a company that is involved in digital identity verification and now trains people to spot identity fraud (Luckie, 2023)

The section above describes two examples of individuals who have been employed for their special ability to identify faces, and there are many other SRs who have been recruited by the police for those specific abilities. Davis et al. (2016) investigated the abilities of 36 individuals who were police staff and had been identified as SRs versus control participants by administering a battery of face identification tests involving memory and face matching. They found that, overall, SRs were more accurate than control participants across the tasks; however, there were large variations in the performance across the tests, with some being more accurate on some tests as compared to other tests. Their findings suggest that the SRs were not a homogeneous group that had a better ability on all the tests. Robertson et al. (2016) conducted a similar study with four SRs who worked for the Metropolitan Police (London), and they were found to outperform police trainees on three tests of face recognition, for familiar and unfamiliar faces. However, there were some members of the control group who performed at levels equal to and in some cases better than the SRs. They point out that it's important to note that SRs' performance is not perfect and that not one individual was 100% accurate on all the face recognition tasks.

Research by Mayer and Ramon (2023) investigated whether SRs who had been identified through face recognition tests in the lab might have transferable abilities when employed in the field using authentic forensic materials that are used to identify criminals. They compared the performance of a group of SRs, who had already classified from previous research (Ramon, 2021), and control participants all of whom viewed videos from CCTV footage and police lineups provided by Cantonal Police. The CCTV footage was of real crimes, two bank robberies, one jewellery robbery and a pick pocketer at an ATM. None of the films depicted physical harm, although the perpetrators did have guns in the bank robberies. They found the SRs were more accurate at identifying perpetrators from the lineups as compared to the control participants and some SRs were more consistent in their performance as compared to control participants. One criticism of this study is that all the lineups they employed were target present and therefore there were no instances where the correct decision was to say that the suspect was not in the lineup, which is the case if an innocent person has been erroneously placed into a lineup. It would be interesting to see if SRs also can make correct rejection of lineups when there is no one guilty present.

Dunn et al. (2023) set up a project to recruit SRs to a specialist unit in a large police force in Australia. To select candidates to join the unit they administered different screening tests, the CFMT +, the GFMT and the UNSW Face Test, to 1600 police officers and found that 38 met the criteria of being super recognisers

They then administered several further tests to those who were classified as SRs and found that although on average they performed more accurately as compared to control participants, none achieved perfect accuracy and there were individual differences between the SRs on matching and recognition tests. SRs were also found to be more accurate at recognising bodies where the face was not visible. Another interesting finding was that SRs were not any more accurate at recalling which visual scenes presented previously with a face; that is they did not remember the context in which they first saw the face. If you remember, back in Chapter 2 I described a phenomenon called the 'butcher on the bus', whereby faces can appear to be familiar but the context in which the face is known is not recalled. Not remembering the context of a face has implications, for misidentifications, as an individual may appear to be familiar, not because they have been seen to commit a crime, but for some other reason. Although SRs are more accurate than the average person at correctly recognising previously seen faces, they may not necessarily be immune from making mistaken identifications.

When it comes to recruiting SRs in specific roles for their abilities, some researchers have been more enthusiastic about SRs being employed at border control and in other security and law enforcement settings (Bobak et al., 2016b; Davis & Robertson, 2020). Other researchers have been cautious to recommend the use of SRs that have been classified via lab-based tests being employed in law enforcement roles, as they may not transfer to the real-life identification skills (Ramon, 2021; Ramon et al., 2019). Bate et al. (2019b) suggest that many of the tests used to recruit SRs do not represent real world face identification tasks; for example lab-based tests often use high quality images of faces where the hair has been removed, rather than images showing natural variation. Furthermore, the Forensic Science Regulator does not consider super recognisers' employment by police units to investigate CCTV images to be a forensic science, as there is no guarantee of impartiality. It's been suggested that SRs employed by the police may have cognitive bias, as they study known offenders and suspects prior to watching the CCTV footage and are primed to make an identification even if the suspects or offenders are not present (Edmond & Wortley, 2023).

Conclusion

Research investigating super recognisers' abilities is still relatively new and there has been far less research in this area as compared to other topics in face recognition (Ramon, 2021). There is still no unified definition of what a super recogniser is, and they do not appear to be a homogeneous group, with some individuals being better at recognition and others at face matching, and some are more accurate overall than others. Much of the early research investigating super recognisers' abilities was based on using only one or two tests for classification and many of the tests were not designed to classify extraordinary face processing abilities. Face recognition tests used to classify super recognisers have also been criticised for the lack of variability in the images and often only having target present trials, which might mean that super recognisers are more biased to choose rather than say a person is not there, and this has implications for misidentifications. Another issue that has implications for potential misidentifications is that although super recognisers are very good at recognising faces, they do not always remember the context in which they have seen a face, so could mistakenly think a familiar innocent person is the perpetrator of a crime (Dunn et al., 2023).

Most of the research investigating super recognisers' abilities appears to demonstrate that they do not process faces differently to other individuals (Noyes et al., 2017), although they may look at the nose area of the face more than control participants (Bobak et al., 2017). Furthermore super recognisers also fall prey to own-group biases and are more accurate with faces from the same age (Belanova et al., 2018; Bate et al., 2020) and racial group (Bate et al., 2019a; Robertson et al., 2020), again lending more evidence that they do not process faces in a qualitatively different way from the general population.

Super recognisers' extraordinary abilities have the potential to contribute to a variety of different security and forensic jobs, such as passport control and forensic facial examiners. Screening for jobs requiring super recogniser skills should use tasks that will represent what the role will involve, e.g. looking at CCTV footage, or matching pairs of faces. Mayer and Ramon (2023) and Dunn et al. (2023) have started to investigate how super recognisers can be employed in the workplace; however, caution should still be exercised as super recognisers are not always 100% accurate.

References

Adcock, B. (2022). 'I'd keep it on the down low': the secret life of a super-recogniser. *The Guardian*, January 15. www.theguardian.com/society/2022/jan/16/id-keep-it-on-the-down-low-the-secret-life-of-a-super-recogniser.

Bate, S., Bennetts, R., Hasshim, N., Portch, E., Murray, E., Burns, E., & Dudfield, G. (2019a). The limits of super recognition: An other-ethnicity effect in individuals with extraordinary face recognition skills. *Journal of Experimental Psychology: Human Perception and Performance*, 45(3), 363–377. https://doi.org/10.1037/xhp0000607.

Bate, S., Bennetts, R., Murray, E., & Portch, E. (2020). Enhanced matching of children's faces in 'super-recognisers' but not high-contact controls. *I-Perception*, 11(4). https://doi.org/10.1177/2041669520944420.

Bate, S., Frowd, C., Bennetts, R., Hasshim, N., Murray, E., Bobak, A. K., Wills, H., & Richards, S. (2018). Applied screening tests for the detection of superior face recognition. *Cognitive Research: Principles and Implications*, 3(1). https://doi.org/10.1186/s41235-018-0116-5.

Bate, S., Portch, E., & Mestry, N. (2021). When two fields collide: Identifying 'super-recognisers' for neuropsychological and forensic face recognition research. *Quarterly Journal of Experimental Psychology*, 74(12), 2154–2164. https://doi.org/10.1177/17470218211027695.

Bate, S., Portch, E., Mestry, N., & Bennetts, R. J. (2019b). Redefining super recognition in the real world: Skilled face or person identity recognizers? *British Journal of Psychology*, 110(3), 480–482. https://doi.org/10.1111/bjop.12392.

BBC News. (2020). Birmingham 'memory cop' Andy Pope spots 2,000 suspects. www.bbc.co.uk/news/uk-england-birmingham-55458847.

Belanova, E., Davis, J. P., & Thompson, T. (2018). Cognitive and neural markers of super-recognisers' face processing superiority and enhanced cross-age effect. *Cortex*, 108, 92–111. https://doi.org/10.1016/j.cortex.2018.07.008.

Bennetts, R. J., Mole, J., & Bate, S. (2017). Super-recognition in development: A case study of an adolescent with extraordinary face recognition skills. *Cognitive Neuropsychology*, 34(6), 357–376. https://doi.org/10.1080/02643294.2017.1402755.

Bobak, A. K., Bennetts, R. J., Parris, B. A., Jansari, A., & Bate, S. (2016a). An in-depth cognitive examination of individuals with superior face

recognition skills. *Cortex*, 82(May), 48–62. https://doi.org/10.1016/j.
cortex.2016.05.003.

Bobak, A. K., Dowsett, A. J., & Bate, S. (2016b). Solving the border control problem: Evidence of enhanced face matching in individuals with
extraordinary face recognition skills. *PLoS ONE*, 11(2), e0148148.

Bobak, A. K., Pampoulov, P., & Bate, S. (2016c). Detecting superior face
recognition skills in a large sample of young British adults. *Frontiers in Psychology*, 7(September), 1–11. https://doi.org/10.3389/fpsyg.2016.01378.

Bobak, A. K., Hancock, P. J., & Bate, S. (2016d). Super-recognisers in
action: Evidence from face-matching and face memory tasks. *Applied
Cognitive Psychology*, 30(1), 81–91.

Bobak, A. K., Parris, B. A., Gregory, N. J., Bennetts, R. J., & Bate, S.
(2017). Eye-movement strategies in developmental prosopagnosia and
'super' face recognition. *Quarterly Journal of Experimental Psychology*,
70(2), 201–217. https://doi.org/10.1080/17470218.2016.1161059.

Burton, A. M., White, D., & McNeill, A. (2010). The Glasgow face
matching test. *Behavior Research Methods*, 42(1), 286–291. https://
doi.org/10.3758/BRM.42.1.286.

Davis, J. P., Lander, K., Evans, R., & Jansari, A. (2016). Investigating predictors of superior face recognition ability in police super-recognisers.
Applied Cognitive Psychology, 30(6), 827–840. https://doi.org/10.1002/a
cp.3260.

Davis, J. P., & Robertson, D. J. (2020). Capitalizing on the super-
recognition advantage: A powerful, but underutilized, tool for policing and national security agencies. https://hdiac.org/articles/capita
lizing-on-the-super-recognition-advantage-a-power
ful-but-underutilized-tool-for-policing-and-national-security-agencies.

de Haas, B. (2022). What's a super-recogniser? *Neuropsychologia*, 166(February), 107805. https://doi.org/10.1016/j.neuropsychologia.2021.107805.

Duchaine, B., & Nakayama, K. (2006). The Cambridge Face Memory
Test: Results for neurologically intact individuals and an investigation
of its validity using inverted face stimuli and prosopagnosic participants. *Neuropsychologia*, 44(4), 576–585. https://doi.org/10.1016/j.
neuropsychologia.2005.07.001.

Duchaine, B., Germine, L., & Nakayama, K. (2007). Family resemblance:
Ten family members with prosopagnosia and within-class object
agnosia. *Cognitive Neuropsychology*, 24(4), 419–430. https://doi.org/
10.1080/02643290701380491.

Dunn, J. D., Summersby, S., Towler, A., Davis, J. P., & White, D. (2020).
UNSW Face Test: A screening tool for super-recognizers. *PLoS ONE*, 15
(11 November), 1–19. https://doi.org/10.1371/journal.pone.0241747.

Dunn, J. D., Towler, A., Kemp, R. I., & White, D. (2023). Selecting police super-recognisers. *PLoS ONE*, 18(5), e0283682. https://doi.org/10.1371/journal.pone.0283682.

Edmond, G., & Wortley, N. (2023). Images, investigators, identification, Code D and the Court of Appeal. *The Journal of Criminal Law*, 88(2).

Growns, B., Dunn, J. D., Mattijssen, E. J. A. T., Quigley-McBride, A., & Towler, A. (2022). Match me if you can: Evidence for a domain-general visual comparison ability. *Psychonomic Bulletin and Review*, 29 (3), 866–881. https://doi.org/10.3758/s13423-021-02044-2.

Hahn, C. A., Tang, L. L., Yates, A. N., & Phillips, P. J. (2022). Forensic facial examiners versus super-recognizers: Evaluating behavior beyond accuracy. *Applied Cognitive Psychology*, 36(6), 1209–1218. https://doi.org/10.1002/acp.4003.

Hammond, C. (2010). Super recognisers. www.bbc.co.uk/sounds/play/b00q3fbv.

Hawthorn, A. (2023). How to tell if you're a super-recognizer. www.psychologytoday.com/gb/blog/the-sensory-revolution/202301/how-to-tell-if-youre-a-super-recognizer.

Jenkins, R. E., Tsermentseli, S., Monks, C. P., Robertson, D. J., Stevenage, S. V., Symons, A. E., & Davis, J. P. (2021). Are super-face-recognisers also super-voice-recognisers? Evidence from cross-modal identification tasks. *Applied Cognitive Psychology*, 35(3), 590–605. https://doi.org/10.1002/acp.3813.

Jones, A. (2015). Meet the 'super recognisers'. www.bbc.co.uk/programmes/p035txs3.

Lee, Y., Duchaine, B., Wilson, H. R., & Nakayama, K. (2010). Three cases of developmental prosopagnosia from one family: Detailed neuropsychological and psychophysical investigation of face processing. *Cortex*, 46(8), 949–964. https://doi.org/10.1016/j.cortex.2009.07.012.

Luckie, S. (2023). A day in the life of a super recogniser at digital identity firm Yoti. https://wearetechwomen.com/a-day-in-the-life-of-a-super-recogniser-at-digital-identity-firm-yoti/.

Mayer, M., & Ramon, M. (2023). Improving forensic perpetrator identification with Super-Recognizers. *Proceedings of the National Academy of Sciences of the United States of America*, 120(20), 1–8. https://doi.org/10.1073/pnas.2220580120.

McKone, E., Stokes, S., Liu, J., Cohan, S., Fiorentini, C., Pidcock, M., Yovel, G., Broughton, M., & Pelleg, M. (2012). A robust method of measuring other-race and other-ethnicity effects: The Cambridge Face Memory Test format. *PLoS ONE*, 7(10). https://doi.org/10.1371/journal.pone.0047956.

Mitchell, N. (2023). Thames Valley Police: 'Super-recognisers' used to patrol for sex offenders. www.bbc.co.uk/news/uk-england-oxfordshire -66609161.

Moreton, R., Pike, G., & Havard, C. (2019). A task- and role-based perspective on super-recognizers: Commentary on 'Super-recognizers: From the lab to the world and back again'. *British Journal of Psychology*, 110(3), 486–488. https://doi.org/10.1111/bjop.12394.

Moshakis, A. (2018). Super recognisers: the people who never forget a face. *The Guardian*, 11 November. www.theguardian.com/uk-news/2018/ nov/11/super-recognisers-police-the-people-who-never-forget-a-face.

Murray, E., Bennetts, R., Tree, J., & Bate, S. (2022). An update of the Benton Facial Recognition Test. *Behavior Research Methods*, 54(5), 2318–2333. https://doi.org/10.3758/s13428-021-01727-x.

Murugesu, J. A. (2020). Some people are exceptionally good at recognising voices. *New Scientist*, 22 January. https://institu tions-newscientist-com.libezproxy.open.ac.uk/article/2230836-som e-people-are-exceptionally-good-at-recognising-voices/.

Noyes, E., Phillips, P. J., & O'Toole, A. J. (2017). What is a super-recogniser? In M. Bindemann & A. M. Megreya (eds), *Face processing: Systems, disorders and cultural differences* (pp. 173–201). Nova Science Publishing.

Phillips, P. J., Yates, A. N., Hu, Y., Hahn, C. A., Noyes, E., Jackson, K., Cavazos, J. G., Jeckeln, G., Ranjan, R., Sankaranarayanan, S., Chen, J. C., Castillo, C. D., Chellappa, R., White, D., & O'Toole, A. J. (2018). Face recognition accuracy of forensic examiners, superrecognizers, and face recognition algorithms. *Proceedings of the National Academy of Sciences of the United States of America*, 115(24), 6171–6176. https://doi.org/10.1073/pnas.1721355115.

Potts, L. (2015). The police 'super-recognisers' putting names to faces. www.bbc.co.uk/news/uk-england-34544199.

Ramon, M. (2021). Super-recognizers – a novel diagnostic framework, 70 cases, and guidelines for future work. *Neuropsychologia*, 158, 107809. https://doi.org/10.1016/j.neuropsychologia.2021.107809.

Ramon, M., Bobak, A. K., & White, D. (2019). Super-recognizers: From the lab to the world and back again. *British Journal of Psychology*, 110 (3), 461–479. https://doi.org/10.1111/bjop.12368.

Robertson, D. J., Black, J., Chamberlain, B., Megreya, A. M., & Davis, J. P. (2020). Super-Recognisers show an advantage for other race face identification. *Applied Cognitive Psychology*, 34(1), 205–216. https:// doi.org/10.1002/acp.3608.

Robertson, D. J., Noyes, E., Dowsett, A. J., Jenkins, R., & Burton, A. M. (2016). Face recognition by Metropolitan Police super-recognisers *PLoS ONE*, 11(2), 1–8. https://doi.org/10.1371/journal.pone.0150036.

Russell, R., Duchaine, B., & Nakayama, K. (2009). Super-recognizers: People with extraordinary face recognition ability. *Psychonomic Bulletin and Review*, 16(2), 252–257. https://doi.org/10.3758/PBR.16.2.252.

Sheridan, J. (2017). The super recogniser. www.imdb.com/title/tt7143362/.

Towler, A., Dunn, J. D., Castro Martínez, S., Moreton, R., Eklöf, F., Ruifrok, A., Kemp, R. I., & White, D. (2023). Diverse types of expertise in facial recognition. *Scientific Reports*, 13(1), 1–16. https://doi.org/10.1038/s41598-023-28632-x.

White, D., Guilbert, D., Varela, V. P. L., Jenkins, R., & Burton, A. M. (2022). GFMT2: A psychometric measure of face matching ability. https://link.springer.com/content/pdf/10.3758/s13428-021-01638-x.pdf.

12 The future of face recognition research

Introduction

When writing any piece of text about the future possible direction of scientific research the aim is to predict the future; however, anything written in hard copy can become out of date very quickly. With that in mind I still thought it was noteworthy to write a chapter on the possible future of face recognition research; nevertheless it could be that by the time you are reading this chapter some of the predicted areas of face recognition research may have already occurred, or changed in unanticipated directions.

In this chapter I will explore some of the research that has investigated methods to improve face recognition accuracy which should help prevent face recognition from 'going wrong' more frequently in the future. The chapter will begin by looking at issues that I predict will focus heavily in the future, such as the increase in deepfake technology and AI imposters and how these might influence when face recognition goes wrong. To gain a wider view of the possible directions of future of face recognition research I have also asked a selection of world-leading researchers what they predict to be future developments in face recognition research and what questions still remain unanswered. To begin, I will revisit face recognition technology, as this will certainly feature heavily in the future of face recognition research.

DOI: 10.4324/9781003177128-12

The future of face recognition technology

Face recognition technology (FRT) is one of the most significant technological advancements of the twenty-first century (Qinjun et al., 2023) and one of the most active areas in computer vision research (Adjabi et al., 2020). FRT has seen great improvements over the last few years with the advance of deep convolutional neural networks (DCNNs) (O'Toole & Castillo, 2021) and can now make decisions as accurately as humans in many situations (Li et al., 2020). FRT has become an integral part of our lives; many people use their face to unlock their phone, computer, and for banking transactions in a banking app. FRT can also be used by drivers to set up specific profiles in their cars, so they can pair their mobile phone to their car and even to open the door without a key (Dron, 2023). FRT provides the means for a person's face to be used for contactless in-person payments, much in the same way as Google Pay and Apple Pay are currently utilised (Lim & Cheah, 2023). In the future, FRT is likely to become even more widespread with the possible implementation of FRT at border control, which might replace the need to present passports, as travellers' faces could be matched with information stored in a central database (Rawlinson, 2024). Does this mean in the future our face will be able to replace items that we might need to carry, e.g. keys, key cards, bank cards or passports? This might sound like a great idea in principle, but what happens when that technology goes wrong or the automatic face recognition (AFR) software crashes? In 2023, the Tesla app that was used by many car owners to open and drive their cars crashed across Europe, leaving many car owners unable to unlock their cars, or check if their battery needed to be charged (Teejay, 2023). Although the software was only non-functional for six hours it did lead to many frustrated drivers. Imagine if you were coming off a plane after a long-haul flight and the border control AFR software is down, and you did not take your passport as you did not think you needed it, or you are buying your groceries in a supermarket and the contactless AFR payment system isn't working and doesn't recognise your face. I personally would not want to rely on using my face in these circumstances and would try to ensure that I had the backup up of identification documents.

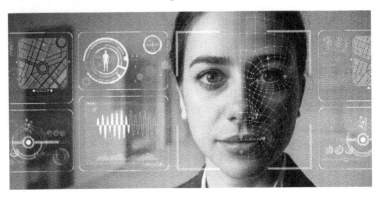

Figure 12.1 Face recognition technology may be used more widely in the future.

Although FRT has some exciting prospects for technological advancements and is considerably faster than humans at examining multiple images, mistakes can still be made, often with serious consequences, and so human oversight is often still needed. Furthermore, in many AFR systems the algorithm examining the face images, doesn't always come up with a 100% match of an identity and therefore a human decision is needed, for example to decide if a match of 80% is an appropriate cutoff to follow up a case. When it comes to including the input from a human operator, their decisions can be biased by contextual information, e.g. an algorithm prediction, which can lead to inaccurate decisions (Fysh & Bindemann, 2018; Howard et al., 2020). Furthermore, there are also large individual differences between humans' ability to match and recognise faces (Fysh, 2018), so future research will need to explore how humans and algorithms can work together effectively.

Hopefully future face recognition research will continue to explore methods to reduce errors and make face recognition more accurate. One method to improve face identification by humans is when people collaborate and work together to make decisions, using the wisdom of the crowd technique (Jeckeln et al., 2018; White et al., 2013). White et al. (2013) found that when responses to a face matching task were aggregated into groups of four they were more accurate than individuals, and in groups of 32 the performance was nearly 100%, while Jeckeln et al. (2018) found that when participants worked in pairs their decisions were more accurate on a face matching task as compared to working alone. Using the wisdom of the crowd technique has also been found to be beneficial when it comes to identifying other-race faces and studies have found that pairs of individuals who were different races (Asian and Caucasian) were more accurate when working together to identify own-race and other-race faces as compared to working independently (Cavazos et al., 2023). It seems that working collaboratively in pairs, groups or even aggregating decisions across several individuals is one method to help prevent face recognition from going wrong, and therefore a noteworthy area for future research. Another method is to employ humans who already have an extraordinary ability to recognise faces (e.g. super recognisers) and then provide them with additional training (Jenkins, 2022).

An alternative method to increase accuracy in face identification is to fuse responses from AFR algorithms and humans together, as this has been found to reduce errors (O'Toole et al., 2007; Phillips et al., 2018). This technique is quite different to a human making a final decision from an output from an algorithm as the decisions are aggregated. The most accurate decisions were obtained by fusing the responses from high ability humans with high-performing algorithms (Phillips et al., 2018) and therefore this certainly has merit for further research in the future. The technique of combining human and algorithms is also predicted to occur more frequently in other areas of research such as consumer behaviour (Mellers et al., 2023).

Research predicts that in the future FRT should continue to improve in accuracy with the increased development of convoluted neural networks (CNNs), and the wider use of diverse training sets (e.g. faces from different backgrounds) should reduce gender and race biases. However, in response to the increase in the widespread use of FRT it is likely that regulations and clear guideline will need to be developed for data handling and storing (Qinjun et al., 2023). Furthermore, the more personal information including biometric information that is collected and stored about all of us from different organisations, increases the risk of our data being stolen by those with nefarious designs. From 2013 to 2023 the total number of recorded data breaches tripled, and these figures are increasing every year, with organisations that store sensitive information such as governments being specifically targeted (Madnick, 2023). Another issue related to the stealing of biometric data including facial images, is what people can do with those images without gaining consent to use them, such as creating deep fake videos.

Deepfake and AI imposters

Deepfake technology is a form of artificial intelligence used to manipulate and generate images and audio content that can be used for various purposes. One of the most common uses of deep fake technology is to digitally alter, or swap the faces from the image of one person to another, and it can also be used to create audio, such as imitating a person's voice. Deep fake technology has become increasingly widespread through the use of easily downloadable apps for mobile phones and software for computers. Unfortunately, some of the individuals who have utilised deep fake technology have done so with malicious intent, such as creating blackmail materials, and/or deepfake pornography, where a person's face is placed on other persons bodies without their consent. In 2023, the UK laws were changed so that it will be easier to prosecute those who have created these types of materials (McCallum, 2023). There are also some positive creations from deepfake technology for entertainment purposes, such as Luke Skywalker's guest appearance on an episode of *The Mandalorian* TV show, and Harrison Ford's younger self in the fifth Indiana Jones movie. Deepfake technology has also been used to create virtual concerts such as the ABBA voyage which depicts the band as avatars as they looked in 1979. Deepfake versions of Tom Cruise and Keanu Reeves have gone viral on TikTok; however, deepfake has the potential to be used to spread misinformation and propaganda.

Deepfake use in politics and war is also increasing. In 2022 deepfake videos were used in the Russian–Ukrainian war. A deepfake video of President Putin was posted online with him declaring peace and also another video of President Zelensky telling Ukrainians to put down their weapons; neither of the

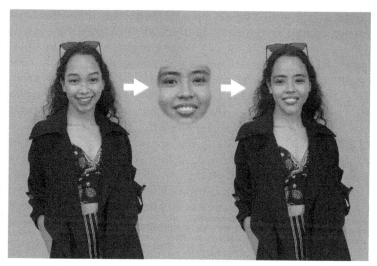

Figure 12.2 Deepfakes often involve face swapping.

videos were very convincing and both were declared as fake (Wakefield, 2022). The videos were removed quickly from social media as it was clear they were violating misinformation policies; however, it's unclear how many people may have seen the videos before their removal. Deepfake videos have also been used in the US presidential elections (Hurst, 2023) and to create fake images of former President Trump being chased by police and arrested (Devlin & Cheetham, 2023). In the UK, both Tory leader Rishi Sunak (Quinn, 2024) and Labour leader Keir Starmer have been victims of deep fake videos (Bristow, 2023). The use of deepfake videos in government elections is likely to increase as they become part of the political propaganda and as another means to spread misinformation (Cohen, 2023). It's also been predicted there will be an increase in the use of deepfake videos for a variety of other illegal activities, such as identity fraud, manipulation of video evidence for criminal investigations, non-consensual pornography, extortion and online harassment (Europol, 2022); it's therefore paramount that deepfake content can be detected.

When it comes to detecting deepfake technology, this is an area that has seen a large rise in research, especially when it comes to automatic face recognition, and some algorithms have been specifically designed to try and spot deepfake videos (Heidari et al., 2023). In 2019, the Deepfake Detection Challenge (DFDC), a global competition, was created to help spur researchers around the world to develop algorithms to detect deepfake videos from the DFDC database of videos (Dolhansky et al., 2020). The competition attracted over 2000 teams from academia and industry, who submitted 35,000 algorithms to try to detect which videos were deepfake and which had not been altered. The most accurate algorithm was able to determine which videos were real or deepfake 65% of the time (Groh et al., 2022), so 35 % of the time even the most accurate algorithm got it wrong and either said a deep fake video was real or vice versa. However, is this any better than humans would perform trying to determine whether a video is a deepfake or not?

Groh et al. (2022) investigated whether humans were more accurate than the leading algorithm at detecting deepfake videos over a series of experiments, using the same materials from the DFDC. In the first experiment participants viewed pairs of videos, and had to decide which one was real and which was the deepfake. They found that 82% of participants were more accurate than the leading algorithm from the DFDC. In the second experiment participants were presented with individual videos and had to respond on a scale ranging from '100% confidence this is not a DeepFake' to '100% confidence this is a DeepFake'. On this task humans performed comparably on overall accuracy with the leading algorithm from the DFDC. There were some differences in decisions, as humans appeared to be less accurate at identifying deepfake videos as compared to real videos; however, when an additional set of videos that included political figures (e.g. Vladimir Putin and Kim Jong Un) were viewed, humans outperformed the algorithm. Their findings demonstrate that semantic knowledge humans hold about real-life people can be beneficial in determining whether a video is real or a deepfake. For example if a famous person depicted in the deepfake is behaving in a way that is unusual for their character, such as Vladimir Putin DJing at a rave, most humans would realise this is fake, but perhaps not all machines! However, the algorithm was more accurate when the video quality was poorer, such as blurry grainy or dark, suggesting it was using visual qualities that humans ignore or cannot perceive. When humans' responses were averaged for each video using the wisdom of the crowd technique, the accuracy for detecting deepfakes was increased. After responding, participants were told the likelihood that the video they had just viewed was a deepfake and were given the opportunity to update their response and this also increased the accuracy of deepfake detection. The study by Groh et al. (2022) demonstrated that humans are not as inaccurate at detecting deepfake videos as first thought, although employing the wisdom of the crowd method and human and algorithm collaboration can increase deepfake detection accuracy.

Another issue that is likely to increase in the future is the use of AI-generated faces that look like real-life people. AI-generated faces are now widely available, and anyone can go online and generate faces using certain websites, and many of the faces are very convincing. Using AI-generated faces has several potential benefits, such as creating realistic foils for police lineups so that a suspect does not stand out in any way. However, they could also be used for malicious intent, on dating websites, or internet scams using fake identities. Research investigating whether people could tell the difference between real faces and AI-created faces found that the AI faces were more likely to be judged as real than those that were actually real-life faces (Miller et al., 2023). On average people labelled the AI-generated faces as human two thirds of the time, and those who were worse at identifying AI faces were more confident in their answers. Researchers have suggested that due to people's poor ability to detect AI-generated faces this means people might be more susceptible to cyber criminals masquerading behind AI identities (Dawel et al., 2023). They have suggested that people need to be aware of their own failings when it comes to detecting AI-generated faces and take additional steps for verification.

There are several benefits that could be gained from using AI-generated faces if they are authentic-looking and indistinguishable from photographs of real persons. They could be employed in police lineups as foils or filler members that resemble the suspect to make lineups fairer and less biased. They could also be used in future research investigating face recognition, as large databases of images of faces of different ages, and ethnicities could be created without the need to take photographs of real people, which can be costly and time consuming. So like many technological advances there are both benefits and potential downsides of the increased use of AI-generated faces.

Asking the experts

So far this chapter has covered topics that I think are going to be important for the future of face recognition research; however, there may be other topics that I have not thought of, so I asked some of the world's leading experts in face recognition for their thoughts. I emailed many researchers from around the globe, and asked them five different questions. Some replied via email, for others we had a chat on a video call and for one person we had a discussion while walking our dogs. I have not been able to include every single answer from every individual, so I have collated the responses in the rest of this chapter.

What do we still not understand about face recognition?

The first question I asked was 'What do we still not understand about face recognition?' and there were some similarities in people's answers. Several academics pointed out we still do not understand how humans recognise familiar faces, such as friends and family and how we learn faces, that is how do humans learn to recognise a face that was once unfamiliar which becomes a familiar face. Mike Burton wrote that 'the basic, fundamental question that drew me to the subject, "how do I recognise my friends?", remains unanswered and surprisingly little studied'.

Graham Hole came at the question from a slightly different, but very interesting perspective:

> In 1963, the ethologist Nico Tinbergen published a paper called 'On aims and methods of ethology' in which he outlined the four major problems in biology: 'What is it for?', 'How did it develop?', 'How did it evolve?' and 'How does it work?' Over the past forty years or so, in the context of face

recognition, I think these questions have been addressed to various degrees and with varying amounts of success.

'*What is it for?*' This is probably the easiest of these questions to answer! If we didn't already know, then studies of the social problems faced by people with prosopagnosia and other face processing disorders would give us a good idea of what face recognition is for.

'*How did it develop?*' This is one of the most intensively researched questions in the face processing literature. We now know quite a lot about the role of experience in the development of face recognition abilities, through the entire lifespan from infancy to old age.

'*How did it evolve?*' has received less attention, at least among psychologists, although comparative studies have shown us that face recognition is by no means confined to humans.

'*How does it work?*' is the question that the vast amount of face processing research has attempted to answer. However, I think we are a long way away from answering it and that's because we still lack a good understanding of the true nature of the 'primitives' for face recognition.

Our lack of understanding of how we recognise familiar faces and how we learn faces also links to another subject that emerged in the answers, and that is the lack in theoretical development since the Bruce and Young model of face recognition, which was developed nearly 40 years ago, and is still the most cited theory in face recognition literature. Both Colin Tredoux and Mike Burton noted there have been relatively few theoretical developments over the last few years, and Sarah Laurence also suggests that 'we need new theories to help the field move forward'. Graham Pike does have one possible explanation for why there has been such little theoretical advancement in face recognition research over the last few decades by suggesting 'understanding the theory of how we recognise faces might not be something that can be verbalised, and that similar to theoretical models in physics it may be understood numerically'. This is a really interesting point, and if this is the case, maybe explains why the theoretical models in Psychology have not developed further over the last few decades and implies that we need to look at this from a different perspective.

Another topic that many of the researchers mentioned is that we still do not know why some people are better at face recognition than others. For example, Reuben Moreton points out:

> We still don't understand individual differences and why they exist. In ten years or so, there's been such a focus on the extremes of the distribution that are two standard deviations above or below the mean, and it can help to research those extremes. But it's not like everyone else is performing in the same way, there's a huge spectrum and we don't really know why that is.

Romina Palermo also points out that 'we don't know what drives individual variation in face recognition ability. This is really the question of why some people are better than others.'

Some researchers also feel there are gaps in knowledge from a developmental perspective. For example Catherine Mondloch suggests:

> We need to pay more attention to how face learning and recognition develop during infancy … We still don't understand how faces are learned and recognised in daily life. We don't know what influences face learning in realistic situations (e.g., in classrooms, in neighbourhoods). These situations provide a rich context for learning, such as social information and motivation, but also lots of competing stimuli.

It seems there is still much we do not know about face recognition, especially when it comes to how we recognise people we know, how we learn faces 'in the wild' and outside a laboratory and why some people are better at it than others. Theory hasn't developed significantly over the last few decades, and this is an area that needs further advancement in the future. I was also interested in what the experts predicted were going to be the paramount areas of research, by asking the following question.

What do you think are the most important issues in the future of face recognition research?

There were several different topics that were thought to be important issues for the future of face recognition research, many of which were related to the first question, and there was also some consensus. Several of the researchers, such as Clare Sutherland, Colin Tredoux and Mike Burton, suggested that how humans learn faces remains an important topic for future research, and we still do not understand how faces become familiar. Sarah Laurence pointed out future research should investigate 'what processes people are using in real world settings – beyond the lab' and Catherine Mondloch concurred with this sentiment.

   Another topic that came up was the issue of individual differences and not only to try and investigate why people differ in their abilities to recognise faces, but to make this information more widely known to the public. For example, Reuben Moreton suggested that end users, such as jurors, or those assessing eyewitness evidence should be aware of the variability in individuals' ability to correctly identify faces. Especially as 'we already know that eyewitness testimony is fraught with risk and is one of the biggest contributors to miscarriages of justice'. Related to the issue of individual differences is face recognition disorders, such as prosopagnosia, and researchers such as Anna Bobak, Sarah Laurence and Romina Palermo suggest this is an important issue for the future of face recognition research. For example, Romina pointed out that 'people who struggle to recognise faces consistently want to know that it is not their fault (i.e., a personal or motivational failing) and how to improve their skills'. Future research should look at ways to help individuals who have face recognition disorders, and develop strategies to aid recognition.

   One topic that was often mentioned by researchers was the increased use of automatic face recognition (AFR) technology and artificial intelligence (AI). Graham Hole said:

> The applied aspects of face processing research are likely to become increasingly important. As AI face recognition

systems become increasingly used by the police and other authorities, it will become increasingly important to understand how they work; how they differ from how we work; and to educate the public (and the authorities) about these systems' limitations.

Reuben Moreton also pointed out the importance of not only AFT itself, but what it is used for and how it is regulated:

I think the other big issue is the proliferation and unregulated use of automated facial recognition algorithms, which is just a huge topic in its own right. And my big concern with that is that in 10–20 years time … along with forensic science and eyewitness testimony, the use of facial recognition algorithm will be up there as a key contributor to miscarriages of justice.

Romina Palermo also points out that when it comes to AI and AFR, 'We must remember that they can be fallible too'.

Several researchers pointed out that AFR systems doesn't tend to work in isolation and that it is important to research the interaction between humans and machines and making the most from these interactions. Eilidh Noyes said:

We need to understand how humans and machines can work together as an effective and reliable face recognition system. This will bring up several important questions, such as what will the role of the human be if face recognition algorithms are more accurate at face identification?

Another subject that was mentioned was the importance of developing neuropsychological models of face recognition. Colin Tredoux wrote, 'it seems undeniable that we will need a neural/brain account at some point'. Mike Burton pointed out:

Given the huge behavioural differences between familiar and unfamiliar face recognition, it is surprising that it has been hard to find a reliable neuroscientific marker for familiarity. Some recent EEG research looks more promising than the techniques applied so far.

This comes back to the issue of theoretical models of face recognition that still need to be developed in the future, and whether neuroimaging technology could help progress this area.

How do you envisage the future of face recognition developing over the next 10 years?

Another topic of interest was what the experts predicted the next ten years of face recognition research would look like. There was a divide in responses to this question, with some researchers being more optimistic about future research, while others predicted that research would go on in the same way as it has the last ten years. A few researchers suggested there would be wider collaborative research, such as Clare Sutherland saying, 'I envisage the future of face recognition involving more team effort: with multi-lab science we can achieve more than we can individually.' In a similar vein Anna Bobak said, 'I'm really hoping that we start to collaborate more, even in adversarial collaborations, and I hope that we all start taking a more holistic approach to face recognition … I think this might just progress the field.' In contrast Mike Burton suggests that 'I think it will go on the same as it has for the previous ten years – we will collect more and more isolated data points, and dodge the difficult theoretical questions. I don't see much appetite for theory.' Sarah Laurence had a similar answer: 'We need some new theories to help the field move forward.'

Several researchers predicted there would be an increase in AI technology and AFR research. Colin Tredoux took this approach:

> The new deep learning technologies will take over for a while, although I doubt that they will last. That is, we will attempt to understand face recognition in terms of convolutional and other varieties of neural network, but since these are 'black boxes' we will rediscover the point of departure of the 'cognitive revolution', who reacted to the 'black box' of behaviourism by arguing for a mental or internal set of causes, and we will similarly argue that the powerful black boxes of AI and deep learning do not tell us much about the mechanisms or processes of face recognition.

The issue of human and AI interactions was also seen as being a continuing area of future research. Eilidh Noyes wrote:

> I think that we will see an increase in algorithm accuracy and a need to develop a framework where we think about how humans and machines might work together. This will bring up big questions for cognitive psychologists and also for law enforcement in order to establish accurate and ethical working practice.

Reuben Moreton also said that the key 'is understanding human algorithm interaction and how they work together'. He talked about the cloud version of AFR algorithms such as Clearview AI, where any law enforcement, government or military personnel can go online and create an account. Reuben said 'If a member of the public had access to those tools, they could just start randomly searching for people and I think that it's just going to become part of everyday life.' He suggests the ARF would benefit from regulation and 'there's still a window of opportunity, to get on top of it, but I think that's diminishing more and more as the technology becomes more available and more widespread'.

Some researchers suggested the developmental and lifespan perspective would also continue to be explored. Clare Sutherland wrote:

> We also need longitudinal studies of face recognisers that start in early childhood and continue throughout the lifespan, to understand how and when we develop face recognition capacity and the diversity of individual differences in the development of this core ability.

Catherine Mondloch also suggests: 'We need to learn much more about the developmental roots of face recognition and how individual differences in early experience relate to later skills in identity matching and recognition.'

Other researchers predicted the increase in neurophysiological measurements to investigate face recognition. Romina Palermo wrote:

I also see growth in the use of EEG (given that these are becoming more cost effective, portable, and measures such as fast periodic visual stimulation [FPVS] can be obtained relatively quickly and without explicit questioning). Intracranial recordings in humans seem to be increasing too.

There were a variety of interesting predictions of future research that were most likely influenced by researchers' specialisms and expertise in specific areas of face recognition. I was also interested in whether the experts would have divergent thinking on what the big issues are that still need to be solved in relation to human and machine face recognition.

What do you think are the big issues we still need to solve to make face recognition more accurate in humans and machines?

In relation to humans, there was some agreement that individual humans' abilities to recognise faces could not be improved, regardless of training. Colin Tredoux wrote, 'Training seems to have little traction for human beings (although we may not have been thinking about this creatively enough.' Mike Burton had a similar sentiment:

> I think there is very little evidence that people can be trained to be better at (unfamiliar) face recognition. As you know, there are large individual differences, but I think these are resistant to training. If you're an organisation relying on human recognisers, select, don't train.

Reuben Moreton, who has previously been employed as a forensic examiner, also suggested that although forensic examiners can be trained to be more accurate:

> Identifying people who are naturally good, so preselection like in super recogniser research, that's one way to ensure that you're picking the right people for the job. I think that's an important point, you could say for making face recognition more accurate in humans is looking at what tasks you want people to do and make sure that they're well suited to those tasks.

In relation to making machines more accurate at face recognition, there was also an agreement that machines have the ability to be very accurate, with new DCNNs often outperforming humans when it comes to unfamiliar face recognition. However, there were still some concerns over AFR systems and their potential uses and the ethics involved. For example, when talking about AFR, Anna Bobak stated:

> I think the big issues are maybe not so much in face recognition, but ethics around the use of artificial intelligence. The algorithms are pretty accurate, but how they are used? I think they should be well-regulated and ethical. So this is a bigger issue than the accuracy when it comes to machines.

Colin Tredoux also wrote about the ethical issues involved in increasing the accuracy of face recognition: 'We need an ethics code, I think that is quite urgent for face recognition and face composite researchers.'

Clare Sutherland took a slightly different approach to AFR by describing the potential for bias:

> We need to look beyond accuracy in terms of sheer numbers or percent correct, and examine demographic differentials. An algorithm or human operator who is more accurate with faces from one group than another (for example, white faces compared to faces of other ethnicities; or male faces compared to female faces) is unfair, and our science, technology, and regulations need to address this unfairness.

Graham Hole also focused on the potential problems of AFR and whether it would be useful to understand how machines can recognise faces. He wrote:

> We need to understand the fundamental nature of human face representations. I'm undecided about how much a study of AI systems will inform us about how humans recognise faces – as with playing chess, computers are likely to use quite different methods from us. However we will need to know a lot about how the computer systems achieve

recognition, in order to be able to evaluate those systems sufficiently critically. Otherwise we run the risk of ending up in a situation where 'the computer says yes' and innocent people suffer miscarriages of justice because the legal system has unwarranted faith in the reliability of computer-based recognition systems – especially if those systems typically out-perform humans (which is likely to be the case given how poorly we recognise unfamiliar faces).

Most researchers agreed that when it came to trying to improve humans' accuracy at recognising faces, even training was unlikely to make any difference and that the best approach is to recruit individuals who already hold superior face recognition abilities. When it came to improving face recognition technology, many agreed that since the implementation of DCCNs, this was now very accurate and in some circumstances surpassed humans' ability. However the issue that needed consideration was reducing the bias of face recognition technology and ensuring it was employed ethically.

If money was no object what would you do to improve the field of face recognition research and to make face recognition more accurate?

My final question was a 'blue sky' question where I was hoping to see if researchers had any wildly creative ideas of how face recognition research could be improved if the constraints of budgets were removed. There was a clear division of two camps of thinking for this answer, with some researchers suggesting ways in which money could help improve the field, while others stated that it's not money, rather a drive to answer the difficult theoretical questions that need to be tackled.

Some researchers did not think having a limitless budget would necessarily answer the big questions in face recognition research that remain unanswered. Mike Burton wrote, 'I don't think money is the problem. I think there is an unwillingness to address the fundamental question – how we recognise the people we know.' Graham Hole also agreed with this sentiment by writing 'I don't think throwing money at the problem will help until we have a better idea of what it is we need to be asking.' Reuben Moreton also suggested that money would not necessarily solve the problems especially in relation to the use of AFR in applied settings:

> I don't know if it's money or like a time machine that you would probably want … If you could go back in time it would be to have some kind of regulatory framework around the use of this technology. Which does not necessarily make things more accurate that's not the problem … the problem for me is making it safe and reliable and ethical.

Several other experts took a different approach and suggested that large multidisciplinary teams of researchers would help advance the field of face recognition research. For example, Catherine Mondloch wrote:

> I would develop teams of researchers tasked with advancing theory based on classic and state-of-the-art findings. The teams would comprise of researchers representing diverse perspectives within the field of face recognition, but also researchers in other fields that I'm convinced would provide important insights (e.g., computer science, language perception, music perception, social psychology, developmental psychology). The aim would not be to collect more data, but to sift through what we already know and develop theory. The teams would be granted time to read outside of their area and to meet in-person for discussion and debate.

Anna Bobak also suggested, 'I would write a massive interdisciplinary grant not only with psychologists, but also with computing, economists who are experts in decision making and people, and it would be longitudinal.' Clare Sutherland stated, 'I would fund big lab science and build an ethical, free to use database of millions of face images which are representative of humans around the world', while Romina Palermo wrote:

> I would personally like to see more large-scale collaborations. I think we could do so much more working together but there are structural barriers in place that make it difficult to organise

and fund large teams. Maybe we wouldn't agree on which type of training or what the diagnostic cut-off should be or something else, but I imagine really large-scale training studies with different groups of participants in different countries etc. Online testing can help this happen. More difficult (but if money was no object!) would be trying to include some neuroimaging measures.

It is interesting that there were differences between these two types of thinking, with some researchers suggesting that money and multi-disciplinary projects could help progress research, while others suggested that theory rather than money needs to be a priority. Perhaps what would progress the field of face recognition is a combination of both ideas where multidisciplinary teams try to tackle the big theoretical questions of how we learn faces and recognise people we know.

Conclusion

This chapter has looked at issues I believe are going to be important in the future of face recognition research, such as the increase in automatic face recognition technology and human and machine cooperation to recognise faces and the dangers of deepfake technology and AI imposter faces. It is reassuring to know that some of these issues were also thought to be important by other world leading experts in face recognition research, and I would like to thank all of the experts for their thought-provoking answers.

When it comes to the big questions, it seems there are still many issues within face recognition research that we do not understand, such as why some people are better at recognising faces compared to others. In addition to understanding why some people have better face recognition abilities, we need to educate the public into the fallibility of face recognition from eyewitness identification and also from machines. As automatic face recognition (AFR) technology is likely to increase in the future, it should be unbiased and accurate for faces from diverse populations. Machine face recognition accuracy is only part of the issue and there are also the ethical concerns of not only how this technology is used, but also storing personal data (face images) of those captured by AFR systems that needs to be considered. Another issue for future research and practice is how humans and machines can work together effectively to prevent face recognition from going wrong.

What I learnt from talking to the world leading experts is we still do not understand how faces become familiar and how people are able to recognise individuals they know such as their friends, neighbours, work colleagues and family. Furthermore, psychology research has been shying away from the big theoretical questions and theory has not developed significantly in the last 40 years. These are areas that need to be investigated in the future of face recognition research.

This book has focused on when face recognition 'goes wrong', and the research cited in this book has explored some very plausible explanations for when faces are not recognised and when people are mistakenly identified as being another person. It seems that one of the big questions that remains unanswered is why face recognition 'goes right', and how humans can correctly recognise faces of individuals they know. It is essential that the future of face recognition research tackles this question.

References

Adjabi, I., Ouahabi, A., Benzaoui, A., & Taleb-Ahmed, A. (2020). Past, present, and future of face recognition: A review. *Electronics (Switzerland)*, 9(8), 1–53. https://doi.org/10.3390/electronics9081188.

Bristow, T. (2023). Keir Starmer suffers UK politics' first deepfake moment. It won't be the last. www.politico.eu/article/uk-keir-starmer-labour-party-deepfake-ai-politics-elections/.

Cavazos, J. G., Jeckeln, G., & O'Toole, A. J. (2023). Collaboration to improve cross-race face identification: Wisdom of the multi-racial crowd? *British Journal of Psychology*, 114(4), 838–853. https://doi.org/10.1111/bjop.12657.

Cohen, B. (2023). How the rise of deepfakes will impact the 2024 presidential elections. www.infosecurity-magazine.com/opinions/deepfakes-impact-presidential/.

Dawel, A., Stewart, B. A., Sutherland, C., Krumhuber, E., & Witkower, Z. (2023). Can you spot the AI impostors? We found AI faces can look more real than actual humans. https://theconversation.com/can-you-spot-the-a

i-impostors-we-found-ai-faces-can-look-more-real-than-actual-humans-21
5160.

Devlin, K., & Cheetham, J. (2023). Fake Trump arrest photos: How to spot an AI-generated image. www.bbc.co.uk/news/world-us-canada
-65069316.

Dolhansky, B., Bitton, J., Pflaum, B., Lu, J., Howes, R., Wang, M., & Ferrer, C. C. (2020). The DeepFake Detection Challenge (DFDC) dataset. https://ai.facebook.com/datasets/dfdc.

Dron, W. (2023). Genesis opens door to keyless car entry via face recognition. *The Sunday Times*, 28 March. www.driving.co.uk/news/
technology/genesis-face-recognition-unlock-gv60/.

Europol. (2022). Facing reality? Law enforcement and the challenge of deepfakes. www.europol.europa.eu/publications-events/publications/
facing-reality-law-enforcement-and-challenge-of-deepfakes.

Fysh, M. C. (2018). Individual differences in the detection, matching and memory of faces. *Cognitive Research Principles*, 3(20), 1–12.

Fysh, M. C., & Bindemann, M. (2018). Human–computer interaction in face matching. *Cognitive Science*, 42(5), 1714–1732. https://doi.org/
10.1111/cogs.12633.

Groh, M., Epstein, Z., Firestone, C., & Picard, R. (2022). Deepfake detection by human crowds, machines, and machine-informed crowds. *Proceedings of the National Academy of Sciences of the United States of America*, 119(1). https://doi.org/10.1073/pnas.2110013119.

Heidari, A., Navimipour, N. J., Dag, H., & Unal, M. (2023). Deepfake detection using deep learning methods: A systematic and comprehensive review. https://doi.org/10.1002/widm.1520.

Howard, J. J., Rabbitt, L. R., & Sirotin, Y. B. (2020). Human-algorithm teaming in face recognition: How algorithm outcomes cognitively bias human decision-making. *PLoS ONE*, 15(8 August), 1–18. https://doi.
org/10.1371/journal.pone.0237855.

Hurst, L. (2023). AI deepfakes are being weaponised in the race for US president – and Trump is the latest target. www.euronews.com/next/
2023/06/09/ai-deepfakes-are-being-weaponised-in-the-race-for-us-p
resident-and-trump-is-the-latest-tar.

Jeckeln, G., Hahn, C. A., Noyes, E., Cavazos, J. G., & O'Toole, A. J. (2018). Wisdom of the social versus non-social crowd in face identification. *British Journal of Psychology*, 109(4), 724–735. https://doi.
org/10.1111/bjop.12291.

Jenkins, P. R. (2022). ETHI Brief: The use and impact of facial recognition technology 1. Summary of evidence. www.ourcommons.ca/Content/
Committee/441/ETHI/Brief/BR11702042/br-external/JenkinsRob-e.pdf.

Li, L., Mu, X., Li, S., & Peng, H. (2020). A review of face recognition technology. *IEEE Access*, 8, 139110–139120. https://doi.org/10.1109/ACCESS.2020.3011028.

Lim, X.-J., & Cheah, J.-H. (2023). Are we ready to adopt facial recognition payment system?: The perspective of cognitive appraisal theory. *2023 IEEE International Symposium on Technology and Society (ISTAS)*, 1–5. https://doi.org/10.1109/istas57930.2023.10305994.

Madnick, S. E. (2023). The continued threat to personal data: Key factors behind the 2023 increase. www.apple.com/newsroom/pdfs/The-Continued-Threat-to-Personal-Data-Key-Factors-Behind-the-2023-Increase.pdf.

McCallum, S. (2023). Revenge and deepfake porn laws to be toughened. www.bbc.co.uk/news/technology-66021643.

Mellers, B. A., Lu, L., & McCoy, J. P. (2023). Predicting the future with humans and AI. *Consumer Psychology Review*, 6(1), 109–120. https://doi.org/10.1002/arcp.1089.

Miller, E. J., Steward, B. A., Witkower, Z., Sutherland, C. A. M., Krumhuber, E. G., & Dawel, A. (2023). AI hyperrealism: Why AI faces are perceived as more real than human ones. *Psychological Science*, 34 (12). https://doi.org/10.1177/09567976231207095.

O'Toole, A. J., Abdi, H., Jiang, F., & Phillips, P. J. (2007). Fusing face-verification algorithms and humans. *IEEE Transactions on Systems, Man, and Cybernetics, Part B: Cybernetics*, 37(5), 1149–1155. https://doi.org/10.1109/TSMCB.2007.907034.

O'Toole, A. J., & Castillo, C. D. (2021). Face recognition by humans and machines: Three fundamental advances from deep learning. *Annual Review of Vision Science*, 7, 543–570. https://doi.org/10.1146/annurev-vision-093019-111701.

Phillips, P. J., Yates, A. N., Hu, Y., Hahn, C. A., Noyes, E., Jackson, K., Cavazos, J. G., Jeckeln, G., Ranjan, R., Sankaranarayanan, S., Chen, J. C., Castillo, C. D., Chellappa, R., White, D., & O'Toole, A. J. (2018). Face recognition accuracy of forensic examiners, superrecognizers, and face recognition algorithms. *Proceedings of the National Academy of Sciences of the United States of America*, 115(24), 6171–6176. https://doi.org/10.1073/pnas.1721355115.

Qinjun, L., Tianwei, C., Yan, Z., & Yuying, W. (2023). Facial recognition technology: A comprehensive overview. *Academic Journal of Computing & Information Science*, 6(7), 15–26. https://doi.org/10.25236/ajcis.2023.060703.

Quinn, B. (2024). Slew of deepfake video adverts of Sunak on Facebook raises alarm over AI risk to election. *The Guardian*, 12 January. www.

theguardian.com/technology/2024/jan/12/deepfake-video-adverts-sunak-facebook-alarm-ai-risk-election.

Rawlinson, K. (2024). Facial recognition could replace passports at UK airport e-gates. *The Guardian*, 1 January. www.theguardian.com/world/2024/jan/01/facial-recognition-could-replace-passports-at-uk-airport-e-gates.

Teejay, B. (2023). Tesla app down: Europe drivers fear not opening car due to outage. www.techtimes.com/articles/287667/20230214/tesla-app-down-europe-drivers-not-opening-car.htm.

Wakefield, J. (2022). Deepfake presidents used in Russia-Ukraine war. www.bbc.co.uk/news/technology-60780142.

White, D., Burton, A. M., Kemp, R. I., & Jenkins, R. (2013). Crowd effects in unfamiliar face matching. *Applied Cognitive Psychology*, 27, 769–777. https://doi.org/10.1002/acp.2971.

Index

For Product Safety Concerns and Information please contact our EU
representative GPSR@taylorandfrancis.com Taylor & Francis Verlag GmbH,
Kaufingerstraße 24, 80331 München, Germany

Printed and bound by CPI Group (UK) Ltd, Croydon, CR0 4YY
08/06/2025
01897003-0001